MURDER ON MARYLAND'S EASTERN SHORE

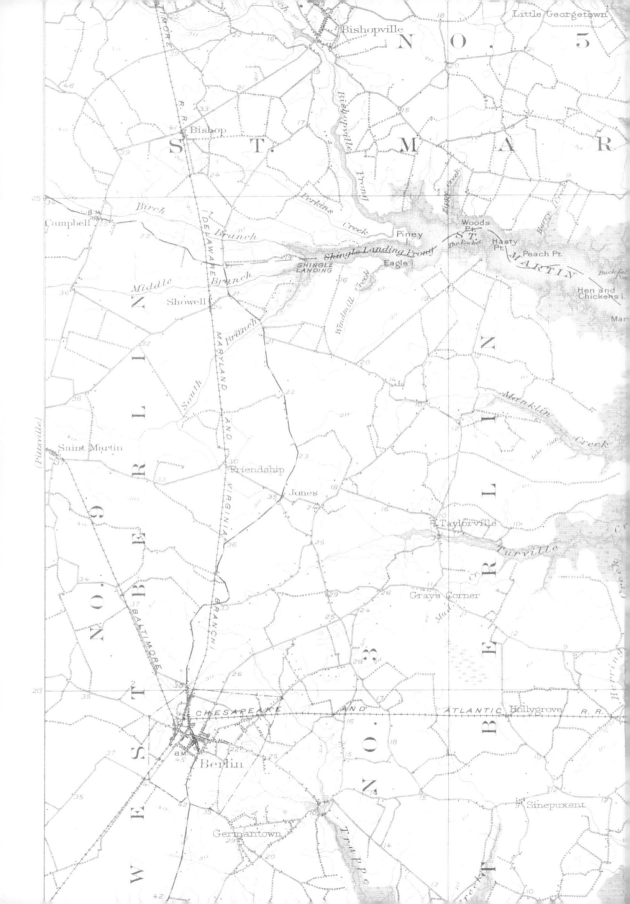

MURDER ON MARYLAND'S EASTERN SHORE

Race, Politics and the Case of Orphan Jones

Joseph E. Moore

Charleston   London

History
PRESS

Published by The History Press
18 Percy Street
Charleston, SC 29403
866.223.5778
www.historypress.net

Front cover image: Orphan Jones was removed from the Worcester County jail in Snow Hill in order to protect him from possible mob violence. Notice the bandage over his left eye, surely a result of being hit during the trip from Berlin to the jail or during the interrogation. *Baltimore* Sunpapers.
Back cover image: The gallows chamber located in a wing of "C" dormitory of the Maryland penitentiary. It was in this foreboding room that Euel Lee was executed on October 27, 1933, the seventeenth man to be hanged in the penitentiary. (Prior to 1923, executions had been held in the county where the crime occurred.) By 1955, when the state mandated that the gas chamber replace the gallows, seventy-five hangings had taken place here. The building has since been demolished. *Courtesy of Maryland Division of Correction.*

First published 2006
Manufactured in the United Kingdom
Second printing

ISBN 1.59629.077.3

Library of Congress Cataloging-in-Publication Data

Moore, Joseph E.
  Murder on Maryland's Eastern Shore : race, politics and the case of Orphan Jones / Joseph E. Moore.
      p. cm.
  Includes bibliographical references and index.
  ISBN 1-59629-077-3 (alk. paper)
  1. Lee, Euel, d. 1933--Trials, litigation, etc. 2. Trials (Murder)--Maryland. 3. Murder--Maryland--Worcester County--History--20th century. 4. Discrimination in criminal justice administration--Maryland--Worcester County--History--20th century. I. Title.
   KF224.L44.M66 2006
   345.752'2102523--dc22
                    2005033309

Notice: The information in this book is true and complete to the best of our knowledge. It is offered without guarantee on the part of the author or The History Press. The author and The History Press disclaim all liability in connection with the use of this book.

Contents

Preface

Iam a native Marylander and a proud Eastern Shoreman. I was born in Berlin, near Ocean City in Worcester County, during the third presidential administration of Franklin D. Roosevelt. My literal birthplace is located in the middle of the town of Berlin, only several yards from the location of the magistrate's office in 1931, which figured in the initial events of the true story that follows. Even though I was not alive at the time of the crime, it is with some difficulty that the tale is told, because of the horrific nature of many of the events which occurred in my home region that I dearly love. The tale recreates the story of a horrible murder in the area, which, because it involved an African American who murdered an entire white family in the segregated, Depression-era Eastern Shore community of Worcester County, caused incredible tensions, racial divisions and turmoil in a normally quiet rural community.

I was elected State's Attorney for Worcester County in 1978, and, after taking office, I stumbled across an old, yellowing file in the clerk's office of the courthouse. This, it turned out, contained the original documents in the case of *State of Maryland v. Euel Lee, alias Orphan Jones*. An ancient telegram struck my eye. Dated October 18, 1931, it read: "AFTER CONFERENCE WITH COURT HERE HAVE DECIDED NOT TO ALLOW ANY COUNSEL APPOINTED OR EMPLOYED BY INTERNATIONAL LABOR DEFENSE TO INTERVIEW EUEL LEE ALIAS ORPHAN JONES UNLESS SO DECIDED BY JUDGE FRANK." It was signed by Godfrey Child, who was, in 1931, the State's Attorney for Worcester County. Intrigued, I inquired of Circuit Judge Daniel T. Prettyman as to whether he would grant me a court order to remove the documents from the clerk's file. His response was typical for him: "Nobody gives a damn, just go ahead and take them." (In the mid-twentieth century, the Eastern Shore circuit court judge was, truly, the "boss" of the county.)

So, I did.

Thus began what turned out to be a twenty-five-year journey through the history of the case of Orphan Jones. I have spent hundreds of hours looking at the records of the Maryland Archives, reviewing the Enoch Pratt library's newspaper files in Baltimore and combing through local histories of the Eastern Shore and documents and historical accounts related to the state of Maryland, visiting the areas where the events took place. With the help of H. Furlong Baldwin, formerly the chairman of the board of Mercantile Bank, and Sandy Levy, the library services director of the *Baltimore Sun*, I gained access to the excellent library of the *Sun*. Sandy also directed me to the repository of the original newspapers of the *Sun* editions at University of Maryland, Baltimore County, where Tom Beck, chief curator of the Albin O. Kuhn Library and his assistant, John Beck (no relation) were unfailingly cooperative and helpful.

Dr. Edward Papenfuse, chief archivist and director of the Maryland Hall of Records, has been of great assistance in achieving the publication of this story. And my introduction, through Ed, to the website of the archives revealed many sources otherwise unknown to me.

Thanks are due to Vincent Fitzpatrick and Ms. Averil Kadis of the Mencken Room, Enoch Pratt Free Library in Baltimore for their permission to use much of Mencken's material that is excerpted in the book.

Jennifer Ketner, Dana Donovan, Kristina Bouton and Sandy Dougan are to be thanked for helping me through the mysteries of computers, recopying text and for formatting this book. Special thanks are due to Mary Humphreys, PhD, for her impeccable and careful proofreading for the second edition of this book.

Janet Ades, the daughter of Bernard Ades, was very helpful in providing me with material that her cousin, James Platt, had found in the National Archives and which I otherwise would not have thought to locate.

The practice of law with its demand on my time has hindered me in the formulation and writing of the book, and my partners and associates in my law firm have put up with literally years of my rambling about the story, normally during our lunch hours together. They really never thought this would ever get written.

My family and friends are to be thanked for their patience and support, especially my daughters Melissa and Jenny and my wife Sue, who have read the manuscript with a critical and unflinching eye toward my mistakes and shortfalls.

I only regret that, during the years, many of the persons who knew the events firsthand died before I interviewed them.

My mother, Bessye Moore, has just (in 2005) celebrated her ninety-seventh birthday, and many of her generation recall the events of this story with startling clarity. Many of them (those who are left) still have an abiding hatred for H.L. Mencken, of the *Baltimore Sun*, because of the vitriolic manner in which he portrayed Eastern Shoremen in general and the events related herein in particular. Mencken harbored an intense dislike for Eastern Shoremen. One of his famous passages (penned well prior to reapportionment of the legislature of the state of Maryland) bemoaned the fact that "the vote of one malarial peasant on the Eastern Shore of Maryland equals that of ten Baltimoreans." To those Depression-era folks still alive on the lower shore, Mencken remains a subject of contempt even today, nearly fifty years after his death.

Elderly Eastern Shoremen also express a dislike for Bernard Ades, the Communist lawyer who defended the accused murderer and the central character of this story, not just because of his unwelcome participation in the defense of the despised murderer, but equally because of his unpleasant personality, his radical politics and his open disdain for the citizens and judiciary on the lower shore. He was, when I began the research into the events related herein, somewhat of an enigma due to his fleeting presence in the lower shore community. Through the years, however, I believe I came to know Bernard, not just because of my perusal of the historical records, but due to my meeting his daughter Janet, who related incidents of his life and personality, and with whom I spent time and of whom I speak in the epilogue. Janet was also extremely helpful in providing me with remarkable material that came into her possession because of her research regarding her father, and some of those materials had been presumed by me to have been lost to history. I am hopeful that Bernard's abrasive personality and remarkable courage will be accurately reflected in this story.

Although he is difficult to like, he is equally difficult not to admire for his persistence and fortitude. As a practicing trial attorney for thirty-four years, I know firsthand the travails of defending a case or client who is difficult, or unpopular. As my mentor, Marcus J. Williams, Esq., once told me as a young lawyer, "Joe, you don't have to love your client, you just have to represent him." Bernard Ades surely espoused this philosophy.

The other central protagonist of the story, State's Attorney Godfrey Child, was a native Worcester Countian who was well respected; an established and genteel lawyer who, during his service as prosecutor, was an effective advocate for the people of Worcester County. He served as a leading figure in the bar, represented the town of Pocomoke City for many years and was later appointed as circuit court judge for Worcester County. He is to be admired for his heroic service to his country during World War I as well as exemplary service to the citizens of his native county.

There are some matters about this story and my portrayal of it that need explaining. First and foremost, the language of characterization related to African Americans in the book does not reflect the nature of my upbringing nor my position on race. It is, however, historically necessary for the reporting of these events in order to reflect the times in which they occurred.

Terminology and race characterization in the 1930s were graphically different than today. Therefore, the categorization of African Americans throughout the book reflects terms that are generally unacceptable in the twenty-first century. I have not intended to offend, and I am hopeful the reader will realize that the language used throughout the book is necessary for the accurate telling of the story.

Secondly, I have felt it necessary to portray the feeling of the community in the context of mid-Depression Worcester County in particular, and the Eastern Shore and, indeed, the country in general, and such portrayal does not reflect either my personal attitude nor the attitude that would prevail today in the same community, including Wicomico and Somerset Counties.

Finally, events in the context of the story that may have been indicative of the community feeling and attitudes at the time and the actions taken then are certainly not the attitudes prevailing in the Eastern Shore today.

I

Horror in the Night

As Charles Johnson walked fearfully toward the neighboring house that was owned by his old friend Green Davis, he noticed that something was ominously wrong. The house had a very strong odor of kerosene oil, the heating fuel prevalent in use in the late autumn days of 1931, and it was as quiet as death.

It had been two days since Johnson had seen anyone at the Davis household, even though the family consisted of Mr. Davis, his wife Ivy and their two teenage daughters. The date was October 12, 1931, and Charles Johnson and his neighbor and friend Sebie Howe were about to discover a grisly scene that would trigger the most sensational murder investigation in the history of the lower Eastern Shore of Maryland.

During the latter months of 1931, Worcester County, Maryland, was a bucolic rural county, with little of the glitter that would come not more than thirty years later due to the tremendous growth of the resort town of Ocean City. Situated on the shore of the Atlantic Ocean, Ocean City is Maryland's only seaside resort. Indeed, Ocean City itself, in those days of the Great Depression, bore little resemblance to its future prosperity, being a mere village with a few rooming houses and a few hotels along its stretch of boardwalk. It was a community that unknowingly awaited the great storm of 1933 to carve out its famous inlet that would open the sleepy resort to the booming sport-fishing industry, gaining the town the nickname, "White Marlin Capital of the World."

Worcester County in 1931 was not dissimilar to many other Southern rural areas, and particularly those counties that composed the Eastern Shore of Maryland. Nine counties lay east of the Chesapeake Bay, divided by that vast estuary from the more metropolitan area of the Western Shore, which included not only Baltimore, but also the sophistication of Annapolis, Maryland's capital, and the communities in the area of the nation's capital. The county in 1931 was staunchly Methodist, strictly segregated and quietly conservative. The county government was totally Democrat, as had been the case since the Civil War, at which time Abraham Lincoln had gotten exactly zero votes from the county voters in the 1860 election. Indeed, within the year the Democratic machine in the county would turn out foursquare for Franklin D. Roosevelt.

Worcester County, as all of the Eastern Shore in this era, however, had a characteristic sadly all too familiar in the rural South. Hand in hand with strict segregation was a prevailing racism generally characterized as "Jim Crowism." This policy is defined in *Webster's Dictionary* as, "a practice or policy of segregating or discriminating against blacks, as in public places, public vehicles or employment."

Horror in the Night

In his book, *Maryland's Eastern Shore, A Journey in Time and Place*, Professor John R. Wennersten writes of the circumstances of Jim Crow in the South. In chapter 8, entitled "Freedom's Ferment," he states the following:

> *Since the Civil War, the history of race relations on the Eastern Shore of Maryland has been a story of struggle and tragedy. Although the Eastern Shore counties are within a two-hour drive of the nation's capital, the communities in spirit and sense of place have been more like the deep South when it comes to racial attitudes. Like slavery, segregation and white supremacy died hard as a sustaining ethos of Chesapeake country life. And it has only been since the 1960s that considerable progress has begun to be made in terms of racial accommodation.*
>
> *By 1904, a new kind of racially repressive system had been installed on the Eastern Shore. In response to changing economic conditions and the growing popularity of political and scientific racism articulated in Southern newspapers and in the state legislatures of the old slaveholding states, Maryland blacks were forced to confront a movement to disenfranchise them and take away what few rights they had. In addition to the growing respectability of white violence as a means of race control on the Shore, blacks were forced to use "Jim Crow" facilities on steamboats and passenger trains. In hotels and other facilities that had never been formally segregated, the new spirit of "separate but equal" prevailed. Unfortunately for Eastern Shore blacks, separate was never equal. Thus it is hardly surprising that after the turn of the century, the Eastern Shore lost over twenty percent of its black adult male and female population.*
>
> *From the turn of the century until the Great Crash of 1929, blacks on the Eastern Shore were influenced primarily by the cycle of economic life in the tomato and fruit canneries and the seafood packing houses of Crisfield, Cambridge, Oxford and Denton. Even before the Great Depression of the 1930s, Maryland's Eastern Shore was one of the most rural and impoverished regions of the state. The Chesapeake Bay and primitive highways isolated the Eastern Shore from Annapolis and metropolitan centers, and few on the Shore at this time spoke out against violence directed at blacks. With the onset of the Depression, struggling blacks and whites competed for jobs on truck farms, in canneries and sawmills, and by 1933 the economic situation for blacks and poor whites generally had become desperate.*

This picture by Professor Wennersten related to the Eastern Shore in general fits precisely the situation in Worcester in the early days of the 1930s.

The county seat was then, as now, Snow Hill, a sleepy little town with the government being virtually its sole enterprise. The red brick courthouse, carefully nestled within a small, tree shaded square where local militia had encamped after the Civil War, represented the tradition of solid, conservative values evident in the area. It was the epicenter of the political establishment that would, by virtue of the impending discovery by Charlie Johnson, be shaken to its very foundation by the upcoming events soon to unfold.

Snow Hill was the county seat—for as much as any other reason—by virtue of its geographical location, settled as it was almost in the exact center of the county. In fact, the location of the county itself is rather unique, being bounded on the north by the state of Delaware and on the south by the Commonwealth of Virginia, thus being the sole subdivision of Maryland sandwiched between those other states.

In the thirties, as today, there were two main routes through the county. Route 213 existed roughly along the line of present-day Route 50, traversing from west to east, and Route 113 extended north to south. The county was sparsely populated, with only four incorporated towns: Snow Hill, Pocomoke City, Ocean City and Berlin. The latter was a rail center located seven miles to the west, a small village that had begun its existence as a way stop on the stage roads of the seventeenth century. Berlin's one claim to notoriety was the fact that Stephen Decatur, the naval hero of the early years of the republic, had been born here, although totally by accident—he was born there simply because his mother was traveling through the area.

The small town had not acquired its name because of any relationship to the capital of Germany, but for a starkly different reason. In the eighteenth century, there had been an inn, or way station, on the road traversing the area, named "Burley Inn." Throughout the years, this appellation had been slurred to "Berlin". In fact, "Burley" was originally a small town in western England, just as "Snow Hill" was derived from an area in London—both reflected the connection of the colonial lower shore populace with their English heritage.

As one traveled south through the county on Route 113, one would go through villages such as Ironshire, Newark, Snow Hill and finally, near the Virginia line, one would arrive in Pocomoke City, formerly called Newtown, which had begun as a port on the Pocomoke River, a tributary of the majestic Chesapeake Bay reputed to be the deepest river in the world for its width.

All of the towns and villages had little activity in the thirties, excepting Ocean City, with its rooming houses, small but charming hotels lining the boardwalk and one or two substantial hotels, all served by the railroad that ended its track in the town. These trains, many filled with excited travelers, would roar across the Eastern Shore peninsula from their beginning station at Love Point on the Chesapeake Bay, stopping periodically at various stations along the route, finally to steam across the rail and auto bridge spanning the Sinepuxent Bay onto the island of Ocean City, and slowly chug up Philadelphia Avenue, two blocks from the ocean, on tracks set into the concrete roadbed where they would hiss to a stop at the spacious terminal. The passengers would alight and walk the few hundred feet up a walkway owned by the railroad onto the boardwalk to the Atlantic Hotel, then the jewel of the fledgling resort.

In Ocean City also in those days was the service facility area, where the servants and hotel workers lived. These were the workers who came to town in order to serve the needs and requirements of the visitors and tourists. African Americans stayed only in areas where the segregated rooming houses, then the accepted standard in the area, were located, tucked away from the view of the resort's white visitors. Indeed, Ocean City in this era was a white person's town. African Americans (other than the workforce) visited only on designated days known as "Colored Days," two or so days set aside after Labor Day during which they were allowed to stroll along the boardwalk and enjoy the sea air.

Henry's Colored Hotel was the only black-accommodation hotel on the island and, indeed, few African Americans chose to reside on the island.

And here into Ocean City, at an unknown time in history, came Orphan Jones.

Jones was a black man traveling from Lynchburg, Virginia, who, for reasons and by means unknown, came to Worcester County. The press would later describe him as a man of sixty years old, of short, heavy build, who had apparently spent most of his adult life wandering from place to place. He had worked at odd jobs—in Boston he had worked as a stevedore, in New Jersey he had been employed as a potato digger and in Baltimore, apparently just before his arrival in these parts, he had worked in a hotel. Perhaps it was this work experience that brought him to Ocean City. Jones was a reticent man, quiet and reserved, as events would strikingly bring forth. When he arrived in town, he took residence in Martha Miller's rooming house, a place for members of the African American race. Martha, known as Aunt Martha, was herself black and had established a reputation for keeping an upstanding and respectable residence.

Again, at an unknown time, Jones acquired employment about four miles west of the island, at Taylorville, a village three miles east of Berlin, as a farm laborer with Green Davis.

Green K. Davis, fifty-five years of age, and his wife Ivy Smith Davis, thirty-eight years, lived at the bend in the road at Gray's Corner with their two daughters, Elizabeth Gertrude, fifteen, and Mary Lee, thirteen. Their house, no longer in existence, was a modest two-story frame dwelling, one not atypical for the area in which families struggled to make ends meet during the Depression. In September 1922, by virtue of a mortgage foreclosure and the public sale that was legally required to be held, Davis was able to purchase the property, which was on a private road adjacent to the property of William D. Pitts, near the Berlin-Ocean City Road, from Calvin B. Taylor, assignee of the mortgage from Wilmer Bodley. The property contained 19.52 acres and was purchased by Davis for $1,800. The house and land was mortgaged by the Davises to the same Calvin B. Taylor, a local banker who, being also a lawyer, had conveyed the property as attorney in the foreclosure.

Davis was a farmer who grew truck crops (vegetables for human consumption) and, in season, peddled fruits from a homemade stand set along the side of the road leading to Ocean City, about five hundred yards south of the Davis house, which was set back a considerable distance from the road. Apparently, just prior to October 11, 1931, Orphan Jones, who had been in the employ of Davis for several weeks, was discharged because of lack of work. Events would bring to light the contention that the farmhand may have been owed some money upon his discharge, a sum noted as one or two dollars.

On Sunday, October 11, the fruit and vegetable stand in front of the Davis property was deserted, even though the weather was fair and clear. It was noted that none of the Davis family was taking advantage of the steady stream of traffic which passed by on the way to Ocean City.

On Monday, October 12, Charles Johnson, neighbor to the Davises, was reminded by his wife that no activity had been observed at the Davis house since Sunday. This was unusual, because the Davis fruit stand was normally in active operation on the weekend days. Thus Johnson, together with another neighbor, Sebie Howe, reluctantly decided to investigate. They walked guardedly over to the Davis property at about four o'clock that afternoon and headed up the long dirt lane toward the residence. Upon their arrival, they peered into the windows but saw no movement. Alarmed, they banged on the door at the side of the house, near the kitchen. No response was forthcoming.

"Do you think anything's wrong?" asked Johnson.

"I don't like it," replied Howe.

"I wonder if we had better break in?"

After a brief conference, the men decided to break into the modest dwelling. An enclosed porch ran along the side of the house, and from there the entrance led directly into the kitchen. There were only two rooms on the first floor, the kitchen and living room. Along the rear wall of the kitchen an open stairway led to the second floor, which also contained only two small rooms, the bedroom of Mr. and Mrs. Davis, and, through a single doorway, the bedroom of the two children. Each bedroom contained a single double bed.

Upon their entry it became chillingly evident to Johnson and Howe that a horrible event had occurred—immediately they became aware of the strong odor of kerosene, and they were assaulted by the sight of overturned furniture and clothing scattered about. A hasty search of the first floor rooms was to no avail, so the two men, with fear increasing, mounted the narrow stairway to the second floor of the house. The sight that greeted the two men there was totally horrifying. Mr. and Mrs. Davis lay in their bed in the blood-spattered bedroom with their heads and faces horribly mutilated. Although sickened and terrified, Johnson and Howe forced themselves to look into the adjoining bedroom. Peering in, they were shaken by the sight of the two young girls' bloody and battered bodies also lying in their bed, brutally murdered. In both rooms, blood was everywhere, even on the walls and ceilings. It was obvious that all four had been shot at close range with a shotgun as they lay sleeping in their beds, and, from appearances, Mr. and Mrs. Davis had been beaten in their faces with some type of heavy object.

Horrified, both men staggered down the narrow steps and Johnson used the wall-mounted telephone to call the authorities. The call went to the local soda fountain, one of the few locations in the small town of Berlin that had a public phone. The call was answered by young Charles Lynch, a teenage soda jerk at the popular location. Local operators (there were no dial telephones at that time in the area) knew to direct emergency calls to that number because there was nearly always someone there who could handle the call or take the message to whomever needed to be notified. Lynch, scared to death by the news he had just been given, raced around the corner and across the street. The police station in Berlin was a small, almost tiny building located on Broad Street, which housed the magistrate's office as well. The constable on duty that afternoon was Fred A. Culver. He was, as one could imagine, totally unprepared for the news that Lynch, breathless, blurted out to him. At first, Culver didn't believe the young boy. It became evident to Culver that Lynch's terror outweighed his own doubts and after a moment's reflection he said he would investigate—but that Lynch was coming with him to the scene and that if there was no truth in the young lad's story, there would be hell to pay.

A quadruple homicide was beyond anyone's imagination in the quiet town of Berlin during the sleepy afternoon of an autumn Monday, or, for that matter, at any time. Culver notified the Maryland State Police and officer H.H. Haines responded to the alarm. Both men, together with a terrified Charlie Lynch, proceeded quickly to the crime scene. Their investigation revealed that there was, in fact, widespread ransacking evident all about the Davis house. It was apparent that robbery may well have been the motive. Furniture was in disarray, clothes were scattered about and the ominous presence of the kerosene splashed about indicated the possible intent to burn the house to cover up the crime.

Although they were law enforcement officers, Culver and Haines realized that this matter was far beyond their capability to conduct a thorough investigation. They had never seen, and rarely heard of, anything resembling the enormity of what they had discovered. Therefore, after their initial look-see, they determined to call in additional help. A call went out to State's Attorney Godfrey Child and Worcester County sheriff Wilmer S. Purnell. Meanwhile, Culver and Haines secured the crime scene upon orders from Child. Young Lynch, who had accompanied them up the stairs and seen the horrid scene, was asked to guard the outside door of the house, alone in the dark. Terrified by the horrendousness of the whole matter, he fled across the field to the road and caught a ride back to Berlin. For years after, Lynch recalled, at his home on Burley Street in Berlin, he would awaken at night, calling out for his older sister, Pauline.

It was determined that the bodies and the home would be left undisturbed until expert help could be summoned, and, due to the bizarre nature of the crime, that help had to come all the way from Baltimore, several hours away. County authorities called in Lieutenant Joseph H. Itzel, a Baltimore detective, and Sergeant William J. Flynn, a Bertillon and fingerprint expert. (The Bertillon system, devised by Alphonse Bertillon, a French anthropologist, was a means of identifying persons by record of individual physical measurements and peculiarities.)

Throughout the long dark night of Monday, a cordon of officers kept a grim vigil around the modest house with its murdered occupants. Early on Tuesday morning, after an exhausting trip from Baltimore—traveling, as was the custom, by train from Baltimore to Wilmington, then transferring to the spur line down through Delaware to Berlin—Itzel and Flynn arrived and began their grisly work.

In the meantime, however, the local authorities had not slackened their efforts at solving the crime. Indeed, clues found at the scene and information provided to the sheriff within three hours of the discovery of the bodies led Sheriff Purnell to order the arrest of Orphan Jones.

Neighbors had advised the authorities that Jones had been working at the Davis farm for approximately three weeks and had just recently been discharged, during which there had been a dispute about wages. Jones was located at the rooming house of Martha Miller and was arrested by Ocean City Police Chief Robert Allen. Jones was brought to the modest police station/magistrate's office in Berlin and was subjected to questioning there. The *Berlin-Ocean City News* , a weekly paper (whose by-line proclaimed, "Devoted to the Interests of the Twin Cities of Northern Worcester County, Maryland") reported in its October 15 edition: "At Berlin, the Negro was searched and on his person was found $84 in cash, a pocketbook and other articles. In his room at the boarding house of Martha H. Miller, negress, the officers found a shotgun, women's clothing and other loot which can be identified as belonging to the Davis family."

According to a report in the *Baltimore Sun*, Jones's arrest went as follows:

The colored man, it was learned, had gone to Ocean City. The Sheriff got in touch with the chief of police Robert Allen of Ocean City and Allen soon located Jones at the home there of Martha Miller, an aged Negro woman.

Told what had been found at the Davis home, Jones protested that he didn't know anything about it. But Chief Allen, searching the farmhand, said he found a Playground Athletic League medal, a billfold bearing Davis' name and a leather money bag containing $84 and a $30 gold piece.

Allen then searched the room Jones rented in the Miller home. He found a watch, a quantity of women's hosiery, several men's shirts, a repeating shotgun, a girls belt buckle and a bar pin. Jones said he had bought the watch at a pawnshop in Baltimore and Davis had given him the shirts.

According to Sheriff Purnell, Miller said: "Orphan came in late last Saturday night with a sack. He went away on Sunday. And came back with another sack. Yesterday morning I saw him cleaning a shotgun out on the back porch. I asked him where he got that and he said he had bought it."

This was the shotgun that had been found in Jones' room and that neighbors later identified as Davis'. The money bag found on the colored man also was one that Davis had carried and the trinkets found in Jones' room had belonged to the farmer's daughters, Mrs. Ethel Hudson and Mrs. Margaret Timmons, who was a sister of Davis, said.

"Did you ever hear Jones threaten the Davis family?" Martha was asked. "I heard him say after Mr. Davis let him go that he was a-going to get even with him," Martha said, according to Robert Lewis, an Ocean City policeman.

The Sheriff repeated this to Jones, who is said to have answered: "I meant that I wouldn't work for him any more."

Charles E. Holloway, Salisbury hardware salesman, told authorities that Davis had been afraid of Jones. The salesman said that while he was talking to Davis last Friday Jones had happened to pass by and Davis had remarked that he was uneasy about the colored man, whom he had caught peeking into windows of the Davis house after his discharge, a fortnight earlier, and that he was going to get a gun.

Looking up Jones' record, Sheriff Purnell learned that he had left Lynchburg, Va. about thirty years ago and moved to Harford County, where he worked on various farms. Last spring Jones went to the Eastern Shore and for a time was hired by a Somerset county farmer.

The colored hand left this employer after an argument, during which Jones is said to have threatened another man with a gun. Jones then went to Taylorville to work for Davis. He slept on the first floor of the farmhouse when he worked there.

Relentless questioning by the authorities ensued. In 1931, there were no legal requirements of notifying a suspect of his Constitutional rights; he had no right to an attorney (if a suspect saw a lawyer, it would likely be in preparation for a trial instead of protecting his right of silence); no comfort was availed a suspect when being questioned—the sole goal of the law enforcement personnel was to get a confession. In this instance, that goal was compounded by the certain feeling in the minds of the officers as to what they saw as the heinous nature of what this black man had obviously done: viciously, mercilessly slain a white, law abiding family in the sanctity of their rural home.

Jones was in deep, serious trouble.

II.
An Ugly Mood

Not only was the weight of evidence against Jones incriminating, but a much more ominous situation began to be evident: the word had spread quickly around the small community in northern Worcester County—citizens spoke of the fact that a black farm worker of no fixed address, with no local connections, had brutally murdered a respected white family in their sleep—in their own neighborhood.

Inevitably, crowds of area residents began gathering at both the crime scene and at the Berlin magistrate's office during Monday night as Jones was being questioned. Murmurs, then talk, of quick justice began to spread. The citizens questioned, Why wait to achieve the justice that he so rightly deserved? Didn't the authorities have ample evidence of his guilt? He had worked for the family hadn't he? Physical evidence had been found in his room hadn't it?

Rumors of a confession began to spread. A gathering takes little conversion to become a mob. In the normally peaceful town of Berlin that night, almost imperceptibly, the ugly underside of society threatened to surface. People who were assumed to be kind to their neighbors, spoke a cheery "hello" on the streets of town, faithfully attended church on Sunday, and led quiet, respectable lives, began to transform their outrage at a horrible crime into a stated intent of seeing retribution, swift and unyielding. In the racial makeup of Worcester County at this time, a black man committing a crime against a white family was not to be tolerated.

To the credit of the law enforcement officials, they sensed this prevailing unrest. It was becoming evident that their neighbors and friends were capable of acts for which the officials could not bear responsibility, nor condone. It was decided, therefore, to remove Jones to the safest place in the county, the jail at Snow Hill. Although for his own benefit, the trip of some sixteen miles from Berlin to the county seat would be a long one indeed for the accused. The road between the two towns was, at that time, narrow and winding, threading its way through flat farmland and two small villages. Jones was wedged into the rear seat of a police car, with an officer on each side. According to Charles Lynch, who was later advised of the ride by officers, the ride was fraught with violence. Lynch recalled that somewhere near the village of Newark, about halfway to Snow Hill, Jones was removed from the car and was beaten by one of the officers, who had finally snapped at the refusal of the man to confess to the crime. Lynch spoke about the fact that, notwithstanding the cruel blows, no admissions from the accused were forthcoming.

At long last, the vehicles rolled into the darkened streets of Snow Hill. At the intersection of Market Street and Washington Street stood the red brick courthouse. Immediately behind the courthouse squatted the jail, a bulky structure, with an office for the sheriff, sparse rooms for the sheriff's staff and deputies and, across a connecting hall, the Worcester County lockups. Large communal cellblocks with several bunk beds and a common toilet for each cell area existed. There were no separate cells in the nature of a modern prison, and all the prisoners in a particular block shared a common living area with tables and benches in the center.

Jones, however, was not placed into the cellblock upon his arrival at the lockup. His grilling was to continue relentlessly, with the law enforcement personnel determined to secure the confession that would seal the making of the case. Throughout the long night, the interrogation proceeded, with officers taking turns in their efforts to break the accused. Over and over, he was questioned as to the items which had been found in his room; again and again, he was reminded of the fact that he had told a person that Davis had "cheated him out of a dollar" when he had been discharged by his employer.

As reported by the *Democratic Messenger*, a county paper whose October 17 headlines screamed:

Quadruple Murder Near Berlin—negro Confesses The Crime

William Green Davis, Mrs. Davis and their two daughters were brutally murdered in their home near Taylorville, last Saturday night, by Orphan Jones, a Virginia Negro, who is alleged to have made a confession that he shot Mr. and Mrs. Davis with a pump gun, and the two daughters with a shot-gun and pistol, his object being robbery. Jones had been employed by Mr. Davis as a farm hand for several weeks, and it is claimed that Mr. Davis discharged the man because he had no more work for him to do. It is said that Mr. Davis agreed to give the man a dollar a day, board and lodging, for his work. In settlement he deducted one dollar for a day that the negro had not worked, and this was the occasion of a quarrel. The negro saw no significance in the fact that he had $80 in paper money and some change on his person when arrested, asserting that he had been accustomed to making "big money."

Only once throughout the hours of merciless grilling under a brilliant electric light suspended from the wall in the kitchen of the jail, did he show the slightest sign of faltering in his determined stand of denials.

Shortly after the telephone bell rang, someone called into the room that it was reported one of the victims was still living. Jones started.

"That's not true, all four of them are dead," Jones spoke loudly.

Then, suddenly realizing how near he had come to stepping into the trap, he smiled and became silent as he often did when he successfully fought efforts to entice him to admit his guilt.

The report of the questioning found in the *Baltimore Sun* was interesting in that it identified the interrogators:

There he was grilled for sixteen hours by Chief of Police Purnell, W.W. Davis, deputy sheriff; Corp. M.B. Brubager [sic], of the State police; Alec Marshall, president of the Board of County Commissioners, and others.

As day dawned and the coterie of officers at the jail increased with the arrival of State patrolmen, Jones showed little ill effects from the ordeal of nine hours of constant grilling. He told his questioners that he was neither sleepy nor hungry.

The stoic demeanor had to end, however. Finally as the *Messenger* reported, "After sixteen hours of grilling by Lieut. Itzel and Worcester County police, Jones broke down and confessed to the murder of Mr. Davis, Mrs. Davis, Elizabeth Davis and Mary Lee Davis."

Another graphically different (and evidently exaggerated) description of the interrogation was reported in the *Afro-American* newspaper, headquartered in Baltimore, one of the premier black newspapers in the entire country. In its October 24 issue, the headlines of the Baltimore *Afro-American* (a weekly at this time) shouted:

> TIE, BEAT SUSPECT—*Say Agonizing Torture Forced Axe Confession. Snow Hill, Md—That Orphan Jones, accused of killing Green Davis, his wife and two daughters on a Taylorville farm, went through the agonies of a Spanish inquisition and collapsed before his alleged confession was forced out of him, was revealed by the statement of a witness in the neighborhood of the grilling, this week. [The "witness" was not identified.]*
>
> *Through the long hours, as grim Eastern Shore prosecutors, constables, and deputy sheriffs "worked" on him, the man's screams of pain could be heard clearly through the open window of the county jail, it is said.*
>
> *When the agonized cries finally died down to choking moans, the prisoner sobbed out, from bruised, battered lips, admission that he had shot Green Davis, 55, his wife, Eva [sic], 48, and their daughters, Elizabeth, 15, and Mary Lee, 13, in their lonely home at Taylorville, near Berlin…The accused man, it is said, was strapped to a chair, manacled and handcuffed from the time he was brought to the jail until he broke, and was given no food or water. Thirst added to the pain of the third degree methods, finally brought the confession.*
>
> *"I worked for Mr. Davis three weeks. I got a dollar a day—seven dollars a week, and my room and board. It rained last Thursday and nobody worked on the farm, but I wanted my dollar a day, and he wouldn't give it to me.*
>
> *"I asked him, Saturday, and he wouldn't give it to me. I was thinking about it and the devil got into me. I got up early Sunday morning before dawn, and walked from Ocean City, where my own home is, and went to the farm. I sneaked in through the back door. Everybody was asleep, but the little dog, Mike, and he knew me and didn't bark.*
>
> *"I got the double-barreled shotgun out of a closet and loaded it. I had my old colt, too. I always carry that. I went to the front bedroom where Davis and Mrs. Davis slept. I fired at them from the door. They never moved.*
>
> *"Then I went into the girls' bedroom in the back of the house. I was crazy then. I pointed the gun at them. I don't know if it went off. But they were still moving. I could see them in the dark under the white sheet. The little girl crawled down under the sheet and the other one leaned over her. I took out my colt then and fired at Miss Elizabeth's head. I fired another shot at Miss Mary Lee through the sheet. They were still moving so I hit them with the gun.*
>
> *"I wanted my dollar. I started out to get it. I found some of Mr. Davis' pocket money and some other money, and I put it in my pocket. I took the rings off Mrs. Davis' hand, and I took the rings off the girls' hands and a locket from Miss Elizabeth's neck. I took some silk clothes too.*
>
> *"I was going to burn down the house so nobody would know. I found some coal oil in the kitchen, and spread it upstairs and downstairs but Mike was barking so much I was afraid somebody might pass and hear him. So I went out and walked to my home."*

Although stated by the *Afro-American* to have been beaten out of the prisoner, the contents of the alleged confession by Jones reported in the paper were, in some part, accurate in describing the nature of the terrible crime. It was not disclosed by the newspaper who related the alleged confession, although it was presented as though Jones had been actually quoted. It was evident, however, that the "confession" contained true details of the events that could not have been known to an innocent black man who had simply been beaten by white officials in an effort to extort an admission to a crime in which he had no part.

[In July 2004, I received a bulky package from Janet Ades, the daughter of attorney Bernard Ades. Bearing a notation of NARA (National Archives Records Administration), the package revealed two remarkable documents: after a futile search of twenty-five years, I was now confronted by photocopies of two typewritten and signed confessions, one of which was the reported confession entitled as follows: "STATEMENT OF ORPHAN JONES MADE ON TUESDAY, OCTOBER 13TH AT TWO P.M. AT SNOW HILL, MARYLAND." The entire confession is reproduced in appendix 1.]

The questioning was conducted by State's Attorney Child, with some interjections by Lieutenant Itzel. The confession, typed, consists of some twenty-seven pages, each of which is initialed "OJ." At the conclusion of the statement is the scrawled signature, "Orphan Jones."

The first notation is as follows:

> Mr. Child: Jones we want you to tell us about the shooting of these four people on Saturday night or Sunday morning but we have nothing to promise you if you tell us and we have nothing to threaten you with if you don't tell us and if you make a statement I want it all to be the truth. Under these conditions are you willing to make a statement?
>
> A: Yes sir.
>
> Q: You are willing to tell us the truth regardless of the fact the what you might tell us might be used against you?

The confession then began in earnest:

> A: I am going to tell you the truth. I don't know what time it was, anyhow it was on Saturday night I went up to Davis' place—I had been drinking and I taken [*sic*] my handbag and my gun.
>
> Q: You mean your pistol?
>
> A: My gun too, and a lot of shells, a Winchester pump gun, and I shoots Mr. Davis and his wife and his children. I takes the cigar box of money. I had $30.00 of my own money and the rest of it belonged to him and the change was in the pouch. I takes these things down to where I stayed and I come back Sunday night and I feeds his stock and watered them and throwed corn out for the chickens the next morning. I left the door not fastened, just pulled it to. I have the key to the little store and I goes down there and packs up a lot of things in a basket I got out of the corn crib and I leaves it there—it is there now. Nobody was with me, I did it all myself. I am sorry. The man was good to me. The whiskey caused me to commit the worst crime ever

been in the history of the world.

Q: Why did you want to kill this man?

A: I don't know except it was mean whiskey and the devil in me. He never done nothing to me, he was a kind man.

Q: When did you first plan to do it?

A: Must have been Saturday because I came out there Saturday and done it Sunday morning just before day, just light enough to see them in their room.

Q: Do you remember throwing coal oil over the place?

A: No, sir. No lamp exploded up there did it? I did not leave no lamp burning, not that I can remember. I remember everything I done because after I did it I was awful sorry and was afraid too.

By Mr. Itzel:

Q: Jones, was any of the bed clothing afire anytime you were there?

A: Yes, sir from the gun. Must have been from the gun because I put out the fire.

Q: Was it a small blaze or a smother?

A: Just a smother in the cotton or wool.

Q: You did the shooting with the pump gun?

A: I shot that gun until it hung up with me.

Q: Who did you shoot with it?

A: I think Mr. Davis.

Q: Anyone else?

A: And his wife.

Q: What did you use when you shot the two girls?

A: I think I must have used my revolver because I did not have but two more bullets in it.

***

Q: Did you not have some difficulty with Mr. Davis about a dollar in your pay?

A: I will tell you how it was. When I went there he promised to give me $2.75 a day, that is, if I boarded myself and if he boarded me $1.75. I worked there I suppose about fourteen or fifteen days and he gave me some money every Saturday night, $8.50, but when he come to settle up I claimed he owed me $12.00 and he said it was only eleven days and he only owed me $11.00. I said, "You owe me $12.00." He said, "I don't think so." I did not say no more about it and when I was going down the road home I come to Mr. Lewis' place…He said, "Are you done work at Green's now?" I said, "No, he has got some more corn for me to cut in two weeks." I said, "I don't know, I guess I will get even with him and not cut the corn." Then I said, "He is a good old scout" and then I went on. On Thursday when I come back to bring some clothes to get them washed I meets Mr. Davis, he had been hauling sand and he said, "Hello, Orphan." He said, "How are you getting along?" I said, "all right." He said, "I want you to come up Thursday or Friday and start cutting corn." That was the last time I laid eyes on him until I shot him. I told him I would be up. How come me to shoot him I cannot say only the devil got in me.

Q: After you shot Mr. & Mrs. Davis, did that awaken the two girls?

A: They were lying down when I shot in there just like their mother and father. I was looking for them to be up.

***

Q: Did you touch any of the bodies after you killed them?

A: No, sir.

Q: Are you sure about that?

A: Yes, sir. I don't remember touching no bodies.

Q: Try to think back now, if you did?

A: When I put out that fire.

Q: Do you remember any clothing lying around there?

A: No, sir.

Q: How old are you?

A: I was born in 1872. Will be 60 years old my next birthday.

Q: Do you recall anything about the coal oil?

A: No, sir. He asked me about that.

Q: Can you account for all the bed clothing lying on the floor?

A: They were searching them.

Q: Can you account for all the clothing, bed clothing and other clothes lying on the floor being saturated with coal oil?

A: No, sir.

***

Q: Was the front door unlocked?

A: Yes, sir.

Q: Did you ever go through that door?

A: He never locked that door day and night.

Q: You went in there and immediately went upstairs?

A: Yes, sir.

Q: Did you drink anything in Davis' home while you were searching?

A: Yes, sir.

Q: What did you drink?

A: Got out some wine. She had given me some before, it was in a closet.

***

Q: Do you assume this entire responsibility?

A: Yes, sir.

Q: Are you alone responsible for this crime?

A: Nobody else but me.

Q: If you are not, we want you to tell us.

A: I would not tell a lie. Nobody responsible but me alone.

Q: Did you use any other instrument, did you use an ax or a hatchet in addition to shooting them?

A: No, sir. The gun was fully loaded. I don't know how many times I shot and I loaded

22

it again. She hung up on me and I took the revolver and the gentleman said the balls out of the gun was in them people.

***

Q: Jones, one of the girls, Elizabeth is the youngest girl?

A: Oldest.

Q: And she was lying on the right side of the bed, the side nearest the door?

A: I don't know which side she was laying on, I did not see.

Q: She had a pair of bloomers on and one leg was out entirely and the other leg in the bloomers, did you do that?

A: No, sir.

Q: Did you take her bloomers partly off?

A: No, sir did not touch none of them, only when that fire was there and I put the fire out.

Q: And none of the four saw you in the room at all?

A: I don't think so.

Q: There was no outcry?

A: No, sir nobody said nothing.

Q: What was your sole purpose in this case?

A: When I heard him snoring the devil jumped in me and said go rob them and shoot them and I did.

So, the horrid tale was told. Even though the confession surely had been coerced, the chilling and accurate details so dispassionately related by Jones certainly proved the involvement of the arrested man.

Just as surely as it was that Jones had been hit, it was also apparent from photos of the prisoner taken the next night that the Worcester County jail had not been a bloody torture chamber that night, as portrayed by the *Afro-American*. The photo of Jones taken by the Baltimore *Sunpapers* at the jail the next night shows only a bandage over his eye; a wound that fit the description of the beating administered on the way to Snow Hill. Nevertheless, he was certainly abused by the Worcester law enforcement officials, in a manner that today would result in recrimination, if not actual criminal charges being brought in response to such action.

On Tuesday morning, back at the crime scene, fingerprints were taken by Sergeant Flynn and autopsies were performed on the victims by Dr. F.S. Waesche of Snow Hill, and Dr. Charles A. Holland of Berlin. It was, for Dr. Holland, a particularly difficult task by virtue of the fact that he was the family doctor for the Green Davis family. Indeed, his daughter Virginia (now Virginia Nicoll) taught both the girls at Buckingham High School. Virginia remembers fondly that Elizabeth's handwriting was so beautiful that she would have Elizabeth put the class assignments on the blackboard.

By this time news had traveled throughout the state. The next report of the crime appeared in the *Baltimore Sun* on October 13. The article gave a vivid report of the events:

Snow Hill, Oct. 13—Activity around the Snow Hill jail, where Orphan Jones is held prisoner, gave rise this afternoon to reports that the Negro had made a statement concerning the murders at Taylorville.

A public stenographer was called to the jail at the time that the officials who have been questioning Jones halted and ordered a meal for the man who had been without food all day.

Thirteen State troopers and a county Sheriff and his deputies today patrolled the walls of the Worcester County Jail at Snow Hill, where Orphan Jones, an itinerant colored farm hand, 60 years old, was locked up accused of murdering a truck farmer, his wife and two young daughters.

Crowds of two to three hundred people gathered from time to time during the day in the vicinity of the Court House where the Worcester county grand jury was about to conclude its October term. The jury remained sitting and prompt action was anticipated pending the verdict of four coroner's juries now conducting inquests.

The bodies of the farmer—Green Davis—and his family, hacked to pieces with an ax, were found late yesterday after noon in their home at Taylorville, a village midway between Berlin and Ocean City. Apparently they were murdered in their sleep, and oil soaked floors, littered with burned matches and scraps of burned rags, indicated that an effort had been made to burn the house.

During the forenoon the four coroner's juries were empaneled at the Davis home. Hundreds of persons milled around the farm buildings.

[At this point in the tale it must be noted that the primary source of information nearly seventy years after the event must necessarily be newspaper reports. In examining the reports of the papers published on the lower shore, and comparing those with the articles reporting the identical incident in the Baltimore papers, one is vividly struck with the phenomenon of editorial license. The local press reported the events with a careful eye on its readers' sensibilities. The metropolitan press was freer with its observations regarding the potential for violence, which, it is apparent, seethed just below the surface. Throughout this book an effort will be made to give the reader the sense of opposition of points of view in the press.]

The report in the *Sunpapers* paints a clear picture of the pervasive restlessness that the horrible event generated among the citizenry, indeed from the inception of realization of what terrible thing had occurred:

Arrested last night at Ocean City, Jones was brought to Berlin and was questioned by county authorities before Magistrate William J. Bratten. He denied that he had anything to do with the murders. Meanwhile a crowd gathered in the street in front of the magistrate's office, where three State policemen and as many deputy sheriffs stood guard.

Another crowd gathered at the Davis home, a two-story weatherboard farmhouse about two and a half miles out the concrete road that leads from Berlin to Ocean City. Bonfires which the crowd kindled to keep warm leaped high in the darkness. But there was no disorder. More State police had been stationed here as a precaution.

News of the crime spread rapidly through the county. Long after the usual Eastern Shore bedtime, persons who had known the Davis family and scores of others who hadn't sped along the roads in their automobiles, some bound for Taylorville and some for Berlin.

Just before midnight the door of magistrate Bratten's office creaked open. The talk in the street stopped. The crowd leaned forward. Sheriff Wilmer S. Purnell stepped out and looked around.

"Folks, we don't want to have any trouble," the Sheriff said. "We don't want to give Worcester County a bad name."

The three State policemen and the Sheriff's deputies cleared a way to the Sheriff's automobile. The Sheriff went back to the magistrate's office and brought Jones out. They got into the automobile. The deputies crowded in with them. The State police got on their motor cycles, kicked down their starters and the prisoner and his guards were off for Snow Hill.

"Well," said a man in the crowd, "I reckon I'll go home and go to bed."

And the crowd broke up quickly.

So, Worcester County began the second day of a new and unfamiliar era. Suddenly and violently, a small, normally peaceful and virtually crime-free area had been transformed by the heinous murders into a fearful, suspicious and unsettled community. The comfortable feeling of trust had been suddenly snatched from the area and was replaced by fear of the stranger, guarded reticence regarding those who were different and, most of all, by a growing and increasing mood of revenge.

The community began to query: Why should the man who had done this deed be spared, even as Green Davis and his little family reposed in the local mortuary, having been violently murdered, mutilated and now awaiting only the cold grave?

There had been, it is true, in the late nineteenth century, mob violence in neighboring counties related to racial incidents, and lynchings had occurred in Somerset and Wicomico Counties in the 1800s. But other than the normally accepted racial segregation and the pervasive community attitude toward African Americans that they had to stay "in their place," Worcester County maintained a stoic and uneventful demeanor toward the racial makeup of the region.

Green Davis, however, had been one of the citizens who deserved better, in the minds of the community. He was a respected, honest and simple man, with a family consisting of females, who never harmed anyone and minded his own business. Therefore, if this horrible fate could befall the Davis family, it most certainly could happen to any of the citizens in the county. Thus, a seething resentment, a sullen loathing, a notion that the person who could do such a thing did not deserve to live, began to formulate itself in the thoughts of many of the people as the news of the event spread by word of mouth that autumn night.

During the early hours of the second day, this unsettled mood was evident to Sheriff Purnell and State's Attorney Child. Their concern increased due to their knowledge that the jail may be too vulnerable to a determined assault by men who intended harm to the prisoner. While the jail was solidly constructed and relatively secure, it was, after all, a combination jail and sheriff's office, not a prison. It was designed to keep prisoners in, not to keep a mob out. Moreover, there had been a steadily growing number of men milling about the courthouse lawn and the adjacent streets, and it was obvious that their mood was not that of passivity. The notion was growing among the law enforcement contingent that Jones should be taken elsewhere for his protection.

It was believed that Jones's absence from the scene would serve to reduce tensions in the entire area. Therefore at about 4:30 p.m. on the thirteenth, Jones was removed from Worcester County.

According to the report of the event in the *Sunpapers*, there was no demonstration at the scene against the defendant as he left the jail in the company of state police and Sheriff Purnell and several of his deputies. "The short, stocky Negro wore a fresh bandage over his left eye when he was slipped out of a side door of the jail and rushed between files of State patrolmen into the car that was to take him to Baltimore. He was handcuffed and wore dark trousers and a soiled work shirt. With him were Sheriff Wilmer S. Purnell, a State patrolman and Lieut. Joseph H. Itzel, of the Detective Bureau, Baltimore. Behind them in another car rode five State patrolmen as an additional escort."

The officers arrived in Baltimore about nine o'clock, and Jones was taken to the Detective Bureau, where he was photographed. Bertillon measurements and fingerprints were made and after about an hour of processing procedures he was delivered into the custody of Warden Harry C. Martin at the city jail.

III.
Ades Emerges

Back in Worcester County, procedures that today seem arcane were taking place. At the scene of the crime, right on the Davis property, a coroner's jury was being selected. The "coroner's jury" was a group of citizens chosen to make a preliminary determination of the cause of death in such cases where the death was either unexplained or violent, and clearly not from natural causes. According to the *Sun*:

> Outside the house, a crowd of farmers, farmers' wives and farmers' children had waited all night beside bonfires to keep them warm. By noon yesterday a hundred parked cars clogged the sandy road up to the farmhouse and the spectators numbered between 300 and 400.
>
> There was a great pushing and stirring to get within the State's Attorney and Sheriff's line of vision when selection of the coroner's juries was begun. As fast as the forty-eight were selected to view the bodies, they took their places at the entrance of a small barn and there up-ended peach baskets as seats.
>
> Some thirty had been picked when officials first took notice of a divergence in the trickle toward the barn entrance. They found their jurors stopping en route at a corncrib to enter and emerge gnawing russet apples with which their pockets had been stuffed. A State patrolman was stationed at the crib to halt this foraging.

Meanwhile Orphan Jones reposed in a basement cell of the Baltimore city jail reserved for "court prisoners." According to Warden Harry C. Martin, he slept soundly the first night in the lockup, had no visitors and had requested to see no one.

Whether Jones wanted to see anyone or not, he was soon to receive a visitor who would shape the events to come in a way not imagined by any of the Worcester County officials who were busy that night determining the process from this point forward. It was widely assumed on the local level that this trial would proceed in the normal fashion on the lower shore—indictment by a grand jury, arraignment, appointment of counsel by the court and a trial that would proceed in a matter of days. The docket of the Worcester County circuit court was not one that boded well for those accused of committing crimes in the community. It was rather typical of a rural court's workload—several mundane matters that could easily be shoved aside in order to accommodate a high-profile case such as the murder of four family members by a black outsider.

It was at this time, however, that a man entered the scene who would shatter all the notions that this case would fit the profile: into the Baltimore jail strode Bernard Ades.

Although Jones was to be assigned counsel in the person of a respected member of the Worcester bar, Franklin Upshur, Bernard Ades was a man on a mission. A member of the International Labor Defense, Ades was at the time twenty-eight years old. He had been educated at Johns Hopkins University and had studied law at the University of Maryland School of Law in Baltimore. He had become a member of the bar seven years before, in 1924. Although his reputation in trying civil cases was good, he had never before tried a criminal case.

Ades was tall, with dark hair and a moustache and, from available photos of the time, was rather handsome in appearance. His personality, however, has been variously described as "obnoxious," "overbearing" and "abrasive," and he would certainly become considered by the Eastern Shore populace as a troublemaker.

Ades was a member of the Communist Party and truly believed that in the courts of the United States it was difficult to achieve justice for members of minority races because, he thought, judges and other officials were usually chosen from the "ruling or favored" classes. (This was a thought that was not an aberration in the Depression era, even though it is evident that many of the people of which Ades thought ill had been elected by the majority of the people they represented.) In a federal court case involving Ades the court remarked that the International Labor Defense, "while not formally affiliated with the Communist party, is officered by Communists and within its scope, has like purposes and beliefs. It interests itself in cases in the courts which involve classes of persons whom it regards as victims of oppression or prejudice, and frequently offers its assistance when such persons are charged with crime."

Ades first went to the jail to attempt contact with Jones on October 13 or 14, but was refused permission to see the prisoner. He was first told that the defendant was receiving medical treatment, but finally the jailers admitted that their refusal came upon the instruction of the Worcester County authorities that Jones could not be interviewed by Ades without the consent of State's Attorney Child. Child was, of course, aware that Franklin Upshur, although becoming more reluctant as time passed, was to be appointed to represent Jones. There was, in Child's notion, no need for some radical outsider to impose himself into the matter. Also, there was the natural aversion of the conservative Child to the whole idea of solicitation by an attorney when no one had indicated that he had any right or claim to intervene. Therefore the State's Attorney promptly advised the jailers not to allow Ades to interview the prisoner. Jones was arraigned before the court, and at that time Upshur made his formal entrance of appearance, agreeing to defend the accused at trial.

Ades, however, was not to be dissuaded from his mission to conduct Jones's defense. For whatever motive ascribed to him, he was determined to give this lonely defendant the best defense that could be had. It is evident in retrospect that Ades did have the best interests of Jones in mind when he persisted in seeing him. Although the International Labor Defense certainly had its agenda in interceding in Jones's case, Ades was to prove an extremely adroit defense attorney who would, in fact, give the man a defense that would not otherwise have been provided had the local bar been responsible for the defense. In the first place, it became evident that none of the local attorneys were anxious to press the issue of removal from the lower shore area.

Under criminal law procedure in a capital case (one in which the defendant faces the death penalty) the defendant is entitled to have his trial "removed" to a jurisdiction other than the county in which the crime occurred, so as to do away with any vestige of prejudice brought on by the close proximity of the trial to the location of the crime.

The local lawyers seemed content to have the trial conducted within the First Judicial Circuit of Maryland, which consisted of Worcester, Wicomico, Somerset and Dorchester Counties. They did not see, or would not acknowledge, that the passions of the event created an atmosphere which would have surely made the empaneling of a fair, dispassionate jury a practical impossibility.

At the time, however, Ades had his work cut out for him just to gain access to the prisoner whom he sought to represent. He was determined that the defense of this man was not going to be denied him, so he began to devise a means of seeing Jones, with or without the permission of the authorities from Worcester County.

Back on the Eastern Shore, however, a solemn and sad event was at hand: the funerals of the family. Green Davis had his family roots at Whaleyville, where his elderly mother and father still lived, and it was to this tiny village four miles west of Berlin that the community now directed its focus. The grim task of burying an entire family of murder victims at one time was something no one in the area had ever experienced.

Following the autopsies, the bodies had been turned over to Mr. Davis's father, William Green Davis, and his sisters, for burial. According to an account published in the *Sun* on October 15,

> *More than a thousand automobiles followed the four hearses this afternoon which carried the bodies of the four murder victims, Green Davis, his wife, Ivy Smith Davis, and their two children, Elizabeth and Mary Lee.*
>
> *Relatives and close friends were allowed to view the bodies as they lay at an undertaking establishment in Frankford* [Delaware] *early this afternoon. At three o'clock they were taken to the Buckingham Presbyterian Church here* [in Berlin] *where services were conducted by the Rev. Dr. J. Russell Verbrycke, pastor of the church.*
>
> *Thousands of persons lined the streets as early as noon today to get a glimpse of the funeral cortege. Threats of violence were heard on all sides as to what should be done with the sixty year old Negro accused of perpetrating the outrage.*

Buckingham Presbyterian Church was then, as now, located on South Main Street in Berlin. At the service, over two hundred girls and boys of Buckingham High School at Berlin, classmates and friends of Elizabeth and Mary Lee, were in attendance, school having been suspended for the day. Boy classmates of the girls acted as pallbearers. Honorary (female) pallbearers for Elizabeth were: Florence Coffin, Cormediah Fleetwood, Etta Lynch, Esther Cooper, Elizabeth Dennis and Grace Thomas. Acting pallbearers were Crawford Holland, Howard Jarman, Roland Trader, James Wooten, Franklin Smack and Elisha Esham. Honorary pallbearers for Mary Lee were Elinor Boston, Marcenia Downing, Dorothy Davis, Marie Valentine, June Purnell, Marion Coffin, Eleanor Adkins and Mary Louise Taylor. Mary Lee's active pallbearers were Percy Holland, Donald Marshall, Carroll Beauchamp, Mitchell Parker Jr., Frank Dodson, Lloyd Godfrey, Robins Gilliss and William Hudson.

The *Sunpapers* erroneously reported that the funerals of Mr. Davis and Ivy were held at Whaleyville at the Davis home. According to the *Sunpapers*, hundreds of farmers and their families gathered at Whaleyville for the services. Automobiles blocked the roads around the home and it was necessary for the authorities to direct traffic in order to get the funeral procession started.

In fact, all four funerals were held in the Presbyterian church on South Main Street. As reported by the *Berlin-Ocean City News*:

> *A throng of persons, estimated at over 2,000 attended the funeral services held on Thursday afternoon at Buckingham Presbyterian Church, Berlin, for the four members of the Davis family, who were slain. The edifice was packed and the streets outside were crowded with those unable to enter the church. Excitement prevailed during the service when Mrs. Ruth Timmons, wife of Harry Timmons of Whaleyville, fainted and had to be rushed from the church to a physician for treatment.*

The sad funeral processions wended their way toward the Odd Fellows Cemetery off Morris Road in Bishopville, in the north edge of the county, seven miles from Berlin. The cemetery is nestled in a small cleared area just adjacent to the small village, and even today the "Davis" headstone with four stones starkly etched with the individual names and the single date of death smites the senses of the visitor.

The funerals were, on that Thursday, sad spectacles that again raised already strained emotions to the limit. The citizens of the area were assaulted by the vision of four coffins being lowered into the ground that early autumn day, and the farmers and their families slowly made their sad way home after the interment of the murdered family was finished.

IV

The Legal Maneuvering Begins

Legal events may have paused during the funeral services for the victims, but they did not wait long. Ades, anxious to receive status in the case, soon decided upon his plan: he issued a press release to the *Sun* in which he stated that Warden Harry C. Martin and other jail officials had advised him that they were unable to allow him access to the prisoner because he must obtain permission from the Worcester County authorities. Ades stated for the record that Sheriff Wilmer Purnell and State's Attorney Godfrey Child had refused to even consider the application of attorneys from the ILD, and on Saturday, October 17, he applied to Judge Eli Frank of the Baltimore City Court for a writ of habeas corpus (literally, "bring forth the body") to bring Jones forth for him to interview. Judge Frank, apparently under the impression that Ades had entered his appearance and was being denied access to his client, issued the writ and set a hearing for Monday, October 19, in Part 1 of the Baltimore City Court at one o'clock.

In the meantime, however, matters were proceeding apace in Worcester County. An arraignment was scheduled and the grand jury was expected to indict Jones on Monday, the same day of the hearing on Judge Frank's writ. Several judicial entities were beginning to get into the act. It was apparent that something had to give. With an arraignment on the same day as the hearing on the writ of habeas corpus, the judges on the shore and Judge Frank conferred, certainly by telephone, in order to work out the conflict. It was agreed that Jones would appear in the circuit court for Worcester County, and that Ades, if he wished, could journey to Snow Hill to await events there.

Also, at this juncture of the case, the Baltimore *Afro-American* newspaper reported an interesting event taking place in the town of Berlin. It reported that, although the mayor of Berlin had stated that there had been no disturbances in the town as had been reported in an Associated Press dispatch, twenty-five "white businessmen" of the town had filed a petition with the mayor and council. The petition protested against the actions of some whites who delegated to themselves the privilege "of driving colored people from the streets." The petition read:

> We, the undersigned, representatives of businesses in Berlin, Md., do most vigorously protest the banishment of the colored race from the streets of Berlin, as occurred on Saturday evening, October 17, 1931. Acts of this nature have occurred many times in the past and we urge that means be employed to prevent a repetition.
>
> The Constitution of the United States makes no distinction in color among its citizens and it grants each and everyone the protection to which he is justly due. Through fear of being molested, the colored

race refrained from entering the business section of Berlin on the aforesaid date: consequently many of them were deprived of food for Sunday. The large majority of our colored population is of a peace-loving nature, respecters of the law, and there should be no reflection on this class for the wrongdoing of a very small minority.

The fair name of Berlin is being smirched, an injustice is rendered law-abiding citizens and the business interests of Berlin suffer if this protection is not afforded. If the Mayor and Council of Berlin find themselves unable to cope with this situation we implore them to invoke the aid of the county and state authorities.

The petition was, indeed, signed by many of the business leaders of the town: Paul M. Rhodes; Burbage, Powell & Co.; American Stores Co.; V.R. Strickland; Joseph Hollins; J.A. Boston; William L. Farlow; E.H. Benson; Paul T. Jarman; John F. Rayne; C&P Hardware Co.; The Woman's Shop; Berlin Hardware Co.; J.M. Bratten; Victor H. Boston; George L. Mitchell; A& P Tea Co.; J.E. Esham; Garfield Johnson; The Purnell Co.; I. Villani; Willette Hat Shop; Pruitt & Timmons, M.T. & C.H. Quigley and Rydia Burbage. If one were to take a census of business and community leaders of Berlin in 1931, the list of signers of the petition would be virtually 100 percent of those people.

The event that had precipitated the unified and commendable petition was reported in the October 23 edition of the *Berlin-Ocean City News*:

Three Negroes were hurt in a street disturbance, perpetrated against members of the colored race by a mob of whites, on the streets of Berlin Saturday night [October 17]. Officers say the outbreak against the Negroes was in reprisal partly over the brutal slaying of four members of the Green K. Davis family in Taylorville by a Negro.

Purnell Leonard, 30, and his wife Mattie Leonard, 28, Negroes of Berlin were attacked by a mob of whites on Gay Street when the racial disturbance began. The husband was severely beaten and both were rescued by officers and later returned to their home.

The disturbance raged for nearly two hours on the streets of Berlin, as mobs of whites thronged street corners on the lookout for members of the colored race.

Buck Mumford, Negro of Berlin, was accosted on William Street by a mob of whites and knocked down. His assailants escaped.

Earl Douglas, another Negro who lives south of Showell, drove into Berlin with a companion during the height of the disorder for a physician. His wife was ill. On Bay Street, near the residence of Dr. Charles A. Holland, the Douglas Negro was attacked by a mob of white youths, one of whom struck him with a brick. Officers rushed to his rescue.

Two aged Negroes sought refuge in a Berlin store from the mob. They were safely escorted away later by officers. One Negro youth who attended the show at the Globe Theater was rushed to his home in an automobile with official protection.

The disturbance was finally quelled by officers and the mob was dispersed after several arrests were made. During the disorder several Berlin residents were sworn in as special deputies.

Thirteen white youths have been cited for hearings before Magistrate William J. Bratten at Berlin, as a result of the disorder. Four were tried Monday and fined $1 and costs. In addition eight other youths are being sought in connection with the outbreak.

Those cited for hearings are: Reese Bradford, Joseph Kelly, Wilson Wilkins, Ernest Williams, Noble Morris, George Aydelotte, Ben Parsons, Henry Truitt, Bert Truitt, Alvin Powell, Vernon Nichols, Fred Hudson, Leon Powell.

Bradford, Kelly, Wilkins and Aydelotte have been tried and fined $1 and costs.

Business in Berlin stores was paralyzed Saturday night as a result of the mob disturbance and by eleven o'clock, P.M. the streets were practically deserted by both whites and Negroes.

With one exception all of the white youths apprehended as members of the mob, are residents of Taylorville and Sinepuxent rural districts.

Meanwhile, on the legal front, another bizarre twist entered the case. Lieutenant Joseph E. Itzel, the original Baltimore investigator, had returned to the Baltimore jail on the evening of October 15 to acquire Jones's signature on the Snow Hill confession, which had now been carefully typed, and to further interrogate the suspect, when he was told a jarring fact: "Orphan Jones" was an alias for the real name of the accused, which was, in fact, Euel Lee.

This second confession also surfaced in the package of documents recorded in the National Archives, and, just as was the initial statement, is a compelling document (see appendix 2). It also brings to light a new and intriguing facet regarding the motive for the killings. The statement was made in the presence of Captain E. McKim Johnson of the Maryland State Police, Warden Harry Martin of the Baltimore city jail, state police corporal M.D. Brubaker, Detective Sergeant William J. Flynn and Joseph Itzel.

Lee related to Itzel that he had been raised in Virginia by a white family. He also advised that, prior to traveling to the Eastern Shore, he had, for a time, been employed as a waiter in an inn at Fullerton, in Baltimore County. Itzel also related that authorities in Detroit had requested Lee's fingerprints in order to determine whether he could be implicated in a murder of a father, mother and their four children in that city two years ago, said to have been committed by a Negro who was never caught. (Nothing ever came from this submission, however.)

The statement is interesting as it brings forth a new and totally unreported (in the press) allegation from the accused. Itzel conducted the questioning:

Q: Jones, you made a statement at Snow Hill, Md. several days ago, both in the form of a confession and a statement. Do you recall that?

A: I do.

Q: Can you read?

A: Yes sir, but not without glasses.

Q: Well, we can save time, I will read it to you and will you follow me carefully?

A: Yes sir.

[*Statement read by Lieut. Itzel.*]

Q: Are these correct?

A: Yes, sir.

Q: No mistakes?

A: No, sir.

Q: Jones, I'm going to ask you if you will sign this statement?

A: Will I sign it? Sure I'll sign it, I was the one that made it. But I never told what caused the whole trouble and what led up to the whole business, I have never said that.

Itzel interrupted him at this point and once again warned him of his rights. The statement then continued.

> Q: What did cause all the trouble?
> A: When I first went there I gave him my money and my gun to keep for me and he said he lost it in the Ocean City Bank, but I knew he didn't lose it, he wanted to beat me out of it.

[In the Depression, banks oftentimes failed due to the loss of faith in the depositors of an institution, causing a "run" on the bank in order to retrieve one's money—in many instances the banks simply didn't have enough cash on hand to satisfy the large demand of ready money demanded by so many customers, so they simply closed their doors. This crisis lasted into the first administration of Franklin D. Roosevelt.]

> Q: How much money did you give to him?
> A: Davis had $250.00. When I went to work for him I had $268.00 and I kept the $18.00 in my pocket and gave him the $250.00.
> Q: Are you sure that was the amount of money you gave him? When did you give it to him to keep?
> A: When I first went there in September, I gave him my revolver and my money to keep. I make my money and I don't want to get done out of it. I always gets work when I am out of money. He told me he lost the money in the bank, he was going to rob me of it.
> Q: According to that, you really had that on your mind when you left Ocean City?
> A: Yes, sir. To collect the money or I was going to fight him.
>
> ***
>
> Q: When did you ask for the money the first time?
> A: On Saturday, October 3rd, he said he would have it for me, so on Monday [October 5] he told me he had lost it in the Ocean City Bank, and I said "What's the use of telling me that, the bank has been busted over a week, and I didn't give you the money to put in the bank, I could have put it in the bank," and it came to me he was trying to beat me out of it.
> Q: Then, when did you go back to him?
> A: I didn't leave. Monday he said he had corn to cut, I didn't know he had another field to cut so I worked Monday, and Tuesday I asked for the money and he just gave me the money I had been working for, he made me sore, he didn't lose my money in the bank, he didn't put it in any bank.

During the course of the statement, Jones repeated the assertion of the loss of his money not less than five more times. It was evident that it was an allegation that he was sticking to, and that it was, according to him, the reason that triggered the crime.

Before too long, Itzel returned to troubling details related to Mary Lee, the younger daughter, which had been referred to in the earlier statement in Snow Hill:

Q: The autopsy shows very distinctly and clear that the younger girl had a fracture of the skull right in front, and shows as if she had been struck by some blunt instrument. Did you hit her with the butt of the gun?

A: No, indeed, I never hit any of them with nothing.

Q: Are you sure of that?

A: Certainly I am sure.

Q: What do you suppose caused the injury?

A: I don't know, I didn't hit her with anything.

Q: She was struck with some blunt instrument.

A: Could it have been a glancing shot?

Q: No, the skin wasn't broken, but the bone was broken in the skull.

A: Maybe the doctor was wrong.

Several pages later, after questioning about timing and other details, the subject again returned to Mary Lee:

Q: Orphan, can you recall if you hit the girl over the head?

A: I can't recall hitting anybody.

Q: If you did hit her you would know it, and you had the presence of mind to know it?

A: I think I would, I don't think I did. Who was the doctor who said that?

Another troubling detail was the presence of coal oil all through the house:

Q: How do you account for the oil being all over the place?

A: I think I must have used the bucket with oil in it and pumped water on top of it.

Q: There were a pair of bloomers lying on the bed, pair of lady's bloomers, lying under the feet of Mrs. Davis, I think they were pink, they were under the comfort or blanket and this blanket or comfort had oil on it from the bloomers and the bloomers were entirely saturated with oil. How do you account for that?

A: I don't know, unless somebody else done it.

Q: Let us assume you took the bucket to put the fire out—the fire on the girls' bed, how do you account for the room being so thoroughly saturated with oil?

A: Search me.

Q: That oil didn't come through the ceiling, there are no marks on the ceiling and the floor down stairs was full of oil.

A: Who found the people?

Q: Some neighbors.

A: Don't you know who the neighbors was, they may have been the ones who put the oil around.

With this simple assertion, Jones had, perhaps inadvertently, given himself a loophole that would be later exploited in his case to a huge degree. Itzel, however, was having none of it.

> Q: Those people got out as quick as they could, they were friends of the Davises, who they were, I don't know, they were neighbors and they had missed the Davis family because they had not opened the store.

Sergeant Flynn then returned to the troubling aspects of the circumstances surrounding the body of the younger sister, Mary Lee:

> Q: This little girl was lying in the bed, and she had a pair of pink bloomers on, her left leg was out of the bloomers and the right leg was in the bloomers and her under gown was up above the navel.
>
> A: I don't know anything about that—I didn't put my hands on anything at all.
>
> Q: The left breast of the girl on the right side near the window, her breast was exposed and the night gown was torn completely away from the breast.
>
> A: I thought you said they were shot through the breast?

Lieutenant Itzel picked up the response:

> Q: Both of the girls were shot directly through the left breast, the older's night gown had a hole just big enough for the shot to go through, but the younger one had her entire breast exposed and the night gown torn away.

Jones was not admitting to anything provocative regarding the lifeless bodies of the family:

> A: It might have been done before, did you look to see if it was a new rent?

Itzel then changed course and explored a new avenue: Jones's admitted intoxication, which had come to light in Snow Hill.

> Q: How much wine did you drink after shooting those people?
>
> A: I didn't drink but very little, I went up stairs to get it.
>
> Q: Did you drink the wine in the same room where the shooting took place?
>
> A: I went downstairs and drank the wine, mixed it with some water.
>
> ***
>
> Q: Did you have anything against these girls?
>
> A: They had too much coon and nigger in their mouths, and they were told by their father they were going to keep my money and say I attacked them.
>
> Q: Did you kill them because they called you nigger, did you kill them for that?
>
> A: No, they were just as nice as could be.

Eventually, Itzel got to a point that, from reading the confession transcript, was obvious he must have known all along. Without any segue, and out of the blue, the questioner changed the subject:

Q: What is your correct name?

A: Orphan Jones.

Q: Were you ever baptized?

A: I must have been baptized when I was a baby.

Q: Nobody baptized you "Orphan."

A: That is my name, the people who raised me called me that.

Itzel was not to be dissuaded:

Q: What is your right name?

Then, as suddenly as the question had come, came the answer:

A: Euel Lee.

Q: What was your father's name?

A: Joe.

Q: Mother's name?

A: Jane.

Q: And, you were born in Virginia?

A: In Lynchburg.

Q: How long have you been using the name of Jones?

A: Ever since I can remember.

Q: Your foster parents' name was Jones, that is why you took it?

A: Yes, they were white people.

Q: Do you consider the white people your foster parents?

A: Yes, sir.

Finally, Sergeant Flynn added a jarring note to the interrogation:

Q: You know they were buried today, all of them, and they couldn't find any clothing for them?

A: God knows they had enough clothing, somebody got the clothing, the girls had all kinds of clothing hanging up there.

Itzel was winding down:

Q: Orphan, we are about to close this statement. Have you anything else to tell us?

A: I understand everything, please don't ask me any more questions, I am satisfied.

The questioning ended at 12:30 a.m. on Friday, October 16, 1931. A series of new insights into the case had come to light. The results of the new revelations would be turned over to State's Attorney Child to use as he saw fit in Snow Hill soon.

Thus, the stage was set for the first confrontation in the case: the attorneys, the public and the accused killer would all meet at Snow Hill on Monday.

Monday, October 19, dawned clear and a bit cold as the normally sleepy town of Snow Hill awoke for a momentous event. It was apparent at once that this day would be like no other in recent memory. As the sun rose over the woods east of town, cars, trucks and farm wagons began to enter the little county seat. License tags indicated that these were not the normal travelers into the small business district. There were visible in the slowly growing stream of traffic, tags from the Eastern Shore of Virginia, the state of Delaware and surrounding Maryland counties. It was still early in the day when the people in Snow Hill realized that there was to be a curious crowd who was intent upon viewing the day's events. It is not clear how word had spread, but it was very evident that the courthouse was to be the focal point of interest for more people than had been expected to show up in town. No one knew quite what to expect; it was rumored that Jones (Lee) was to be returned to the court for a formal hearing, and the more informed among the gathering people had become aware of the intrusion of a very different type of person: a Communist lawyer from Baltimore. This would not be a legal proceeding like what the townspeople had been used to, where a local court-appointed attorney would enter his appearance and everything would proceed under the judicial eye of the locally respected judges. No, this was somehow different—there was in the atmosphere a vaguely unsettling notion that this proceeding was not under the control of the county officials.

There was, therefore, the restless murmur of discontent: the "confessed killer" was possibly not going to be quickly dispatched with a speedily resolved trial after the clearly expected indictment by the grand jury, which was shortly to be convened in the jury room on the second floor of the courthouse. There was, instead, the possibility that the turn of events would be quite different—the result could be a delaying strategy on the part of the outside lawyer, if in fact, the judges would allow him to intervene.

Surely, the community thought, the local judges would be able to control such matters and relegate the interloper back to the city where he belonged. No big-city lawyer from a Communist organization would impose himself in this matter, which was solely of local concern; one which the local system could handle. Now that the accused killer was back on the shore, the local justice system would regain all of its influence and banish Ades from the scene.

In fact, State's Attorney Child was making every effort to do just that. Over the weekend Child had been busy, first succeeding in having Judge Frank, in consultation with Judges Joseph Bailey and Robert Duer, waive an immediate hearing on the Baltimore writ of habeas corpus; then arranging with the Baltimore jail warden to allow the transfer of Lee to Worcester County in the custody of Sheriff Purnell; and, finally, continuing to block Ades's efforts to see the prisoner.

At 11:34 a.m., a Western Union telegram was sent from Child in Pocomoke City to Mr. Ades at his office in the Baltimore Trust Building, Baltimore: "AFTER CONFERENCE WITH COURT HERE HAVE DECIDED NOT TO ALLOW ANY COUNSEL APPOINTED OR EMPLOYED BY INTERNATIONAL LABOR DEFENSE TO INTERVIEW EUEL LEE ALIAS ORPHAN JONES UNLESS DECIDED BY JUDGE FRANK. GODFREY CHILD." If Ades insisted on intruding, it would be on Child's turf in Snow Hill.

At about ten o'clock at night on Sunday, October 18, Lee was removed from the Baltimore jail by Sheriff Purnell and a Worcester deputy after arrangements for his transfer had been worked out in phone conferences between Child and Judge Frank. During these calls, Child informed the

Baltimore judge that, even though Lee had previously been removed from Snow Hill for his own safety, the threatened mob action would not materialize and that Lee could be returned to Snow Hill safely now. Judge Frank relented and waived his scheduled hearing on Monday afternoon, giving way to the pending Worcester County proceedings.

Consequently, the sheriff, his deputy and the prisoner left Baltimore quietly late that Sunday evening, proceeded to Annapolis, crossed the bay on the early morning ferry and motored unobtrusively down the shore toward the awaiting events in Snow Hill.

With all the clamoring that had gone on regarding the case, and with the threat of violence so prevalent, one may inquire as to the propriety of the action of the sheriff—why, indeed, would he, in the presence of only one deputy, undertake the journey with a hated and threatened black man who had already been effectively convicted in the court of public opinion in the sheriff's native county? In answer, one only has to place himself into the context of the time.

Wilmer Purnell Jr. was a native born Worcester County man; his father, Wilmer Purnell Sr., had gone south during the Civil War, as had a large number of Worcester County men, and had served honorably with the First Virginia Cavalry in Company K, consisting nearly completely of Maryland men. Wilmer Sr. had been captured by Union troops and imprisoned for a time at Ft. McHenry in Baltimore, a post that, ironically, his son Dr. Harry Purnell, the sheriff's brother, would command during World War I when it was a military hospital. Company K had been with J.E.B. Stuart at the site of his 1864 mortal wounding at Yellow Tavern, near Richmond, and after the war, Purnell's father had returned to receive the respect and accolades of the citizens of Berlin and the county. Wilmer Jr. had run for the influential office of sheriff and had been easily elected to the high office.

Together with the State's Attorney, the sheriff embodied the concept of law enforcement—a matter, in the early years of the new century, which was held in utmost respect by the citizens of rural Maryland. The sheriff of Worcester County presumed he had nothing to fear from its citizens. He felt he was in control of all matters of concern to his office and he would not be intimidated or dissuaded from the duty of his office. It was clear to Sheriff Purnell that the prisoner, no matter how hated, no matter how highly emotions ran against him, would be safe in Purnell's presence.

So it was that the sheriff, his lone deputy and Euel Lee, surely frightened, entered Snow Hill that Monday morning. There is no contemporary account of the sheriff's thoughts as he drove over the Pocomoke River bridge into town, but he must have been alarmed at the incredible number of cars and the crowds of people lining the courthouse green and the normally quiet streets of town that early morning. It is certain that he quickly drove to the jail and speedily took Lee into the relative safety of the lockup. It is also almost certain that he communicated with State's Attorney Child upon his arrival so as to receive any instructions on how to proceed to get Lee arraigned in the courtroom that morning with the proper protection and without any violence.

The modern town of Snow Hill is remarkably similar to the way it was seventy years ago. It is a small, compact town, more in the nature of a village, with the county government its only viable business. The courthouse, unlike those in many larger jurisdictions, still has the basic semblance of its 1930 configuration. It sits, now as then, within a compact green square, bounded on the front by Market Street, on the north by Washington Street and on its south by Franklin Street. The only edifice which is no longer there is the jail.

In 1931, the jail sat chockablock against the main building, right near the rear door of the courthouse. In fact, only a narrow walkway separated the two buildings. The trip from the cells to the courtroom was a matter of minutes in the stern company of a deputy sheriff.

The courtroom in which Lee was shortly to be arraigned on October 19, 1931, is still the same courtroom in which the circuit court for Worcester County holds court today. Although now one of three trial courtrooms, it is in essentially the same configuration as it was seventy years ago. As one enters the front door of the courthouse, there is a large, wide hall traversing the entire length of the courthouse. The clerk's office is directly on the right, and the Register of Wills is on the left. To the right, just past the entrance to the clerk's office, an unmistakable focal point is a large imposing staircase, which winds to the second floor. At the top of the stairs, one arrives at a foyer-like area, and then, through two double doors, one enters the courtroom. The ambience of the room is different now, after a major renovation in 1968; solid mahogany wall paneling and heavy burgundy carpet now give a muted, respectful tone to the room.

It is, however the very same room in which the events of this story unfolded. There was, in 1931, no resident judge from Worcester. The chairs that First Judicial Circuit Court Judges John Pattison (the chief judge, from Cambridge in Dorchester County), Joseph L. Bailey (from Salisbury, Wicomico County) and Robert F. Duer (from Princess Anne, in Somerset County) sat on, are still arranged behind the bench, though today, except for ceremonial functions, only one judge occupies the tall-backed chair; the other two remain empty. It is not hard to imagine, though, the imposing presence of three judges sitting at the bench; indeed, by their very presence, they surely impressed anyone in the courtroom with the solemnity of an occasion that necessitated the appearance of not one but three jurists. In front of the bench, prior to the renovation, there were two oak tables of imposing length, at which counsel sat. There were several captain's chairs lined up behind the tables, and to the left of the bench, as the judges faced, a dais where the clerk of court or staff member sat. In 1931, the clerk of court was Bessie Bowen, perhaps the first elected female official in Worcester County history. (Sue Collins, who preceded Miss Bowen, was the widow of Oliver D. Collins, the former clerk who died while in office, and therefore was unelected.).

In the left of the courtroom (to the right of the judges) was the jury box, and to its immediate rear, the jury room where deliberations took place. Behind the bench was an unobtrusive door that opened into the judges' chambers. The bar separated the lawyers' area from the public space where there were seats for about one hundred observers. The courtroom is sixty-five feet across and about fifty feet deep. It was then, and it is now, an imposing room.

It was in this room that Euel Lee, Godfrey Child and Bernard Ades first came together. Before they appeared, however, the room was packed with ordinary citizens who had come to view the proceedings, of which they had little if any understanding. They knew that the murderer was to be brought among them and they wanted to see what manner of man was this person who stood accused of the brutal killing of an entire family.

The grand jury for Worcester County had met early on this Monday in order to consider the request of the State's Attorney to indict Lee. The grand jury, as petit or trial juries, then consisted of white men only. Black men were not chosen for jury service, and women were not allowed to serve on juries in the state of Maryland until the Women's Jury Service legislation was passed in the late 1940s. It had been stated for years that women could not serve on juries because of the lack of ladies' restroom facilities in all of the courthouses of the Free State. (There was also concern among many men that allowing women would eventually lead to the removal of spittoons from all the courtrooms.)

In the tradition of the county, the names among the panel were, in most respects, well known to the citizens of the county, as many prominent men were chosen to serve. The grand jurors were: John W. Humphreys, (foreman), Clarence W. Dryden, Richard Leake, Joseph Hudson, Harry J. Cropper, James Kelly, Elmer A. Brittingham, Raymond Hancock, Clarence Brittingham, Pemberton Hickman, Barney F. Sturgis, Peter S. Truitt, James M. Bratten, Avery Palmer, Clarence W. Pilchard, Fred J. Dukes, Harry Davis, Francis S. Carey, James Savage, Monroe Howell, Marion W. Landing, Joseph A.J. Stanford and Horace Lynch.

There were only three witnesses presented to the panel: Robert J. Lewis of Berlin; Dr. F.S. Waesche, who had performed the autopsies; and Lieutenant Itzel. In a bare minimum of time, the grand jurors returned four identical indictments, in numbers 21, 22, 23 and 24 Presentments for the October Term, 1931:

> *The Grand Jurors of the State of Maryland, for the body of Worcester County, upon their oaths do present that Euel Lee, alias Orphan Jones, colored, late of the County and State aforesaid, on or about the eleventh day of October, in the year of our lord nineteen hundred and thirty-one, at the County and State aforesaid, feloniously, wilfully and of deliberately premeditated malice aforethought did kill and murder Green Davis, Ivy Smith Davis, Elizabeth Gertrude Davis and Mary Lee Davis; contrary to the form of the Act of Assembly in such case made and provided, and against the peace, government and dignity of the State.*

The documents were signed by Godfrey Child and John W. Humphreys, the foreman of the grand jury.

Immediately a capias (a writ requiring an officer of the law to take a defendant into custody) was issued to the sheriff, ordering him to bring Lee forth. In its formal legal language, the court ordered:

> *To the Sheriff of Worcester County, Greeting:*
> *You are hereby commanded to take Euel Lee, alias Orphan Jones, late of Worcester County, if he shall be found in your bailiwick, and him keep safe, so that you have his body before the Circuit Court for Worcester County immediately to answer unto the State of Maryland in a plea of and upon a certain presentment and indictment for Murder.*
> *Hereof fail not at your peril and have you then and there this writ.*
> *Issued the 19th day of October, AD 1931.*

The sheriff returned the writ marked simply, "Cepi" (meaning, "I have taken"). Thus the defendant was brought forth.

Nellie Gibbons, a lifelong resident of Snow Hill, and later an employee of the clerk's office, remembered the day. She was secretary in a nearby law office and she recalled that she was given time off to go over to the courthouse to see the accused killer. She recalled that the courthouse square was full of people and that there was standing room only in the second-floor courtroom. It is interesting that she recalled that the defendant was only a secondary presence to the attorneys, and that she had no lasting impression of him except that he was morosely silent. She was not to observe the real drama of the day, however; that event took place out of the public eye.

V.

Ades vs. Worcester County

Bernard Ades had, indeed, come to Snow Hill in order to interject himself into the case. No matter that State's Attorney Child had successfully thwarted his efforts to see Lee; Ades was determined to gain control of the case. There was one problem—the matter of the court-appointed attorney, Franklin Upshur. Mr. Upshur was in the court that day also. He was to formally enter his appearance at the arraignment, and the judges seemed in no mood to have him shunted aside by Ades. The judges did, however, on the bench in full view of the public, express their willingness to allow Lee to speak with Ades in order to determine whether he could become a part of the defense team (no reaction from Child is noted for history).

"There is present in Court," said Judge Bailey, "a representative of the International Defense League [*sic*], and attorney, Mr. Bernard Ades, who desires an interview with you and the Court is willing to grant this interview now."

Lee's reply was, "If he wants to talk with me, all right, but I don't see any use."

The court recessed in order for Ades, who was accompanied by Louis Berger, secretary of the ILD, to speak in private with the defendant. (One can speculate that they were given an area off the judges' chambers to the rear of the courtroom, out of the public areas, in order to confer.)

Ades was afforded the opportunity to speak with Lee by virtue of the telephone conference between Judge Joseph L. Bailey and Judge Frank over the weekend, in which Frank's habeas corpus hearing gave way to Bailey's arraignment, upon Judge Bailey's assurance that Lee would be given an opportunity to speak with the representative of the International Labor Defense. It is apparent that Judge Frank had advised Judge Bailey that the writ had been requested by the league only in order to allow their representative to ask whether Lee wished their representation.

It is not clear whether Mr. Upshur was present during the conference. What is evident from the newspaper reports is that Lee was ambivalent as to Ades representing him. In a later court determination as to Ades's propriety in the case, the court noted that Ades had never tried a criminal case, and in all likelihood, at the time of the Worcester County arraignment, Lee inquired as to Ades's qualifications; if Ades was honest, he surely stated his lack of experience. Lee must have considered carefully the request to place his fate in the hands of this inexperienced man, enthusiastic as he may be. He was surely also aware that he had another lawyer in the person of Franklin Upshur, and in his ability, the court had evidenced its approval.

After a period of over an hour, Lee and Ades reentered the courtroom. The court received the not-guilty pleas from the defendant in the presence of both Ades and Upshur as to the charges of murder, but did not make a determination with regard to the matter of representation or the exclusion of either attorney. The newspaper accounts reported at the arraignment that the judges appointed Mr. Upshur and Mr. Ades as co-counsel. The reports described Ades as "voluntary assistant counsel." This arrangement, however, was certainly not to Mr. Ades's liking and would, if he had his way, soon change. After the official proceedings, it was decided, prudently, that Lee would not remain in the jail but would be transported to another facility. The Dorchester jail in Cambridge, about fifty miles away, was decided upon. Lee was whisked out of town, even as the crowds still milled about the area of the courthouse. It was intended that Lee be housed in the Cambridge jail until Thursday, at which time the trial would commence in Snow Hill.

At the close of the hearing, State's Attorney Child was quoted by the *Berlin-Ocean City News*: "In my opinion the Labor Defense League is an organization of Communists, who have interested themselves in the Jones case, merely to secure publicity that may tend to promote the League through membership in Baltimore." He hinted at his notion that the intervention of the Communists would likely cause racial hatred in Worcester County and said that he very much regretted their intervention in the case at all.

Events would once again transpire, however, that would keep Lee from reaching the jail in Cambridge. There came a rumor that several cars filled with neighbors of the Davis family were passing through Salisbury, about halfway to Cambridge, intent upon seizing the prisoner. Chief Judge John R. Pattison of the First Judicial Circuit advised Lee's removal back to Baltimore and, under the cover of darkness and in the presence of several state policemen, Lee was transported by boat across the bay to Baltimore, arriving at the city jail at about 6:30 a.m. on Tuesday, October 20.

In Baltimore, the International Labor Defense was busy. Mr. Berger advised that Ades had gone to Snow Hill for the purpose of seeing that justice would be done, and was critical of State's Attorney Child who, Berger said, by emphasizing that a speedy trial was necessary, had indicated that Lee would be subjected to community prejudice.

In fact, Child was simply reacting as any politician would; he had a defendant in the most high-profile case in memory. The populace, the press and the facts of the case demanded quick closure of this sordid event. Indeed, in the county in this period of history, it was a common practice to indict, arraign and try a defendant within a matter of days. The scheduling of Lee's trial for Thursday, October 22, after an indictment dated Monday, October 19, was not at all out of the ordinary. It was the normal course of procedure and it was expected—particularly by virtue of the fact that the accused had confessed. What was there to prevent the quick resolution of this "open and shut" case? Certainly the Worcester Countians who were present at the preliminary hearing could not provide any negative answer. And just as certainly, Godfrey Child, elected by them to the highest law enforcement post in the county, was not going to allow any matter (or any lawyer) to interfere with their belief that he should—and could—get this murderer to trial quickly.

Meanwhile, Franklin Upshur was in a spot. He had to defend a man who was the most hated figure in the community within anyone's memory. He surely didn't want the job, but the judges had said he had to do it. Now, to make matters infinitely worse for Upshur, along came Ades, who was not going along with the notion of perhaps a fair, but certainly a swift and local, trial. Ades insisted that the community—Upshur's community—was incapable of rendering a fair verdict.

Maybe Ades didn't care about public opinion but Upshur sure enough did. As a lawyer whose livelihood depended upon good will and respect, he had to carefully consider how he handled himself in this case. A resident of Berlin, he had to face everyday the very same people who had lined the streets for the grim funerals, who had clamored to become members of the coroner's inquest and who daily received more information (both true and untrue—accurate and sensational) regarding the brutal crimes and the confession rendered by Upshur's client. It really put him in an untenable position: as an attorney, he had a professional obligation to defend his client to the best of his ability, but as a citizen of the area, he faced condemnation from his neighbors and friends who were outraged by the crime.

Then along comes a Communist lawyer from Baltimore, reminding Upshur of the rules of procedure in Maryland law—if a motion is filed in a criminal case with the capital penalty of death, the court is obligated to remove the case. And yet there was Godfrey Child publicly stating that the defendant could receive a fair trial in Franklin Upshur's community—how could Upshur respond? He would have to challenge his friend's assertion, and do so at the peril of offending community opinion.

It was apparent that Ades was going to hound the court for a removal from Worcester County, and surely Upshur saw the merit of this move. Therefore, after the appearance in court, he announced that, indeed, a motion for removal was being considered by the defense team. That motion would be made at the date of the trial.

Immediately after the proceedings, Ades left town and shortly thereafter journeyed to New York to confer with the officials of the Labor Defense League. While there, he telegraphed Mr. Upshur in Snow Hill, protesting against the trial, which he had been informed from a newspaper report was set for October 22. He also insisted upon a change of venue to the Western Shore of Maryland. Upshur replied to Ades that the trial had not yet been set, and that Ades could interview Lee at the Baltimore city jail. He then added the news that Ades was surely awaiting: with the consent of the court, he would withdraw from the case. It is reported that Upshur withdrew due to the pleading of his family and friends, and that citizens had made threats against him if he remained as counsel for Lee. Mr. Upshur later denied the threats, but not the pleas.

In any event, he shortly withdrew, and on October 28 the court appointed F. Leonard Wailes, a member of the Wicomico County bar and a resident of Salisbury. The *Sunpapers* of that date reported that the court's efforts to obtain counsel from Worcester County were unsuccessful and "the jurists were obligated to turn to the adjoining county to find someone to defend [Lee] by appointment." Mr. Wailes was considered one of the leading lawyers in the state. He had practiced for more than thirty years, and had been elected president of the Maryland Bar Association. He promptly went to the jail in Baltimore to interview Lee. It was apparent that Wailes did not then know of Ades's involvement in the case.

Meanwhile, on October 30, there was filed in the circuit court the following: "I, Orphan Jones, hereby retain Bernard Ades as my sole attorney to defend me in the above action, to investigate the case, to appeal it and to do any and all things which he may consider necessary to my defense. I do not desire any other attorney." It was signed by Lee in the name of "Orphan Jones," and was witnessed by one Harry C. Martin, the warden of the city jail.

VI

Not on the Eastern Shore

It appeared that at long last Ades was in control of the defense. However, it was also apparent that he at least recognized that his inexperience at the bar might be aided by the presence of a lawyer of Wailes's ability. Accordingly, he wrote a letter to Wailes, a copy of which is extant. It is truly remarkable when one realizes that it was authored by an inexperienced young lawyer to the former president of the Maryland Bar Association, who had extensive trial experience. Dated October 29, 1931, it reads, in part:

> *Dear Mr. Wailes,*
>
> *I note from the local newspapers that Associate Judges Robert F. Duer and Joseph L Bailey have appointed you as defense counsel in the matter of the* State of Maryland vs. Orphan Jones.
>
> *After Jones was indicted and when he was about to be arraigned Judge Bailey asked whether he had counsel and he replied that he did and designated me as his counsel. Judge Bailey then undertook to appoint Mr. Franklin Upshur as Jones' counsel announcing that I would be Jones' counsel as a volunteer and that Mr. Upshur would be his counsel as the Court's appointee. I do not consider myself as a mere volunteer in the case but as Jones' chief counsel. Nevertheless, I raised no objection to the appointment of Mr. Upshur.*
>
> *I intend to remain as Jones' sole counsel but nevertheless invite you to the defense on condition that you care to defend the case along the lines which seem to me to be the most conducive to a fair trial. In this connection I think it proper to acquaint you with the proceedings thus far.*
>
> *Jones was arrested on the afternoon of Monday October 12th. He was immediately subjected to a barbarous torture, all of the details of which were known to the States Attorney, Mr. Godfrey Child. On Tuesday morning, after sixteen hours of the third degree which included threats of immediate lynching as well as actual black-jacking, Jones, in order to save his life (literally and not figuratively) invented a story and "confessed."*
>
> *On account of the threats of mob violence and of the protests of the International Labor Defense to Governor Ritchie and to Sheriff Purnell, Jones was brought to Baltimore on Tuesday night. On Wednesday, Thursday and Friday I was consistently refused permission to see Jones on the instructions of States Attorney Child and while Jones was thus being deprived of his constitutional rights by Mr. Child this same Mr. Child, whose sworn duty it was to prosecute the torturers of Jones, was getting a new confession from Jones under less obvious but equally illegal conditions.*
>
> *On Saturday morning, I obtained a writ of habeas corpus requiring that Jones be in Court here on Monday. Mr. Child immediately activated himself and demanded that Jones be in Snow Hill on Monday.*

I therefore went to Snow Hill on Monday morning where Judge Bailey promised to let me interview Jones as soon as he arrived. This promise was not kept and Jones was brought into court to be arraigned at which time Judge Bailey asked him, under conditions calculated to bring a denial, whether he wanted to see me privately. I did see Jones privately (after ejecting a policeman from the cupboard where he was concealed and where he could overhear what Jones had to say) and I then conferred with Judges Duer and Bailey at their request. They determined to appoint two legal counsel to defend Jones in spite of my protests and it was only at the request of Jones that my appearance was entered at all. Moreover, Judge Bailey intimated that the trial ought to be held in Worcester County, a proceeding which I consider manifestly improper.

When Mr. Child announced on October 13th that the trial would be held within a week, no objection was made by the Court to what must have appeared, even to them, to be the railroading of a prisoner to the gallows.

When Jones left the courtroom on October 19th he was taken to Cambridge for safekeeping but a lynch-mob being reported on its way there, Judge Pattison ordered Jones' removal to Baltimore. On October 26th there was a rumor that Jones was in the Snow Hill jail and that night a mob, variously estimated as having from 300 to 700 members, composed from elements from all over the Eastern Shore, surrounded the jail and actually gained entrance, conducting a thorough search for Jones. Neither Mr. Child, the warden nor the Sheriff has started any prosecution of these would-be lynchers who invaded the jail. Nor has anything been done looking towards a prosecution of the police officers who tortured Jones.

For these reasons the defense not only objects to a trial in the first circuit with either Judge Duer or Judge Bailey on the bench but objects to a trial anywhere on the Eastern Shore and demands a removal to the Western Shore, preferably Baltimore. It is also the intention of the defense to attempt to eliminate all questions of race prejudice by demanding that Negroes be included in the jury that is to try Jones.

It is the contention of the defense that the whole case is a frame-up and that if wagon-loads of the Davis possessions were found in Jones' lodgings as the police say, then the police themselves put it there.

If you can agree with me on these points I would appreciate your immediate assistance in the matter of getting a copy of the coroner's report and your advice as to whether autopsies were made or can now be made. It is also necessary that a day be set for the argument on the motion for a change of venue as Mr. Child declines to agree to a removal from the first circuit.

I am awaiting your reply.

Very truly yours,

Bernard Ades

Needless to say, Wailes, a shoreman and a respected and experienced attorney, took this insolence with a moribund eye. He must have thought that here was a young, inexperienced attorney from Baltimore, dictating the course of a capital trial in Wailes's territory. Not only that, but the trial tactics of this young interloper included, as an essential ingredient, a castigation of law enforcement, the State's Attorney, the sheriff and the judges. The entire legal system in Wailes's area was being taken to task, if this young lawyer had his way.

Apparently holding his temper and maintaining his composure, Wailes simply wrote Ades that they should meet in Snow Hill on November 4 so that the court could determine their respective roles in the conduct of the defense. At that time, Wailes could see whether the court envisioned that primary role of defense being within the control of this twenty-seven-year-old upstart or the former president of the Maryland Bar Association, who lived in the area of the crime.

Meanwhile, the publicity of the impending trial had been causing problems in Snow Hill. On Thursday, October 22, it had been thought that the trial was to begin in Worcester County on the next day. Thinking that Lee was surely back in the county jail, a crowd of men decided to take action. In the darkness of the night, more than three hundred men assembled on the courthouse green. What surely must be described as a mob came that night to take the law from the duly established system and into their own hands, and to begin the process which would, surely, cause the legal process to be removed from the local authorities. The *Sunpapers* reported the scene:

> *Snow Hill, Md, Oct. 22—More than three hundred men assembled on the Courthouse green here tonight and demanded proof that Yuel Lee* [sic], *indicted in the killing of a family of four, is not being held in the jail behind the court building.*
>
> *It was only after Warden Ernest West had permitted seven men from the crowd to search every foot of the jail that the throng, which gradually worked its way to the doors of the jail, broke into little groups and then dispersed.*
>
> *The men came by automobiles—almost 200 out-of-town cars were counted on the streets surrounding the green—from many parts of the Eastern Shore. Most of them arrived, as if by prearrangement, about 3.*
>
> *They appeared to be leaderless, however, and there were no speeches or demonstration of any sort. They stood around the green and on the street in front of the courthouse for half an hour.*
>
> *Then, seven men, who had no apparent claim to leadership, made their way to the door of the jail, summoned Warden West and demanded to know if the 60 year old Negro was within. The Warden told them he was being held at the Baltimore City jail. Not satisfied, the self-appointed delegates of the crowd asked permission to search the jail. This was granted.*
>
> *After the search, four automobiles bearing members of the crowd left Snow Hill for Pocomoke City, home of Godfrey Childs* [sic], *States Attorney for Worcester county, from whom they said information would be demanded as to the whereabouts of the Negro.*
>
> *Today, scores of country folk, crowded into the small courtroom, expecting the opening of Lee's trial, were surprised when Judge Joseph L. Bailey adjourned the court until November 4. No date for Lee's trial was set.*

As Ades had related in his letter to Wailes, the quiet town of Snow Hill was beginning to be overcome with impending indications of violence. And the events were being noticed throughout the state. Because of the notable newspaper reports, the case was getting the attention of the governor and the attorney general of Maryland. The case was becoming a larger-than-life event, and one which was not to be limited in its scope to the counties of the lower shore. Attention was being focused on the small rural Worcester community; and that attention was not going to be appreciated by the folks in Snow Hill.

In the interim, Ades, armed with the hand-signed appearance certification executed by "Orphan Jones," was getting busy with the preparation of the case. His tactics, however, were anything but laudable. He decided to focus on Martha Miller, the landlady of Lee's rooming house, located near the ice plant and railroad station on Philadelphia Avenue at Worcester Street in downtown Ocean City. His tactics with regard to Martha were unfortunate in that he decided to engage in a strategy which today would be called "witness tampering." He sent a young woman to various places related to the crime who represented herself as a saleswoman. On November 3, she called upon Martha Miller, who was described in the language of the times as "an elderly colored woman of the old-fashioned type." It can be presumed that the young woman attempted to have Martha shade her impending testimony. She was implored to state that the police could have placed the incriminating evidence in Lee's room, and when she did not come across with the shade of testimony desired, she was persuaded, with some difficulty, to journey to Baltimore to meet with Mr. Ades.

That night, Martha arrived in the office of Mr. Ades in the Baltimore Trust Building in downtown Baltimore. Apparently indefatigable, Ades interviewed the elderly lady right then and there, and suggested that she should not say that Lee had brought the articles to the room, but should merely testify as to how the goods were found. Examined and cross-examined on the point, the story she told the investigator in the first instance could not be shaken. Disappointed, Ades realized that his female investigator had not produced a witness who would shake the State's case and determined to let Martha go. Ascertaining that a round-trip bus ticket was $7.50, he gave her the money and turned her loose to find her daughter, who resided in the city.

However, Martha's husband had told certain people of her trip to see Ades and the word got to the Worcester County authorities, who, being of a mind to thwart Ades's every effort, sent Baltimore detectives to find Martha in the city. The report of Sergeant William Flynn, written to Lieutenant Itzel, stated the circumstances:

> Sir; At 2:30 P.M., this date, Mr. Godfrey Childs [sic], States Attorney, Worcester [sic] County, Md. Called by phone and informed me that a woman (WHITE) in an automobile, has been seen loitering around OCEAN CITY Md. for the past two days. This morning at 11:00 A.M. this same automobile with the same woman (description of both unknown) pulled near the home of Martha Miller (C) and Martha Miller (C) entered the automobile in the company with the white woman. Mr. Childs states on information received that they are on their way to Baltimore to the home of Martha's daughter Matilda Johnson (C) #632 Vine St. Mr. Childs feels that something is behind this move and thinks it's a case of stealing a valuable witness. He instructs that Martha Miller (C) be picked up and held for the Worcester County authorities for safe keeping.

In fact, State's Attorney Child sent a telegram to Captain Charles Burns of the Baltimore City Police: "ARREST AND HOLD MARTHA MILLER COLORED AS MATERIAL STATE WITNESS MURDER CASE NOW PENDING IN THIS COUNTY STOP LT ITZEL AND SGT FLYNN YOUR DEPARTMENT HAVE ADDRESS AND KNOW PARTY STOP WIRE ME IN POCOMOKE WHEN PARTY IS IN CUSTODY." Succeeding in their quest, they took Miller to police headquarters and interviewed the obviously tired and bewildered lady further.

Her statement was recorded on Tuesday, November 3, 1931, by the ever-present Lieutenant Itzel and Sergeant Flynn. According to the transcript, Martha's statement was as follows:

> The lady first came to my home in Ocean City about 10:00 o'clock this morning. She came alone. She asked if I was Martha Miller and I said "yes." She said she wanted to talk to me and I invited her in

and we sat in the kitchen when the lady said, "I don't want to sit here because I am afraid somebody will see me," so we went to the bedroom and the lady told me to pull down the curtains so no one could see her. I pulled down the curtains.

She asked if Jones lived in my house, and I told her he did. She said, "Do you remember when the officers came to your house and went up stairs?" and I said "yes." Then she said, "Did they have anything in their hands when they came in, and did they have anything in their hands when they went upstairs?" The gentlemen asked me if they could go upstairs and I said "yes" and I went up first ahead of them and I said, "You gentlemen come on up." The lady asked me about 3 times if the men had anything in their hands and I said, "no." She said, "Are you sure?" and I said "yes, I am sure they had nothing in their hands." I told her that when they came down from up stairs they had something in their hands and that was the things that they found in Orphan Jones' room. She asked me what they found in the room and I told her that we found a big scarf with flowers, lady's bloomers, stockings, one little ring, another gold band ring, a ring that looked like a lodge ring, a locket, pearl beads, a watch, wishbone pin and some other things.

Several other questions regarding the possessions of Orphan Jones at the time followed and then Martha stated:

The lady told me I had to go to Baltimore today to see a lawyer and I said, "I can't go until tomorrow." She said I must go today, she said the lawyer who wanted to see me had to go to Snow Hill tomorrow and that is why it is necessary for me to go to Baltimore today. The lady said I would get back to Ocean City tomorrow or Thursday. She was talking to me about 20 minutes in my home and asked me where she could use a telephone and I sent her over to the depot and I followed her up. I went to the ice house to see my husband and told him I was going to Baltimore and when I had done this the lady went with me. We left Ocean City about 11:00 o'clock this morning or somewhere around that time. We came over on the ferry and got to Baltimore about 5:00 o'clock. We drove up near the hospital near Green and Lombard Sts., and the lady got out of the car. Some man came and got in the machine and they took me to some office in a big building. There they called some other man and a tall man came into the office, when they questioned me the tall man wrote everything down, and I told him everything I had told the lady and everything I had told the officers in Ocean City and told it the same way because when you tell the truth you can tell the same thing a thousand times and always the same way.

Of course, the "tall man" was, indeed, Bernard Ades.

Satisfied that she was sticking to her original story, the officers let Martha go to her daughter's house. Martha Miller was still a beneficial and steadfast witness for the State. Godfrey Child tucked this information away for his case against Ades; there would, if Child had his way, be a day of reckoning for this lawyer.

VII

The Snow Hill Mob

On November 4, 1931, in Snow Hill, the court was set to straighten out the matter of the defendant's trial counsel. Leonard Wailes had been appointed by the court after Upshur's resignation, and, in the meantime, on October 30, the clerk had received and filed the signed request by Lee (in the name "Orphan Jones") that Ades would be his sole attorney. The matter of the attorneys' conflicting positions in the case needed to be resolved.

The warden of the Baltimore city jail, hearing that Ades was intending to journey to Snow Hill, warned him that if he went there, it was likely that he, in addition to his client, would be lynched. Nonetheless, on the appointed date, Ades set out for the town, in the company of a male attendant, Oscar Rabowsky, and Helen Mays, his young and very attractive female investigator, the same lady investigator who had whisked Martha Miller off to Baltimore. (Mays was identified as such by Ocean City Police Chief Robert Allen.)

Whatever motives one ascribes to the lawyer, it is inescapable that his courage is to be admired. Knowing that he was detested by the citizens and disdained by the county officials, Ades nevertheless headed into an unknown and uncertain circumstance. His physical safety was indeed in jeopardy as he traveled to the courthouse that day. He apparently did not demand protection for himself, nor did he rail against the surely awaiting difficulty. He simply decided to face whatever adversity awaited.

And indeed it did await. Anxious for any news of the upcoming trial, there was, once again, a large crowd of men present at the courthouse. They were in a mood to affect whatever they could in the case—unable to achieve their goal of having at the defendant, the crowd on this date decided to have at the lawyer.

The mood was surely ugly on that late autumn day as the mob stayed around the courthouse seeking to control events. After an appearance of the parties in court, the proceedings were adjourned in order to have lunch. In a lunchroom directly across Market Street from the courthouse, Ades and Helen Mays were accosted by a group of men that had followed them into the establishment. One man stepped forward and brazenly told Ades that he should leave town. The proprietor of the establishment advised that he was closing the restaurant and refused to serve Ades and Mays. It was necessary for sheriff's deputies to rescue the pair and escort them back to the sheriff's office behind the courthouse. Deputy Sheriff Alonzo Blades was assigned as a guard to Ades and Mays.

That morning, Ades and Wailes had met in the courtroom in order to attempt to resolve the ongoing controversy about who would be Lee's lawyer. Wailes, one could imagine, was not enthralled with the whole case, but was duty bound to accept the appointment of the court. Ades, however, armed with the entry of appearance signed by Jones, was clearly becoming a force to reckon with.

Meanwhile, the local press had their own take on the events of the day. In its November 7 issue, the *Democratic Messenger*, published in Snow Hill, was hardly reticent in its account of the day's events. Under a headline that proclaimed: "ADES' WOMAN DEFENDER WITH GUN, RESPONSIBLE FOR MOB ATTACKS!" the account read in part:

> There was great excitement in Snow Hill late Wednesday afternoon, when a mob composed of people from Delaware, Virginia and Worcester County attacked and beat up Bernard Ades, counsel of Yuel Lee [sic], alias Orphan Jones, indicted for the murder of the Davis family. Helen Mays and Oscar Rabowsky, who came here with Ades, were also beaten up, the woman receiving blows intended for Ades. Officers rescued the trio from the mob and placed them in jail, from which they [were] afterwards taken out of the county. They went to Wilmington the same night.
>
> Considerable resentment has been aroused among the people of Worcester County against the Baltimore attorney, on account of his intrusion into the case as a self appointed associate counsel of the confessed murderer, and on account of statements attributed to him, as reported in some city papers. It is felt here that the Court, the State's Attorney, the counsel for the defense, and other officials are capable of handling the case, and are officials of such well known integrity that they will see that the prisoner will have a fair trial, and that justice will be done without the intervention or assistance of a foreign element, "red" or communist.
>
> When Ades and his woman companion left the Court room to get some lunch, they were followed by a small group of people to the restaurant. While Ades and Miss Mays were seated at the counter sipping coffee, a delegation of three citizens entered the room and accosted Ades. He was told that his intrusion onto the case was resented by the people of Worcester County, and that his presence here was unwise and undesirable from every standpoint of view. He was requested to leave town and the county within a stated time. At this point, it is claimed that the woman, Miss Mays, arose and made a threatening gesture, asserting that she had come to protect Ades. Miss Mays carried a purse clasped in her hands, which it is said were folded across her breast. As she nervously fingered the purse, it is declared by bystanders that the clasp became unfastened and the purse flew open disclosing a pistol concealed within its sides. It is also asserted that the purse touched, or came perilously near touching the breast of one of the delegation, who had issued the warning to Ades.
>
> In the meantime the rumor that Miss Mays was carrying the pistol reached the officers and she was taken in custody on the charge of carrying a concealed weapon. She was carried before Justice Walter W. Price, but waived a hearing and asked for a jury trial. Justice Price placed her under a $500.00 bond for her appearance in Court [Friday] morning. Bond in the required sum was posted by Ades, who is a registered lawyer of the Baltimore City bar.
>
> By early afternoon, a large number of people had assembled in Snow Hill and when it became known that the Mays woman had come here carrying a concealed weapon, the temper of the crowd changed from a tone of mild protest to one of deep indignation. One could sense the feeling of unrest with which the crowd was teeming, although there was no concerted action on the part of individuals. What took place later should be attributed to mob psychology—the onrush of feelings and passions which had been long pent up, but which broke forth at last in an avalanche of emotional activity, sweeping everything in its path. Carrying the figure of speech still further, the avalanche bore down on the man Ades, the woman Mays, and the foreign nomenclatured Rabowsky, as the trio emerged from the Court House after adjournment of Court for the day.

The trio was escorted by Judge Bailey, Sheriff Purnell, Deputies Davis, West and Blades, Chief of Police Randolph Purnell and other officers, toward the car in which the Baltimore trio had motored to Snow Hill. They were followed by a large number of people gathered on the Court House lawn, while hundreds more continually swelled the crowd, milling their way from the Court Room and streets into the seething throng. Judge Bailey was in the thick of the affray and made a valiant effort to maintain order, but he was brushed unceremoniously aside. The officers gave what protection they could, but when the car, parked in front of the Methodist Protestant Church, was reached, violence could no longer be averted and pandemonium broke loose. The temper of the crowd throughout the fracas was marked by a feeling of quiet determination and strong resentment. There were no missiles thrown, and no shots fired, the assailants being satisfied in the application of man power.

The trio was finally rescued, many of the erstwhile leaders of the crowd pleading with the others to desist. They were lodged in jail and a short time afterwards were released without being molested and taken to Wilmington under official escort.

In the same issue of the *Messenger*, this editorial appeared:

MOB VIOLENCE

When Yuel Lee [sic] was taken to court two weeks ago, after his indictment for the murder of the Davis family—father, mother and two daughters—the Court room was packed with people from all sections of the county who expected the negro to receive a speedy trial. He had admitted the crime and gave as his reason that he was angry with Davis for not paying him money. Nothing would have happened to Lee had he been put on trial here, but counsel for the defense delayed the trial and from time to time has been quoted as asserting that this self-confessed negro murderer of four people could not get a fair trial in Worcester County or on the Eastern Shore. The neighbors of the murdered family are now possessed with a fear that by some hook or crook the perpetrator of the horrible murder will escape the gallows. They have read that the negro was insane when he committed the crime, and they know different. They have read that he has been tried before for murder and that witnesses for the state were spirited away, enabling him to get off with a few years in jail for larceny, instead of having his neck stretched for murder.

All this has tended to make the people of Worcester County suspicious that Baltimore Reds are at work to save, in any way, Lee from the gallows, and to stir up race prejudice and obtain as members of their organization innumerable ignorant negroes. The intelligent, well-thinking negroes of Worcester County are as strong in their condemnation of Yuel Lee as are the white, and there is not one of them who desires to serve on a jury.

The mob which attacked Ades and his compatriots in Snow Hill last Tuesday was composed of men from three states, who believed that a citizen of Snow Hill had been threatened with a gun by a woman who claimed to be Ades' protector, and no power could stop them from doing what they did.

The people, preachers, laymen, editors, merchants, farmers, mechanics—everybody, resent the International Defense League's interference with the case of Yuel Lee, and the attempts of the counsel to stir up race hatred where there is none.

When one reads this missive from a distant and dispassionate perspective, the editorial is graphically and blatantly unfair in its content and conclusions. It is, perhaps, somewhat understandable that the passions and prejudices of the rural Worcester County perspective were clearly at work. However, it is jarring to read such a clear, oppressive and obvious call to prejudge the guilt of a yet unconvicted, though charged, defendant in the criminal justice system. So much for a fair press, intent upon a fair trial, in Worcester County, Maryland.

The event was not lost on the national press, either. In the *New York Times* edition of November 5, on page twenty-two, the following article appeared:

> *MOB BEATS COUNSEL OF NEGRO SLAYER OF 4: Liberty Defense League* [sic] *Attorney and Two Aides Are Forced to Leave Snowhill* [sic]*, MD.*
>
> *A Worcester County mob, thwarted in three attempts to seize Yuel Lee* [sic]*, confessed Negro slayer of a family of four, turned its wrath today upon Bernard Ades of Baltimore, attorney for the International Liberty Defense League and voluntary counsel for Lee. Twice during the day, Mr. Ades and two companions, one of them a woman "protector" were attacked by the mob. After the second attack, Mr. Ades and his companions left Snowhill, promising never to return. The second and most serious demonstration came as Mr. Ades, with Helen Mays and Oscar Rabowsky, attempted to leave the court house as circuit court was adjourned. The mob attacked the trio and beat them severely before they were rescued by Judge Joseph Bailey. Taken to the court house, the two were placed under protection. A loaded pistol was found in the woman's possession, and charges of carrying a deadly weapon were brought against her by a committee of citizens headed by Mayor J.O. Byrd of Snowhill. She was released in $500 bail furnished by Mr. Ades, whom she said she was hired to protect.*

The spotlight, and not an especially favorable one at that, was beginning to focus on the ugly side of events in the case.

VIII

The Shore vs. the Communists

Not to be outdone, some of the local politicians got into the act. On Thursday, Mayor J.O. Byrd of Snow Hill felt compelled to issue a stern warning. He placed the blame for the Wednesday mob squarely on its victims: "We are a law abiding and peace loving community," the mayor intoned.

> We believe in justice to all regardless of color or creed.
>
> A terrible murder has been committed. The criminal has been arrested and has confessed. Our people feel that justice has been delayed by the interference of the International Labor Defense League, which they deeply resent...The mob, I don't believe wanted to injure Ades very badly, as I am told some members of it attempted to protect him, after they felt that sufficient warning had been served that the league has no place in Worcester County.
>
> The criminal in this case will be given fair and impartial trial[!]
>
> If, as Louis Berger, the league's secretary says, its members attempt to march into Worcester County, they will be met at any border by Worcester County citizens. I can advise Mr. Ades to stay away from here with his organization. He is not wanted.

As all this rhetoric unfolded, the legal system of the county was attempting to function with a semblance of order. Godfrey Child needed to get the case to trial, however, and this prospect was dimming as Ades continued to throw obstacles in the way. Child needed a local lawyer to take charge, but that was also proving difficult. It was thought that Wailes, with his widely respected reputation, could get the job done, but no one countenanced Ades, the young, brash city lawyer. Now Lee was apparently bending to the will of this radical.

In Child's perspective the trial needed to get scheduled and fast, and it also needed to remain here in the county where the crime occurred. The Baltimore Reds were intent upon getting the proceedings out of the area, indeed, off the shore, and that boded ill for a fast and expeditious end. However, the judicial community was equally intent upon not being interfered with by these radical outsiders. The judges were in control, and, regardless of the efforts of the Communist militants, they would remain in control.

The day after the mob violence, November 5, the International Labor Defense sent a telegram to Judge Pattison, chief judge of the circuit, naturally denouncing the mob violence toward Ades and his companions, the arrest of Miss Mays and the alleged campaign of torture, and the efforts to railroad and lynch Lee on so-called framed-up murder charges. The judge was called upon to immediately halt the unlawful acts, and a change of venue to Baltimore and a trial by "a jury composed one-half of negroes" was demanded.

On the same day, however, the Baltimore *Sunpapers* reported that the judges had again announced that no lawyer for the International Labor Defense had any standing in the circuit court for Worcester County, and that Ades would no longer be recognized as counsel for Lee. It quoted Judge Joseph Bailey as saying, "No representative of an organization like the International Labor Defense League has any standing in court, and he had no business here in the first place." Not to be outdone, Ades, when informed of the judge's statement, replied, "No jurist who would make a statement like that has any business on the bench." So, once again in accordance with the bench's determination, Ades was barred by the warden of the Baltimore city jail from seeing Lee.

In Worcester County, efforts were being made to get the case to trial. Once again Mayor Byrd made a statement; he advised the press that he had been given fifteen state policemen to patrol the roads and that any person not giving a satisfactory explanation of his purpose would be arrested and held until after the scheduled trial on November 6. However, it was indeed uncertain as to whether this trial would actually take place. Even though Ades was temporarily out of the picture, Wailes announced that he would seek to have a removal of the case to Cambridge, in Dorchester County. If the venue change were granted, as it was obligated to be, the trial could be delayed several days.

The Worcester County authorities were not rid of their nemesis so easily, however. Ades was not to be denied the participation in this case which he had so arduously sought. He announced that he would travel back to the shore in order to participate in the defense. In fact, if necessary, the whole International Labor Defense membership would come to the county. The confrontation that everyone dreaded was about to happen.

Events were quickly moving beyond the precincts of the Snow Hill streets and the headquarters of the ILD on East Baltimore Street. The Maryland governor's office had been requested by the league to offer protection in Worcester County. Maryland governor Albert C. Ritchie had certainly been made aware of the circumstances and was mindful of the previous disturbances. He was, however, an official who believed in the sanctity of the local governments, and was therefore loath to act in the face of local assurances. So he sought counsel from the local officials. He was surely made aware of the local opinion that Ades was an interloper who had not gotten the sanction of the court in his quest to represent the defendant. It is likewise certain that the local jurists assured the governor that all could be handled quite legally on the local level. (It is interesting to note that, by all indications, the local officials seemed to honestly believe that the defendant could receive a fair trial in Snow Hill if only the local system was left alone to deal with the situation.)

Receiving assurances from the judges and satisfied that Ades had no true standing, Ritchie relented. He came down on the side of the local judiciary and the prevailing opinion of the lower shore. He recognized only Wailes, who was appointed by the court, as the defense attorney, to the exclusion of Ades, "who has not been engaged by anyone in authority to represent Orphan Jones." Ritchie went on in his dismissal of Ades:

> *I have heard that Mr. Ades contemplates going back to the county tomorrow. I know of no reason why he should do this. The only matter before the court is an affidavit to remove the case from Worcester County and I understand that has been filed. It can be acted upon by the judge without the necessity*

of Jones' attorney being present and certainly without the necessity of the presence of some one who simply constituted himself Jones' attorney, while Mr. Wailes, Jones' real attorney is in the county.

However, Mr. Ades ought to be permitted to go wherever he wishes and without molestation, and in view of what happened yesterday, I thought that I should telephone the authorities in Worcester county to find out whether there was any assistance which would be needed from me.

The highest official in the Free State had come down on the side of the locals and against the interference of the outsiders.

IX

A Picture of the
Maryland Communists

It is perhaps appropriate, at this juncture, to give a picture of the status of the Communist Party in Maryland during this period of time. In his treatise, "The Communist Party, Anti-Racism, and the Freedom Movement in Baltimore, 1930–1934," published in *Science and Society* in 1997, Andor Skotnes provides a well-researched and interesting view of the party in those times:

> Baltimore was, by 1930, a major industrial region and huge port—the seventh and third largest in the country, respectively—with a multi-ethnic working class that comprised about seventy percent of its population. It was also a Jim Crow "border" city with weak traditions of radicalism. African Americans, who made up eighteen percent of Baltimore's population, were subjected to a racial segregationism that, while not as terroristic as that of Deep South, was deeply rooted and omnipresent. As the Urban League's Charles Johnson put it a few years before, "In its industrial development Baltimore is northern; in its social customs it is more southern than Virginia."
>
> Furthermore, the Depression rapidly and deeply disrupted Baltimore's economic life, demoralizing its people, and amplifying racial-ethnic antagonisms. It left those social movements that did exist in disarray. In 1930 and 1931, the Baltimore Afro-American repeatedly complained that the city's traditional freedom organizations were doing nothing and demanded that they "justify their existence" through action. Similarly, the Baltimore Federation of Labor, which led the small local labor movement and which was dominated by the often-racist craft unions, seemed helpless in the face of mounting unemployment.

Skotnes then relates a series of *Afro-American* editorials praising the action of the "Ready Reds," including the statement that, "Reds as courageous as the Minute Men or the volunteer firemen seem everywhere ready of a demonstration against race prejudice," and, "The Communists appear to be the only party going our way. They are as radical as the N.A.A.C.P. was twenty years ago. Since the Abolitionists passed off the scene, no white group of national prominence has openly advocated the economic, political and social equality of black folks. The Communists are going our way, for which Allah be praised."

Skotnes relates that his research, oral histories and interviews with the editor of the *Afro* revealed that between 1930 and 1934, the Baltimore section of the Communist Party profoundly affected the social struggle in the city, especially the fight against racism. In the early 1930s, Skotnes says, "Baltimore Communists were not just a small group—they were an extremely small group." Their numbers were probably only in the dozens at the beginning of the decade. Membership was mainly working class, and as the local organization grew, the ethnic make-up gradually changed. The traditional membership base of European immigrants was falling in number relative to the number of native-born Americans, specifically African Americans. According to Skotnes, one military intelligence reports black membership as much as 60 percent in 1932 (though he allows for some exaggeration).

Skotnes goes on to describe the party's growing influence as the Depression deepened in the Baltimore area:

> *Despite their small numbers, and in striking contrast to other social activists who suffered deep discouragement, Communists in Baltimore were remarkably energetic in the wake of the Crash. Communists in places like Baltimore tended to view themselves, not as a handful of revolutionaries lost in a vast dispirited population, but as members of an international revolutionary army whose time was approaching.*
>
> *The outlook of the Baltimore Communists was also deeply influenced by the Third Period position on the "Negro Question." Adopted in 1928, this position proposed that Black Americans were a distinct people, an oppressed nation…the Black liberation struggle was seen as a discrete and central component of the coming socialist revolution, and participation in this struggle—and in the broader struggle against all forms of racism—was the revolutionary duty of all Communists, regardless of their racial-ethnic background.*

With the party-led International Labor Defense League, local activist groups got directly involved in the African American freedom movement. The Baltimore ILD focused on anti-lynching laws and legal defense work, giving life to the local freedom movement. Across the nation, ILD branches were seeing results from their legal efforts. This prompted the Baltimore branch to investigate and intervene in the Orphan Jones case.

> *By October 1931, the ILD in Alabama had been involved in the famous Scottsboro Boys case for over five months and stopped the initial attempt to railroad the accused into a legal lynching. During that month, the Baltimore ILD, drawing on the Scottsboro experience, began to investigate the case of Euel Lee [sic] to see if racism was involved.*
>
> *As was typical of Communist defense work during the Third Period, the Euel Lee campaign was fought on two interrelated fronts, a legal front and a mass action front. The premise was that litigation in the "bourgeois courts" was most successful when it was backed by mass struggle, and that such litigation was an excellent opportunity to build the broader mass movement. On the legal front, the Baltimore ILD's strategy was to focus, not on the judicial question of Lee's guilt or innocence, but on the political fact that he could not get a fair trial because of a whole system of racial discrimination. Therefore, while the ILD continued to press for a change of venue, it also demanded that African Americans be included on Lee's jury, and that the Jim Crow jury system be abolished.*

So it was that Worcester County, the Eastern Shore and the entire state of Maryland became targets of the Communist efforts at mass action, directed on behalf of the indigent African American then reposing in the Baltimore city jail.

X

The State is Invited Out

Governor Ritchie had been assured by both Judge Bailey and State's Attorney Child that the trial could be handled by the local authorities. He accepted these assurances and was willing to leave the matter in the hands of the Worcester County officials. He had stated that he would not accede to the demands of the Labor Defense League that he see to the prosecution of those members of the mob who had attacked Ades and his companions on the previous day, again expressing confidence in the local authorities. Ritchie stated, "Whether those who did the molesting can be identified or ascertained or not, I do not know. Both Judge Bailey and State's Attorney Child told me they doubted this could be done. However that may be, I do feel that if any proceedings of this kind can and should be taken, that I can rely on the judge and the State's Attorney taking them in view of the fact that they were present at the occurrence."

Upon being made aware of the statement of the governor, Ades naturally took issue. "I have been appointed by Lee to defend him and I will be there when the case is tried to assert my rights as his attorney. The judge's action is a clear invasion of Lee's prerogatives."

In view of the appearance filed in court on October 30, signed by Lee, it would appear that Ades was precisely correct. However, it should be noted that Lee was also signing documents prepared by Wailes. On November 4, as Ades was filing an affidavit petitioning a change of venue to the Western Shore, Lee had signed one prepared by Wailes asking removal to Dorchester County. The petition prepared by Wailes had been delivered to Lee by Warden Martin of the Baltimore city jail, and he confirmed that Lee in fact had signed it. "Lee is no fool," the warden said, "He knows how they feel toward him on the Eastern Shore. He reads and almost everyone in his tier gets newspapers, so I guess he's aware of the troubles down there."

If, as Martin said, Lee knew of the trouble on the shore, one must wonder at him signing the Wailes petition, which merely moved the case from one area of the lower shore to another. Ades's petition would have been more effective for the protection of the defendant as it sought the sanctity of the Western Shore. Nevertheless, at this time Wailes had the recognition of the prosecutor, the judges and, indeed, the governor of the state. Ades would need to secure a reversal of Lee's apparent intention in order to remain a factor in the case. So he went to the press.

In an article in the *Sunpapers* dated November 7, Ades once again took the offensive. Asserting that Judge Bailey had failed to use "proper discretion" in ordering the removal of the case to Cambridge, Ades threatened an appeal to the Court of Appeals, Maryland's highest court. Ades pointed out that in his motion for removal, he had requested that Lee's trial be moved to Baltimore, or at least the Western Shore. He also asserted that Lee could not receive a fair trial in Cambridge, which he pointed out was in the First Judicial Circuit, just as was Worcester County. Ades also answered the statement of Governor Ritchie by asserting that he had, on Thursday, filed a retainer signed by Lee in which he was described as Lee's sole attorney. Ades said he had kept a photostatic copy of the document. [The original document is in fact in my possession, over seventy years later, having been retrieved from the court file.]

Ades further advised that he would continue his efforts to see Lee at the Baltimore jail (he had once again been barred by an order of the Worcester County State's Attorney). Ades had again sought the intervention of the Baltimore City Court, entreating first Judge Frank and then Judge Walter L. Dawkins. Although it is not certain that either refused to sign the writ, they did make it plain that they would rather not sign the document (apparently in deference to Judge Bailey's order and the governor's stated position of support for the Worcester authority). Each judge made it clear that the issuance of the writ would only trigger a hearing as to whether Lee was being held illegally and would not gain the stated objective, that Ades be able to see Lee. They suggested that, instead, Ades seek a writ of mandamus from a court in Baltimore City directing the warden to allow his interview of the prisoner. Finally, it was decided among the lawyer and the two judges that Ades should appeal to Chief Judge Pattison of the First Judicial Circuit to influence Child to withdraw his order to Warden Martin. Such action should have been unnecessary, as Ades now had the signed retainer. However, Child did not relent.

The trial was scheduled to go forward the next morning, November 6. There was still no final determination regarding the removal of the case, as the dilemma of the defendant's trial representation was still present, so it was apparent that Lee would be in Snow Hill on the next day. As if by a signal, a steadily increasing volume of traffic began entering the sleepy town during the evening hours of November 5.

Cars and wagons chugged and rumbled slowly into the area of the courthouse, from over the Pocomoke River bridge and from Salisbury to the west; from the south and north; from the direction of Stockton and Virginia's Eastern Shore below the state line; and from Berlin, Newark and points north. The evening drew on and grew cold as the normally quiet streets of the county seat filled. The atmosphere of the scene was graphically captured by a *Sunpapers* staff correspondent:

Snow Hill, Md. November 6. The hands crept around the illuminated face of the clock on the Courthouse tower—12 o'clock on the courthouse tower—12-and business was still booming in Washington Street. It was the biggest night's business since the last Presidential election.

Snow Hill—or a large part of it—yet was staying up to await the return from Baltimore of Euel Lee, alias Orphan Jones, colored farmhand accused of having murdered the family of Green Davis at Taylorville last month.

"They are bringing him down tonight," said a man in the crowd that thronged the streets.

"Look," and he pulled a pistol butt out of his coat pocket.

The oyster house, the poolroom, the barber shop and the three restaurants between the hotel and the courthouse were crowded with men.

There were a few women, too, most of them young girls with carefully marcelled hair, bright skirts and fur coats, but the men outnumbered the women almost a hundred to one.

The cold night air was occasionally perfumed by the unmistakable odor of country corn whiskey.

Three motorcycles stopped opposite the Mason Opera House and three State policemen got off and walked across the street to Brimer's restaurant. "Yaay Ho!" shouted someone in the crowd. As the State policemen went into the restaurant, pulled off their gauntlets and ordered hot coffee. "No road cop are gonna lock me up," murmured a man in the crowd out front.

Eight other State policemen appeared. They followed Chief of Police Randolph Purnell down Washington Street to the courthouse square.

The crowd closed in around the head of the little column; one man somewhat unsteady on his feet and inarticulate in his speech, stepped up to one of the officers.

"No road cop is going to do anything to me," he said.

"Why don't you go home and go to bed?" the State policeman asked good naturedly.

"Nobody's going to tell us to go home and go to bed," said another man in the crowd.

Chief Purnell stepped up on the low-stone coping of the courthouse terrace.

"Now, boys" he said to the crowd, "you help us and we'll help you. All we want you to do is to keep quiet," said the chief. "There are some people in town who want to sleep, you know. They'll get up when it's time, you know how it is," continued the chief.

"We don't want you to make any noise. You can stay here all night if you want to." He turned toward the front door of the courthouse and the police followed him.

The chief unlocked the door and the police followed him.

"I don't vote in Worcester county, but I want my rights!" cried a man in the crowd.

"We're going to have our rights!" shouted another.

"You're going to get them," said the chief. "You're going to stay here all night and help me," the chief added tactfully, "I know there isn't one of you boys in the crowd who wouldn't help if I asked him to."

"That's right, chief, you can count on us," came a reply as the chief squeezed inside the courthouse door and closed it behind him. A night latch on the door clicked.

Lights were burning in the clerk's office, but the inside shutters were closed. The crowd pushed its way up on to the pretty little Georgian portico of the courthouse and peeped in through the glass panels on either side of the door. "What are they doing?" asked those in the rear. "Watch them!" Agile youngsters clambered up the iron bars on side of the windows and peeped through the slats of the inside shutters.

"He's taking their names," they reported, but as a matter of fact, Chief Purnell was swearing in the State policemen as special county officers. The portico was still crowded when the police came out. "I'm glad this happened this week," the chief laughed. "I want to go rabbit hunting next week."

"Where have you been?" asked a man in the crowd who wore a hunter's license pinned to the back of his canvas hunting jacket, "I've been shooting rabbits for a week."

The State police strolled to a restaurant, went inside and hung their Sam Browne pistol belts on a hatrack.

A man in a ragged overcoat spun the cylinder of a revolver. Some one turned out the lights of the barber shop. The darkened shop was still crowded with a group that sang "John Brown's Body." One or two automobiles started up and pulled away.

"I'm getting tired of this," said one of the marcelled ladies. "When's something going to happen?"

In the restaurant the State police finished their coffee and lit cigarettes.

"Grease a rail. Get some tar and feathers and let's give somebody a ride. This Ades can't come here."

The State police pinched out their cigarettes, buckled on their guns and went out on the street.

The courthouse clock struck 2. Rumors appeared that Jones would arrive between 2 and 4 o'clock and had passed a police station near Wilmington bound for Snow Hill.

"When he gets here," it was whispered, "they're going to sound a fire alarm so everybody in town will know he's here."

Chief Purnell showed his restlessness. He had to be back in court at 9 o'clock. The crowd dwindled. The Courthouse Square was almost deserted. The tower clock struck five times. The sky turned faintly grey. There remained only four of the State police.

XI

The Saga Shifts to Dorchester

On the morning of November 6, Judge Joseph Bailey signed an order removing the trial to Dorchester County. The judge announced that the trial would probably be heard during the week of November 16. The judge was questioned as to the status of Ades and he advised that the lawyer's standing would now be resolved in Cambridge, if Ades even showed up to defend Lee. The courtroom in Worcester County was jammed with people as the judge made his ruling. All had come in a vain attempt to glimpse the defendant or his city lawyer, but neither was present.

The judge announced that he had before him two petitions for removal, the one filed by Ades and also Wailes's. "There are two petitions here asking a change of venue," Judge Bailey announced. "The removal of the trial is mandatory because the defendant has asked it. The petition will be granted and an order entered removing the case to Dorchester County." As was sometimes the custom, Judge Robert Duer sat with Judge Bailey during the proceedings. Judge Duer announced that it was to be noted that State's Attorney Child was not responsible for the delay in the trial. Unfortunately, the *Sunpapers* report of the proceeding contained a typographical error and printed that the judge had said Mr. Child *was* responsible for the delay. Beset with the political situation in his own county, Child had a fit. The *Democratic Messenger* reported his response: he sent a telegram to the *Baltimore Sun* demanding an immediate retraction. His message read, in part: "Printing this [statement that Child was responsible for the trial's delay] either constitutes gross negligence or malicious untruth, for Judge Duer announced that I was not responsible for any delay. I demand that a correction be made on the front page of your edition coming to the Eastern Shore of the *Evening Sun* today, the *Sunday Sun* tomorrow, and the *Morning Sun* on Monday. Wire what you intend to do. Do not phone, as I want everything a matter of record." To the paper's credit, the retraction was prominently displayed in the next edition. With all the murmuring in the community about the delaying tactics of Ades, the communist city lawyer, Child didn't need the impression afoot that he was unable to push the case forward. He was frustrated enough by this man who just wouldn't go away.

At last, he thought, now there would be a trial, and it would start within a matter of days. How wrong Godfrey Child would prove to be.

As soon as the change of venue was announced, Child at once conferred with James McAllister, the Dorchester County State's Attorney, who would, according to protocol, sit with Child in the prosecution of the case in McAllister's county. On November 9, the new term of court opened in Dorchester County.

Lee, even though he was becoming notorious, would most likely have to wait in line to get a trial date. J. Fred Dunn, clerk of court, announced that the court had a full docket and the Lee trial may have to be postponed a week or more. This would give Ades some more time to make his next move, which was not long in coming.

On the same day that the November term opened in Cambridge, Ades announced that he had spoken to Leonard Wailes by telephone and sought his opinion on Child's refusal to allow Ades to speak to Lee. Wailes demurred, saying that he didn't think Child would be amenable to reversing his edict, and that he didn't wish to become involved in the controversy. Ades decided that he would thereupon apply immediately for a writ of habeas corpus and a writ of mandamus. He stated that it was evident that Lee could not be placed on trial until the issue of representation was finally resolved.

While these events were going on, the November 10 *Baltimore Sun* reported that "Baltimore Communists today sent Governor Ritchie and Judge Joseph L. Bailey, of the First Judicial Circuit, protests against what they called the 'frame-up' of Lee. The protests were approved by the Communists Saturday night at a meeting at the Polish Hall, 510 South Broadway, to celebrate the fourteenth anniversary of the establishment of the Soviet Union." Worcester County had certainly never seen the likes of these events.

On November 12, the *Sun* issued a special dispatch from Cambridge:

> *Yuel Lee* [sic], *alias Orphan Jones, colored, charged with the murder of four persons at Berlin, probably will be tried in the Circuit Court for Dorchester County here next Thursday, it was indicated today by State's Attorney James McAllister of Dorchester County, who will aid Godfrey Child, State's Attorney of Worcester County, in prosecuting Lee.*
>
> *Captain Edward McKenna Johnson, commander of the Maryland State policemen, conferred with State's Attorney McAllister here yesterday and offered to provide fifty policemen to assist local authorities in maintaining order during Lee's trial.*

Meanwhile, in Baltimore, Ades was finally getting his way with regard to seeing Lee. After seeking to see Lee for nearly two weeks, he proceeded to the jail on November 14, accompanied by the Baltimore assistant State's Attorney, John A. Sherman. Sherman had been brought into the case after a conference between Baltimore City State's Attorney Herbert R. O'Conor, Ades and Judge Eli Frank. There was obviously some indication that Ades had grounds to see Lee, or the prosecutor's office would not countenance the interview. In any event, Sherman proceeded to interview Lee and Ades still did not get to speak with the prisoner.

However, Judge Frank had scheduled a hearing on November 18 for Ades to present his mandamus writ. At that hearing Judge Frank was obviously impressed with Ades's case, as he ordered that Ades be recognized by the authorities as Lee's counsel. Immediately, Ades advised that he, as counsel now, would ask the Worcester County court to reconsider its removal order and send the trial, at last, to Baltimore. He maintained that Lee could not receive a fair trial anywhere on the shore. When Ades was asked what the defense of his client would be, he snapped back, "That he didn't do it." He reasserted that the confession had been obtained under duress, and that if the State had any evidence they would have to prove it. Ades then advised that he intended to see Lee that very day at the jail and informed the press that it would be the first interview that he would have had with Lee.

"I've got an awful lot to do today," said Mr. Ades, "I have to see Lee at the jail and then I've got to prepare the motion for transfer of the case. I don't know whether I'll have time to get the motion sent off or not. If the court grants my request for change of venue, I will go ahead with my plans for the defense of Lee. If it does not grant the request, why, then, I'll go ahead with defense plans anyway."

Good to his word, on November 20 Ades filed a motion containing seventeen separate allegations of error in the court's requiring the case to go to Dorchester County. The allegations were all those that Ades could think of, including the complaint that Ades had not been allowed to inspect the record before the removal and that the defendant could not receive a fair trial in any county on the Eastern Shore. He also asserted that Lee had been subjected to brutal torture and beating by the officials of Worcester County which torture and beating lasted sixteen hours and that during that time your petitioner was allowed to have neither food nor water; that a mob led by well known citizens of Worcester County were, on October 13, 1931, preparing to lynch the defendant; that, after being removed to Cambridge, a mob gathered in Snow Hill and started for Cambridge with the purpose of lynching the defendant; that the defendant had been saved only by virtue of his removal to Baltimore, and no member of the mob had been prosecuted; that on October 26, 1931, a mob in Worcester County surrounded the jail and gained entrance for the purpose of searching it with the intent to lynch the defendant; that on the night of November 5, a mob in Worcester County, being of the opinion that the defendant would be in Snow Hill, waited until 3 o'clock in the morning on the streets of Snow Hill, and that the normal two-man police force was extended to ten deputy Sheriffs and twenty-five state policemen; that the animosity of the people of the Eastern Shore was such that in Chestertown, a mob surrounded the jail searching for George Davis, a Negro, with the purpose of lynching him, and that Davis had to be, likewise, taken to Baltimore in order to save him.

Ades further noted that the State's Attorney for Worcester County had prohibited Ades from seeing his client; that the now infamous telegram had been sent from Godfrey Child to the warden of the Baltimore jail barring Ades from seeing Lee; that after the withdrawal of Franklin Upshur from the case, the court was unable to secure the appearance of any other Worcester County attorney and had to go to the neighboring county of Wicomico; that one of the judges had stated that no representative of the International Labor Defense had any business in Worcester County in the first place; that Ades had to resort to a writ of habeas corpus in order to see his client in the Baltimore jail; and there were to be two hundred national guardsmen "armed with bayonets, machine guns and gas bombs ordered to Cambridge for the purpose of guarding the Court House and the Court Room in which it is intended to try this case."

Ades concluded with a flourish:

> *That the intimidations and threats of bodily injury to your petitioner and to his counsel, should this trial be held on the Eastern Shore of Maryland, and the intimidation and duress on the minds of the residents of the county who may be called for jury duty will be such to deprive your petitioner of a fair and impartial trial by a jury of his peers and to deny to your petitioner the due process of law guaranteed by the Constitution of the United States and of the State of Maryland.*

The simple fact is, Ades was precisely right.

The atmosphere of the community on the shore was totally inflamed. Whether the populace had good cause because of the instigating rhetoric coming from the Labor Defense League was really not the point; the possibility of a fair and untainted trial evaporated with the first intimation of mob psychology on the streets of Snow Hill. A jury had to be chosen from among the citizens who had been inundated with the inflammatory press, the inciting shouts of the communists and the provoking actions of the crowds demanding retribution on the defendant. Ades was right: there was no possibility of pure justice in the real sense on the shore.

The problem was, the judges could not bring themselves to confront the situation head on. For them to acknowledge the inherent unfairness of the trial atmosphere was, indeed, to repudiate their own community. Therefore they set out to do what they could to see that the trial was held in the fairest circumstances possible. They conferred and came up with a novel idea of protection for the prisoner. There is no doubt that the judges and, indeed, all the law enforcement officials were intent upon the protection of Lee and Ades. Judges Pattison, Bailey and Duer normally labored assiduously to ensure that no stain of injustice would be seen in their counties; the simple fact, however, is that they were unable to stand off and look at the terrible situation dispassionately. They should have bowed to the inevitable conclusion that Lee deserved the solace that distance brought, and he should have been granted the right to be tried in Baltimore.

Such was not the case, however. The judicial system of the Eastern Shore determined that Lee would be tried by its own citizens.

On November 27, Ades filed a motion to reconsider the removal of the trial to Dorchester. In that document he again requested that the case be sent to the Western Shore, reiterating that Lee could not get a fair trial anywhere on the shore. The judges, in due time passed their order. They advised that the petition and the State's answer had been "carefully considered."

Their ruling stated,

> The question presented is whether the defendant can have a fair and impartial trial in the Circuit Court for Dorchester County and unless the Court can properly reach the conclusion that the defendant cannot have such a trial in said court, then the case should be tried in the Circuit Court for Dorchester County to which it was removed.
>
> We have very carefully investigated the conditions, not only in Dorchester County, but in other sections of the shore wherein the conditions there found may have some bearing upon the question, whether the defendant can have a fair trial in the Circuit Court for Dorchester County, and as a result thereof, we have been unable to obtain information which would lead us to believe that the defendant could not have a fair and impartial trial in the last named Court.
>
> It is therefore ordered this 30th day of November, 1931, that the above mentioned "suggestion, petition and motion" be, and it is hereby dismissed, and the Clerk of the Circuit Court for Worcester County is hereby directed to forward the Transcript of Record of the above entitled case to the Circuit Court for Dorchester County, for trial in compliance with the original order of removal in this case.

The order was signed by all three judges.

There were, necessarily, extraordinary measures extended for the trial. If it was indeed to be held in the midst of the area of most concern, it would need to be safe for the defendant. The *Sunpapers* reported on November 17:

A detachment of National Guard, under command of Adj-Gen. Milton A. Reckord, will deliver the Negro, Yuel Lee [sic], alias Orphan Jones, to Cambridge for trial on the charge of murder at 9 o'clock on Thursday morning. The detachment will remain in Cambridge and protect the Negro during the trial.

State policemen will augment the National Guard force.

The manner in which the Negro will be taken from the City Jail where he now is to Cambridge has not been disclosed. It is reported that he will be placed aboard a boat of the oyster police in Baltimore and transported to Cambridge.

Gov. Albert C. Ritchie said today when he was asked about these arrangements: "All I can say is that the Negro will be adequately protected."

Adjutant General Reckord said, " I have been ordered to protect the Negro in his removal from Baltimore to Cambridge and during the trial. An adequate force of the National Guard and the State Police will see that he is taken to Cambridge and delivered to the court for his trial at 9 o'clock on Thursday morning."

General Reckord would not say whether a squad or a regiment would guard Lee.

Though the atmosphere was not considered volatile enough to warrant the removal of the trial, a contingent of the Maryland National Guard was dispatched to guard the defendant. One must carefully contemplate that fact, as viewed from the perspective of history.

Cambridge is sited on the south bank of the Choptank River, a large tributary of the Chesapeake Bay. It is a water-oriented town, with water-related vocations providing its principal means of economy. In 1931 Cambridge was a compact town on the shore of the river. As was reported, Lee would be brought by boat to the scene. Thereafter, for the duration of the trial, he would be kept aboard the vessel in the Choptank so as to afford a means of protection during the proceedings. Each morning, Lee would be shuttled ashore, and then in the evening, he would be carried back aboard the official boat so as to harbor him from any mob. The spectacle of National Guardsmen shuttling a defendant back and forth from the protective asylum of a moored boat so as to prevent a lynching somehow did not seem to register with the jurists who had claimed the venue safe and fair.

Dorchester, as had Worcester before it, now prepared for the wind-up of the Lee saga.

XII

The Shore's Terrible Retribution

In the meantime, however, a horrifying event occurred in yet another of the counties on the lower shore. Just days after the *Salisbury Times* headlines blared out the news "LEE TO BE TRIED ON SHORE TUESDAY," an enigmatic headline appeared in the Friday, December 4 edition: "NEGRO SLAYS D.J. ELLIOTT AND SELF: Motive for Slaying is Not Known." The article continued:

> *Daniel J. Elliott, prominent crate and basket manufacturer, was shot and killed in his office at 2:15 this afternoon by a negro employee, who then turned the pistol on himself.*
>
> *There were no eyewitnesses to the shooting but moments later James Elliott, a son, entered the office. The elder Elliott was slumped in the chair at his desk. The negro, Mack Williams, 35, was lying on the floor in a pool of blood.*
>
> *A hurried effort was made to place the manufacturer in an automobile to rush him to Peninsula General Hospital.*
>
> *While this was being done, Williams staggered out of the office into the lumber yard. James Elliott ran into the office, seized the negro's pistol that had been left lying on the floor and fired at the man. It was later found the bullet barely grazed William's head.*
>
> *The negro was taken to the hospital and died a few minutes later.*

What in fact had occurred was much different. In an apparent effort to correct the vastly erroneous account of December 4, the *Salisbury Times* reported in its Saturday edition, in small-type headlines only on the right column, "Coroner's Jury to Investigate Slayer's Death—State, County and City Officials Co-operating; Mayor Expects No More Trouble."

The story continued:

> *Matthew Williams, confessed slayer of D.J. Elliott at his office yesterday afternoon, was removed from the Peninsula General Hospital last night and hanged in the Courthouse yard. The hanging was witnessed by hundreds of people.*
>
> *An investigation of the entire affair is being conducted by local authorities who had not progressed sufficiently to make any statements at press time.*
>
> *The opinion prevails that many of those participating in the actual hanging came from other sections of the peninsula and that their actions were prompted by events that have occurred in their own communities.*
>
> *States Attorney Levin C. Bailey said a coroner's jury, composed of leading citizens, will be summoned this afternoon, and later adjourned until a later date for a hearing.*

"All evidence that can be collected will be placed before the jurors whose duty will be to fix responsibility for the death of Mr. Williams," Mr. Bailey said.

After a special meeting of the Mayor and Council this morning in City Hall, Mayor Wade H. Insley issued this Statement:

"A careful investigation shows that everything is quiet and no further trouble is anticipated. There is no indication of tense racial feeling and what has happened can safely be classified as indignation directed only toward the individual concerned. There never has been any trouble between the races here and there is not going to be now."

Governor Albert C. Ritchie returned hurriedly home from New York and began a thorough inquiry.

The Eastern Shore, for the first time in over twenty years, had been host to a lynching.

The details of the actual event are too grotesque to imagine from the perspective of seventy years of history. It is evident that the accused was taken to Peninsula General Hospital for the treatment of his wounds. Once there, he was set upon by a mob, according to one report, dragged to a window and heaved out into the waiting custody of the incensed crowd gathered below. He was removed to the front yard of the Wicomico County Courthouse where a young man shinnied up a stately tree on the lawn and swung the rope over a branch. Williams was then lynched and his body was cut down, mutilated and set afire. His burned body was then dragged the length of Main Street, through the business district of town and across the Wicomico River into the black section of town. There the mob left the charred body for the observance of the black community.

It was surely one of the most shameful hours in the recent history of the shore. Dozens, if not hundreds, of seemingly upright and respectable citizens had taken the law in their own hands and had, during the frenzy of the moment, cast a shadow of repugnant lawlessness over the region. There was no explanation that made sense, but the cry was that Euel Lee had not been tried in a speedy fashion and that the same delay of justice would not occur in the case of Williams.

The lower shore sought a scapegoat for its terrible acts and the "blame" was placed upon the International Labor Defense and Ades. There was no remorse or shame to be admitted, no blame to be accepted. The community would find other reasons, other excuses, other causes for its violent acts, and such causes were laid at the feet of the hated Communists and their predominant personage, Bernard Ades.

In Baltimore, across the bay, however, the circumstances regarding the account of the events in Salisbury were markedly different. The headline of the December 5, 1931 edition of the *Sunpapers* shouted out the horrid facts: "SHORE MOB LYNCHES NEGRO." Just below was the damning subtitle: "SALISBURY KILLER IS HANGED FROM TREE AT COURTHOUSE," and then the grotesque finale: "BODY IS THEN BURNED ON LOT AT EDGE OF COLORED SETTLEMENT." The event was starkly and vividly portrayed in the following article:

Salisbury, Md., Dec. 4— Matthew Williams, Negro, who killed Daniel J. Elliott, prominent box manufacturer, in his office this afternoon, was hanged from a tree in the courthouse green here at 8:05 o'clock tonight and twenty minutes later his body was cut down and burned on a vacant lot on the edge of Salisbury's Negro settlement.

A few minutes before 8 P.M. six men entered the Peninsula General Hospital, where Williams was under treatment in the Negro ward for a self-inflicted wound, lifted him from his bed and ordered him to walk with them into the street.

There more than 300 men and women surrounded the Negro and walked with him to the courthouse green at Main and Division Street, three blocks distant.

One of the crowd had obtained a rope while the mob was moving toward the green. Several men flung it over the limb of a tree, about twenty-five feet from the ground, and two others tied one end of it around the bandage-swathed neck of the Negro.

The men holding the rope tugged the Negro about fifteen feet above the ground as the mob, which had grown to about 2,000, applauded.

The Negro was raised and lowered several times as the mob's shouts rose and fell. Finally the rope was secured and Williams [was] left hanging in the green.

He was suspended in the green for about twenty minutes as the mob, constantly swelling, looked on. Then several men stepped forward, slashed the rope, and picked up the Negro's body, shouting to the mob to follow them.

G. Murray Phillips, Wicomico County Sheriff, stepped forward and ordered the men to drop the Negro's body, but he was brushed aside by the mob, which had started to close in.

They dragged the body to a lot on Poplar Hill avenue, within easy view of scores of Negro homes, and, after drenching it with gasoline, set it afire.

More than 2,000 persons, most of them members of the mob which had witnessed the hanging, but many new recruits, grouped about the pyre. They did not disperse until the last flame had flickered out.

The *Sun* also recounted the preliminary actions of the crowd, and one must contrast the apparent lack of fortitude of the law enforcement officials that evening with that of Worcester's sheriff, Wilmer Purnell, during the violent events in Snow Hill:

The lynching spirit was raised suddenly in the town a half hour before the hanging. Several men, standing near the courthouse green, who apparently had been discussing the killing of Mr. Elliott, raised the cry: "Let's lynch Williams!"

As they walked toward the hospital they repeated that cry, and scores of men fell in behind them; the mob members appeared from stores, side streets, corners, and when the crowd reached the hospital there were about 300 closely grouped.

The crowd was orderly and stood by without a shout or untoward movement while six men attempted to enter the front door of the hospital.

Police chief N.H. Holland and Deputy Sheriff John Parks, guarding the entrance, refused to let them pass. The delegation fell back, considered the situation a moment, and then went around to a side door of the hospital and entered.

The mob's representatives, it was reported later, went directly to the hospital superintendent, Miss Helen V. Wise.

One of them said to her, "Shall we take him quietly?"

She is reported to have replied: "If you must take him, do it quietly."

They reappeared in a few moments with the Negro, whom they had taken from his bed in the Negro ward on the first floor. Williams' head was so heavily bandaged he could not see, and he was guided to the center of the mob and then escorted to the courthouse green.

Neither the police nor any of the citizens endeavored to dissuade the mob or halt the lynching.

It was manifestly evident that a not insignificant number of Salisbury citizens had participated, either as passive, non-protesting bystanders or, indeed, as mob participants in this savage event. Yet there is only Johns Hopkins faculty member Broadus Mitchell's account of the events that would indicate that anyone—civic leader, clergy or law enforcement official—did anything, even to raise the most timid protest to the hanging. He stated that Mr. Alexander Grier, a Salisbury businessman, tried to halt the mob procession from the hospital, but to no avail, and that Mr. John Downing "at peril to himself" tried, after the lynching, to get the mob to turn over Williams's lifeless body to the sheriff, who was also trying to prevent "further action."

The events of that night, however, would not escape the glare of outrage. Those people not in close proximity to the community had the right and inclination to express their revulsion to the foul event. In its Saturday, December 5 edition, the *Evening Sun* went on to expose further shameful details of the horrid event and the plans for investigation and punishment of the instigators. A detailed account was printed beneath the headlines "PROMPT PROSECUTION OF MOB PROMISED" and "RITCHIE AND LANE OPEN LYNCHING INVESTIGATION":

Salisbury, Dec. 5—Immediate prosecution of the leaders of the mob which hanged and burned a colored prisoner here last night and of every member of the mob who can be identified, was promised today by State's Attorney Levin C. Bailey.

"There will be no more delay than necessary for the identification of those who took part in this crime," Mr. Bailey said in announcing his plans, "I plan to prosecute this case very vigorously, stopping not at the leaders, but carrying it to every other person who took part and who can be identified. I have arranged for an immediate conference with Sheriff G. Murray Phillips and Chief of Police N.H. Holland, who saw the mob in action, to obtain from them the names of all the persons they recognized and the extent of participation of each."

An investigation of the failure of the local police to halt the lynching was started by Mayor Wade H. Insley, who called upon the Chief of Police and the members of the force who were on duty at the time for detailed written explanations, especially in reference to reports that three uniformed patrolmen were directing traffic on the fringes of the mob while the hanging was in progress.

Attorney General William P. Lane, Jr., telegraphed to Mr. Bailey an offer of assistance of his office in the prosecution. The telegram said: "The facilities of my office are at your disposal for any assistance you may require in connection with the lynching last night."

"It isn't necessary for me to say that I am shocked," Mr. Lane said. "It comes back to a question of any influence that the lynching may have on the case of Orphan Jones. I have already said what I have to say about that."

The Attorney General referred to a letter he sent to the prosecuting authorities on the Eastern Shore in the Orphan Jones case stating a conviction that "this case ought not to be tried in Dorchester County and should be removed for trial to some other court of this State sitting in a community free from the influences that have manifested themselves in Worcester and Dorchester counties."

Mr. Lane's Statement was followed by reports of a projected meeting of the three judges of the First Judicial Circuit to consider the impending trial in Cambridge of Yuel Lee [sic], alias Orphan Jones, in the light of last night's events here. Lee is charged with the murder of a family of four in Worcester County.

The judges, John R. Pattison, Joseph L. Bailey and Robert F. Duer, ruled last week in Snow Hill that there was not a sufficient threat of mob violence to prejudice Lee's chances for a fair trial on the Eastern Shore.

This county, Wicomico, is part of the circuit in which Judges Pattison, Bailey and Duer sit. Judge Bailey, whose home is in Salisbury and who is the uncle of the State's Attorney, termed the lynching "an awful shakeup," and Judge Pattison spoke of regret at the occurrence.

A telephone call to him at Nanticoke, twenty miles away, brought the first information he had of the activity of the mob, the State's Attorney said, in expressing regret that he was not in Salisbury at the time to do what he could to halt the lynching and to gather first hand information concerning the mob's membership.

As soon as he heard that the mob had formed and had dragged the prisoner from the Peninsula General Hospital, Mr. Bailey drove to Salisbury at top speed, but the crowd had broken up when he arrived.

"From Chief Holland and Deputy Sheriff John Parks, who were on guard at the hospital, I learned that there seemed to be six leaders of the mob of 200 to 300 men," Mr. Bailey said.

Chief Holland told the State's Attorney that he and Parks were at the main doorway of the hospital, about one-fourth of a mile from the courthouse and county jail, when a mob that appeared to number about 150 surged over the hospital lawn at dusk.

"I stood in the doorway with Parks," the chief of police said, "and some of the men came up. One of them said, 'Where is he?' and I told him that I didn't know. Another man spoke up and said, 'I know where he is, all right.' Parks and I warned them to get away, and while we were holding them off a small group went around to the rear of the hospital. They entered by an emergency exit, went through the basement and to the Negro ward on the first floor.

"As soon as I saw this going on I left Parks on guard at the door and telephoned to the Sheriff's office for help. While I was telephoning, I heard a commotion in the hospital and a nurse told me that the men were taking the Negro out. I ran back to the Negro ward in time to see Williams being lifted out of the window and dropped to some other members of the mob waiting outside.

"I can't remember whether any of them threatened me because everything happened so fast. I remember thinking that if I pulled out a gun it might start a riot and other patients in the ward might be shot. There were four other Negro patients in there and I was afraid they might take them too.

"Through the window I saw them start toward the Courthouse, half carrying and half dragging the man."

It was related that a Negro workman passing along the sidewalk beside the hospital saw the mob with its victim coming toward him and broke into flight, leading the procession until it disappeared from sight of those at the hospital.

Holland said that the authorities had no indication that a lynching was planned and that his investigation during the night produced evidences that the mob developed spontaneously, when a small knot of men near the Courthouse, apparently discussing the murder of Mr. Elliott, suddenly raised the cry "Lets lynch Williams!"

They started toward the hospital where the man had been taken after his arrest. Along the short march to the hospital the leaders were joined by groups who ran from stores, from offices and from dwellings.

Chief Holland said he followed the mob after it left the hospital and found Williams hanging from a tree, his head swathed in bandages and his white hospital gown flapping in the night wind.

"There was no use for me to try to arrest anybody," Holland said, "because I was outnumbered too much. There was too many of them for one man to handle."

He reported to the State's Attorney that Williams was suspended from the tree for about twenty minutes, after his body had been raised and lowered at the end of the rope several times. The man, apparently dead, was then lowered, and the crowd, which then numbered 2,000, marched away behind a group that was carrying the body toward the Negro section.

On the way, the leaders stopped at the garage of the Red Star Bus Line and from a watchman demanded gasoline. The watchman protested that the pumps and tanks were locked and he could not open them, but this statement was met by a threat to break the locks. He then opened the pumps and the mob filled buckets and marched on to a vacant lot on a hill above the section where most of the Negro populace lives. The gasoline was poured over the man and lighted.

Flames leaped up for a few minutes and the mob then picked up the body and started again to the courthouse. Near the center of the city a rope was thrown over a guy wire on a telephone pole and the body pulled into the air again. It remained there and the mob dispersed. Sheriff Phillips cut the body down later.

Sheriff Phillips reported to the State's Attorney that he was knocked down and trampled by the mob when he tried to reach the tree from which Williams was hanging.

"I was in my office when a telephone call came that a mob was gathered around the hospital," he said. "I got into my automobile and started to drive there, but the streets near the hospital were choked with parked automobiles and I got out and ran to the entrance. When I got there and asked what the trouble was, somebody yelled 'You're too late Sheriff, they've gone with him.'

"As soon as I found the direction the mob had gone, I started at a run after them, but when I got to the Courthouse green the man was already hanging from a tree. I tried to get through, but was knocked down and walked on. I don't think the mob recognized me. I didn't recognize any of them and it seemed to me that they must have come from all around. There were a lot of women in the crowd.

"When the mob started away from the body I went to my office to get assistance. As soon as we were able to get the body we put it in a truck and hid it until the mob broke up and then turned it over to an undertaker."

The sheriff said that the crowd at the courthouse when he tried to break through numbered at least 1,000.

"Most of the time while the lynching was underway," witnesses told the authorities, "you could have heard a pin drop." The hanging occurred, old residents recalled, within forty feet of the spot where the last lynching in the history of this county took place, far back in the last century."

The *Sunpapers* also expressed outrage in its editorial of Saturday, December 5. It was entitled "DISGRACE" and read, in part:

The Eastern Shore has reaped its reward. For four weeks its restless elements have proclaimed mob law. For four weeks its officials and its responsible citizens have yielded ground. They started with their minds fixed upon law as the means of dealing with crime, however atrocious. But they have increasingly wavered. In the Yuel Lee [sic] case the court could find last Monday no conditions which would prevent a fair and orderly trial at Cambridge, although no more than two weeks ago the same court and the State's Attorney had petitioned the Governor for troops and for police "armed for any emergency." That judicial finding, so strangely in accord with popular clamor, so hazardous in the view of observers, was hailed on the Eastern Shore as a vindication of the dignity of the people! And as if in logical sequence, last night a mob in Salisbury heeded the law not at all, but instantly wreaked barbarous vengeance upon a Negro murderer.

We say the Eastern Shore has had its reward. Whether the reward takes the form this morning of satisfaction or shame we have no way of knowing. We do know that the Eastern Shore's reward is shame for the state of Maryland. It has been twenty years since Maryland has been disgraced by this savagery. We had supposed the freedom from disgrace was permanent. And it had not been supposed that in any old and seasoned community of the State, decent and intelligent people would throw wide the gates to the mad and unreasoning and bid them take command. It was a false pride and a false security. The lowest and least civilized elements did take command and that remains true whether or not men of position participated in the Salisbury lynching or tacitly approved it.

There will be hope that this upsurge of barbarity will bring intelligent men on the Eastern Shore to their senses, and that they will take whatever steps need to be taken to assure respect for the law in the cases of the two Negroes yet to be tried for serious crimes. But there is a duty beyond that. There is a duty upon the officials of Wicomico county and upon Governor Ritchie to seek out the members of the Salisbury mob and to punish them. It must be admitted that there is no great hope that the county officials will do so. The size of the mob and the manner in which the lynching was carried out point to official indifference and complacency. That, however, makes it the more imperative that the Governor use the full power of his office and that he permit no technicalities to stand in the ways of ruthless prosecution.

XIII

Mencken Weighs In

The *Evening Sun* would strike a further and indeed mighty blow against the senseless violence that had occurred in Salisbury. On Monday, December 7, 1931, Henry L. Mencken mused at the events, then sharpened his sarcasm and vitriol to a fine honed edge. He would stay silent no longer. The barbarity of the incident overwhelmed him and he used his unparalleled power of the word to strike back.

Born in Baltimore on September 12, 1880, Henry Louis Mencken had carved a meteoric career in journalism. In the1920s he had been an editor of the *American Mercury* magazine, a fashionable periodical for the sophisticated all over the country. Although the *American Mercury* was published in New York as a joint venture with Jean George Nathan, Mencken had faithfully and fastidiously remained a steadfast resident of Hollins Street, a middle-class neighborhood in west Baltimore (his carefully maintained house remains today as a faithful but seldom visited shrine to his memory).

Mencken, a strident intellectual, had gained national fame when he covered the 1925 "Scopes Monkey Trial" in Dayton, Tennessee. This internationally renowned trial in which the fundamental Christian movement and its champion, former presidential candidate William Jennings Bryan, clashed resoundingly and famously with the ideals of Clarence Darrow, the nationally famous liberal trial lawyer (who was portrayed impeccably by Spencer Tracey in the movie *Inherit the Wind*), over teaching evolution in schools gave Mencken a nationwide audience. He quickly became a celebrated and respected American journalist.

By 1931, Henry Mencken had settled into a regime of esteemed journalistic tenure with the *Baltimore Sun*. He was an editor with a byline, which assured the *Sun* of a wide and respectful readership. Mencken was the star of the *Sunpapers* show. Although not at the pinnacle of his national prominence, he was still a formidable presence in the literary world. Therefore, when Henry Mencken wrote, people read and paid close attention.

On December 7, the *Evening Sun* published his article on its front page for all the world to read. Entitled "The Eastern Shore Kultur," the article fairly spat the contempt Mencken felt:

> *Not many observant Marylanders, I take it, were surprised by the news of last Friday's extraordinarily savage and revolting lynching at Salisbury. Something of the sort has been plainly hatching down in that forlorn corner of the State for a long while. There was a time, years ago, when it was the seat of an urbane and charming culture, dominated by an enlightened and public-spirited gentry, but of late it has succumbed to its poor white trash, who now determine its ideas and run its affairs. The Ku Klux Klan, which was laughed at in all the more civilized parts of Maryland, got a firm lodgment in the lower counties of the Shore, and the brutish imbecilities that it propagated are still accepted gravely by*

a large number of the people, including not a few who should know better. The whole area is a lush stamping-ground for knavish politicians, prehensile professional patriots, and whooping soul-savers. It is, quite naturally, a stronghold of Prohibition (and of the rot-gut liquors that go therewith), and within its bounds tin-pot revivalism is making its last stand in Maryland.

Certainly it would be silly to think of the lynching as if it were an isolated incident. It was, in fact, nothing of the sort. It was the natural culmination of a degenerating process that has been in progress for years. At least since the World War, the lower Shore has been going downhill mentally and morally. It has been sliding out of Maryland and into the orbit of Arkansas and Tennessee, Mississippi and the more flea-bitten half of Virginia. Time and again the whole State has been menaced by the particular swinishness of its boozing-dry politics, and now it holds us all up to the contempt of the nation and the world by staging a public obscenity worthy of cannibals.

In the immediate premises, unfortunately, not much can be done. The gallant Wicomiconians, having butchered a wounded and helpless black man, seem very likely to get away with it. Governor Ritchie says that he has confidence in the Hon. Levin C. Bailey, the county State's Attorney, and no doubt it is justified, but Mr. Bailey can accomplish little if anything in the face of the prevailing public opinion, which supports the lynchers almost unanimously. If anyone wanted to arrest them, they might have been taken on the spot. They have made no efforts to disguise themselves, and every child in Salisbury knows who they are, and duly admires them. The difficulty is that the running of things in the whole unhappy region has passed into the hands of ninth-rate men. So it has become an Alsatia of morons, which is to say, of lynchers.

What it cries for without knowing it is more attention from the rest of the State. We have let it sweat in its own juices without paying anything more than casual attention to it. We have even allowed it to arrogate to itself a political power and importance altogether out of line with its state of civilization. Baltimore City sends one delegate to Annapolis for each 22,300 of its population, but Wicomico county sends one for every 7,800. Baltimore with 805,000 population, has six State senators, Wicomico, with but 31,600, has one. In other words, the vote of the president of Johns Hopkins University or of the Baltimore & Ohio Railroad, when it comes to electing the lower House of the Legislature, is worth but one-third as much as the vote of one of the Salisbury witch-burners, and when it comes to electing the upper House, but one-fourth as much.

The Salisbury lynching, at least in some part, was a gesture to that end. It was the local morons' answer to the effort of city men to make them behave with common decency.

The Cambridge Daily Banner, foaming in bad English, seeks to put all the blame for the sorry business in the Sunpapers, and hints broadly that it has turned Communist! My own suspicion is that Judge Ulman really had more hand in it though he acted quite innocently. When he intervened in the Yuel Lee case against the Snow Hill Dogberry he set the whole lower Shore afire. The lynching of poor Williams, dragged to death blind and in bandages, was no more than a melodramatic demonstration that the brave fellows of the region were not to be intimidated. They proved it as such poltroons always do—at odds of 1,000 to 1.

Certainly it would be irrational to ask for enlightenment in communities whose ideas are supplied by such pathetic sheets as the Cambridge Daily Banner and the Salisbury Times. Even the burning Baptists of rural Georgia are better off than that.

So I call for volunteers. The first should come from the lower Shore itself. Let its small minority of educated and civilized young men bestir themselves, lest their people be lost altogether.

The Sage of Baltimore had weighed in, and the shore, in response, attempted to rise to the challenge. There was a problem, however—it was hopelessly outclassed by the starkly simple fact that the event was indefensible. However offended the citizens of the lower shore were, the inexorable fact existed: Mencken was right. He had spoken out in his inimitable way against a savage lynching and there was no getting around it. The brutal, senseless killing could not be rationally defended.

Nevertheless, the shore newspapers tried. The *Cambridge Banner*, in its article entitled "The Finishing Touch," said in part:

> *Having fired a number of blasts at this paper, its editor, and the people generally on the Eastern Shore of Maryland,* The Sunpapers *have now turned us over to the tender mercies of Mr. H.L. Mencken, and Mr. Mencken in yesterday's issue of* The Evening Sun *proceeds to tell us what he thinks of us individually and collectively and, apparently, he does not think much of us.*
>
> *We feel rather complimented that to Mr. Mencken should be given the job of putting the final touch on this fair community. In fact, we recall that several years ago he wrote something along the same line (possibly worse) about the Presidents of the United States, beginning with George Washington, the first President and continuing down the line to Woodrow Wilson, and he paid no compliments to any of them.*
>
> *We suggest that the* Sunpapers *publish the article for, no doubt, many persons have forgotten it, especially that portion of the article which referred to William Jennings Bryan, whom he would have taken to the top of the Washington monument in Washington, disemboweled and hurled his remains into the Potomac River, possibly a rather polite form of lynching.*

(Mencken, although he professed to not recall what the *Banner*'s article referred to, had, indeed, suggested such a fate for Bryan in a burst of hyperbole in an article published in the *Evening Sun* on April 11, 1926. At that time, obviously in jest, Mencken had stated, "[The country] is damaged far worse when a Bryan hoists the black flag and declares a holy war upon all intelligence and decorum. That damage goes with the Democratic system. Is there no way of escape? I offer one at once. Let us have a Constitutional amendment providing that every unsuccessful aspirant for the Presidency, on the day his triumphant rival is inaugurated, shall be hauled to the top of the Washington Monument and there shot, poisoned, stabbed, strangled, and disemboweled and his carcass thrown into the Potomac.")

In its December 10 edition, the *Salisbury Times* reported on another consequence of Mencken's censure:

> *Resentment over the nature of criticism directed at the Eastern Shore from Baltimore has assumed the form today of a wide-spread move to bring "economic pressure" to bear upon Baltimore business interests to obtain from certain newspapers and others in that city a public apology to the people of the Eastern Shore.*
>
> *Businessmen throughout the Eastern Shore are severing connections of many years standing with the retail and wholesale houses and the industries in Baltimore. These Baltimore concerns are being told not to send their salesmen to make their periodic calls since there will be no orders placed with them.*

Within 48 hours Salisbury business interests have canceled orders placed in Baltimore valued at approximately $140,000, it was stated.

In these days of economic stagnation, the loss of Eastern Shore business may mean the difference between profit and loss for many Baltimore businesses and the severing of such relationship will be sufficient pressure to change the attitude of influential Baltimoreans toward the Eastern Shore.

In its edition of Saturday, December 12, the *Salisbury Times* prominently displayed on its front page a banner reading "The Eastern Shore Speaks," under which it published a series of articles reprinted from various shore newspapers. It reported the following from the *Federalsburg Times*:

The injustice in the article is plainly evident, when he [Mencken] refers to the section as the land of "poverty"…And if the rest of the state believes all that was in that article, which insinuated that the rest of Maryland would be better off without the Eastern Shore, then we are ready and willing to sever what broken ties remain with the Western Shore and Baltimore city and form a state of our own across the bay.

And, the following from the *Centreville Record*:

All we ask of the Baltimore press is to give us proper publicity and not to exploit unduly the crimes on the Eastern Shore any more than they do the banking and financial happenings in Baltimore city, and we will see that justice is meted out properly to those accused of crimes and without mob violence.

The *Chestertown Enterprise* had stated:

The Eastern Shore wants nothing more at this time than to be left alone in the settling of its problems. Outside interference which caused the delay in the case of the Worcester murderer of four was directly responsible for the deplorable lynching in Salisbury.

Lee, the Worcester murderer, and Davis, the Kent ravager of motherhood, were spirited here and there by the Shore police authorities that justice might be done. And all to what end? The chance for a Baltimore Communistic lawyer, interested in the Negro law trade because of his connection with a firm dealing in financial loans to Negroes, to gain columns of personal publicity at the expense of hampered and delayed justice.

So, without too much effort, the circle had come around to Bernard Ades. The lynching in Salisbury had been laid at his feet, and the blood of Matthew Williams had been placed on his hands. Euel Lee's case and its delays were cited as the reason for the violence at the courthouse lawn in Salisbury, and the violent, lawless death of a black man.

Bernard Ades however, was having none of it. He was not going to let his client, black and indigent as he was, succumb to the Eastern Shore mobs. His determination to see to it that the trial was removed from the entire shore was now more focused than ever. Williams's death was a stark realization of what could happen to Lee if his trial was held anywhere near the site of the lynching.

Joining Ades in his feelings regarding the shore was H.L. Mencken. Anything but cowed by the diatribes from the Eastern Shore press, Mencken hove to and unleashed another broadside.

In an editorial published in the December 14, 1931 *Evening Sun*, he let go another salvo directed at the shoremen:

> What with their grandiose effort to stampede and paralyze Baltimore with threats of boycott, ruin and desolation, their even more grandiose efforts to terrify the sinful *Sunpapers into* leaping to the mourners bench and accepting lynching as a Christian sacrament, and their announced determination, come what may, to save the Republic and the True Faith from the hellish conspiracies of the Russian Bolsheviki, the Salisbury fee-faw-fums are giving a very gaudy show—so gaudy, indeed, that I marveled to see Baltimoreans so indifferent to it. The local papers of the lower Shore, for a week past, have been bursting with incandescent and highly instructive stuff. They have not only mirrored faithfully the emotions of a pious and patriotic people at an heroic moment, they have printed a number of new facts about the sublime event of December 4. [Mencken then reported several items of local papers describing the lynching.] I reprint these brief extracts from a diatribe that runs on to a column because they serve very well to show what effect the lynching spirit, if it is allowed to go unchecked, has upon the minds of simple people—even upon the more literate minority thereof…The question before the house is thus quite simple. It is whether the Salisbury lynchers will be permitted to escape punishment for their crime, and so inspire a long series of like atrocities among similar town boomers, or whether the decent people of the lower Shore will band themselves together effectively and see that the guilty are brought to heel.

Aside from Mencken's formidable contempt, Ades's quest to secure an effective removal of Lee's case from the entire shore was an admirable effort, and one which was essential to his client's safety. His redemption, if it came, would be in the appellate court, not in the caldron of public clamor on the Eastern Shore. He would turn to Annapolis for justice.

XIV

The High Court is Heard From

In 1931, the Maryland Court of Appeals was located on State Circle in Annapolis, just across the street, and in the shadow of the State House. It was a conservative place, and the building reflected its conservative aura. The building was square, constructed of brick and an imposing edifice, as befitted the judicial branch of the state government. The courtroom was at the top of an impressive staircase, and had as its focal point a ceiling made of Tiffany glass. The Court of Appeals was Maryland's supreme court and there was no higher state authority. The court was removed from the political storms and had no constituency, unlike the judges on the lower shore. The judges of the appellate court were surely aware, however, of the notorious events taking place in the Lee case and on the shore. It is certain that the loud headlines caught their collective eye, as hardly a day went by without the *Sunpapers* and several other state dailies reporting the news in detail. The judges observed the events on the shore with alarm. They did not recognize the clamor or the emotion of the citizens in Worcester; they were only intent upon seeing that the law was complied with and observed.

Ades, therefore, determined upon the only course he knew that could secure an audience of judges outside the contentious area: he would file an appeal from the refusal of the lower shore jurists to heed his request to get the case away from the uproar. On December 10, 1931, Ades filed an appeal from the circuit court for Worcester County, which became docketed as Number 105, October term, 1931. His appeal had one salient point to make: his affidavit and offer of proof (rejected by the lower court) showed conclusively that the events which had already transpired on the lower shore precluded a fair and impartial trial.

There was a problem, however; Ades had filed his appeal prematurely. A case cannot be reviewed by the Court of Appeals until a final judgment is entered on the original case. Until the trial was held in Cambridge, no appeal could lie. Until there was a resolution of the guilt of the defendant, the Court of Appeals had nothing to review.

At this time, however, a startling turn of events occurred. The attorney general of the state of Maryland weighed in on the side of the defense. At the oral argument before the Court of Appeals held on December 16, Attorney General William Preston Lane joined defense counsel in arguing that the trial of Lee should, indeed, be removed from the shore. No doubt the events in Salisbury had great influence on his decision. If a black man could be publicly lynched in Salisbury, what would prevent such an occurrence to be repeated in the adjoining county of Dorchester? Ades, of course, had been expected to argue that the lower shore was not a fit place to hold the trial, but the attorney general, the highest law enforcement officer in the state, joining in on that key created a highly charged situation. Lane declared in his argument that "events which took place subsequent to the filing of the appeal have indicated the existence of a state of feeling in certain communities of the first circuit similar to that which caused this court to reverse the circuit court in another case in Talbot County. If the trial of this case proceeds in Dorchester county, and if it is necessary to have the militia and a force of police in order to protect the traverser, such a course may form the basis of a further appeal to this court and possibly to the Supreme Court of the United States." One can discern from the words of the attorney general that he had been swayed by the Salisbury lynching to abandon Godfrey Child and the Worcester County judicial system.

Later that afternoon, back in Pocomoke City, when Godfrey Child found out about Lane's stance, he hit the ceiling. (It is evident that Lane had not personally told Child of his flip-flop.) Child expressed astonishment when advised of the argument, saying that it had been his understanding that Lane would urge the upholding of the lower court decision, so he had decided to not go to Annapolis to argue the case, confident that the attorney general was going to support the State's position. Actually, Child had reason to be upset. It was, and is still, the function of the attorney general to uphold the position of the State in such matters. At least, if Lane was going to do a turnabout, he should have had the courtesy to advise Child so that he would not be blind-sided. In fact, said Child, Lane had promised Child a copy of the brief he filed, but no copy had been forthcoming.

Meanwhile on the lower shore, events were proceeding apace. Taking only a day off to argue in the Court of Appeals, Lane resumed his efforts to achieve an effective investigation of the Williams lynching. It must be noted that in 1931, as indeed today, the office of State's Attorney is one of the most powerful in the state of Maryland. The county prosecutors, in fact, have more untrammeled discretion in the matters of their authority than do judges. There is no review of the determinations of the prosecutor under the Maryland Constitution. While judges faced review by higher courts, no such examination of the State's Attorney's discretion existed at the time nor does it exist in Maryland today. Therefore, Levin Bailey, not William Preston Lane, was in control of the events in Salisbury.

Scream as the *Sunpapers* did, shout as H.L. Mencken may and appeal as Lane might, the decision rested with one man only. Lane, knowing this, apparently decided to ascend the bully pulpit. The *Salisbury Times* reported in its December 18, 1931 edition:

> *Seeking some definite information on which to base action, Attorney General William Preston Lane, Jr., left Baltimore today to return to Salisbury to resume his investigation of the lynching there two weeks ago of Matthew Williams, negro.*
>
> *Mr. Lane, accompanied by one of his assistants, G.C.A. Anderson, left shortly after he concluded a series of conferences with Levin Bailey, State's Attorney for Wicomico county who came to Baltimore for the purpose...*
>
> *Mr. Lane already has spent two days in Salisbury this week in carrying out Governor Ritchie's orders that he conduct a thorough inquiry into the lynching...*
>
> *Mr. Lane's inquiry into the mob action was suspended while he appeared before the Court of Appeals at Annapolis in its hearing on the appeal by attorneys for Yuel Lee, confessed negro Worcester county slayer, from the Worcester circuit court in its refusal to transfer the Lee trial to the western shore. The state's highest court has not yet given a decision on the appeal.*

On December 19, the *Salisbury Times* reported that the coroner's jury was focusing its attention in the case of the death of Williams on an unlikely personage. W. Arthur Kennedy, the foreman of the jury, stated that he wished to have a subpoena issued for none other than Henry L. Mencken, himself. The impetus for this action was, undoubtedly, the editorial the previous day found in the *Salisbury Times* entitled, "Hint To Mr. Bailey." The editorial espoused the complicity of Mencken in the matter:

> *In a perfectly inexcusable editorial, the* Sun *yesterday resurrected the ghost of Matthew Williams and repeated what has already been said a thousand times: That a thorough investigation should be made into the hanging of the confessed murderer here on December 4.*
>
> *But the* Sun *goes farther than many of us. It says the leaders of the mob are known. In this respect,* The Sun*'s editor has us one up…*
>
> *Now if the* Sun *is really serious in wanting to have a thorough investigation, why does not its editor give the information in his possession to States Attorney Bailey or Attorney General Lane?*
>
> *And Henry L. Mencken, whose scorn for everything that is of the Eastern Shore knows no bounds, writing in the* Evening Sun *has twice said that every school child in the city knows the names of the mob leaders. Has he, or* The Evening Sun*, made this information available to the investigators?*
>
> *We suggest that Mr. Bailey issue a subpoena for Mr. Mencken and the unnamed editorial writer of* The Sun *and demand them to testify under oath before the coroner's jury.*

In the January 24, 1932 issue of the *New York Times*, Virginius Dabney, the respected editor of the *Richmond Times-Dispatch*, wrote as an editorial correspondent:

> *One of the liveliest controversies of recent months, a controversy in which H.L. Mencken and the* Baltimore Evening Sun *have been arrayed against the citizenry and press of the eastern shore of Maryland and Virginia, is gradually simmering down, with all hands apparently tired of dipping their pens in vitriol, after some weeks devoted to hurling epithets back and forth across the Chesapeake.*
>
> *The fun began when Mr. Mencken wrote an article for the* Evening Sun *on December 7, three days after the lynching of a Negro at Salisbury, on the Maryland eastern shore, in which he took some ferocious wallops at the state of culture on the lower portion of the Maryland shore. The blast contained such phrases as "poor white trash," "knavish politicians," "prehensile professional patriots," and "whooping soulsavers," "an Alsatia for morons," and "simian self-seeking in public office," all of which he had applied with gusto to the region and its inhabitants.*
>
> *The reaction beyond the Chesapeake was immediate and unmistakable. There was an instantaneous outburst of recrimination in the press, and Mr. Mencken and* The Evening Sun *were roundly scored. At the same time a large quantity of business with Baltimore houses was canceled by Salisbury business men—no less than $150,000 worth in one day according to apparently reliable estimates.*
>
> *An idea of the sort of thing which appeared in the newspapers of the lower Maryland shore may be gleaned from the editorial columns of the* Worcester Democrat, *which opined that "Mencken's soul, if he has one must have come from a hyena, a rattlesnake or a skunk," while the* Cambridge Daily Banner *made the discovery that Mencken himself is "a lyncher" since he once proposed to take William Jennings Bryan "to the top of the Washington monument in Washington, disembowel him and hurl his remains in the Potomac."*
>
> *In the meantime Mr. Mencken was having the time of his life belaboring the Salisbury lynchers. His article in the* Evening Sun *of Dec. 7 was followed by another of Dec. 14, despite the cancellations which were coming in, and there was a third broadside on Dec. 27.*

For more than a month after the appearance of his first article there was an almost continuous flood of protesting letters from the shore to the editor of the Evening Sun. *The shoremen have long looked upon the wet and libertarian city of Baltimore with decidedly fishy eye anyway, and the Menckenian gibes were more than they could stand. "I could not face my God if I should let such insults go unanswered," wrote one correspondent. "The men of the eastern shore are God-fearing, red-blooded men," wrote another.*

As for the lynching itself, the authorities of Salisbury have been spending so much time in denunciations of Mencken and The Sun *that they have neglected to bring the lynchers to justice. Nearly seven weeks have passed and no arrest has been made, although many of the participants in the crime are said to be known. Governor Ritchie and Attorney General Preston Lane have done all they are empowered to do under the state Constitution. If no member of the mob is brought to trial, the responsibility will lie at the door of the Salisbury authorities.*

Once again an unflattering light was cast on the area, this time by the respected *New York Times*.

It is true that, finally, the fiery outrage against Mencken eventually died out, perhaps because of the simple exhaustion of the issue after so much vitriol. (It is equally certain that some resentment against him has remained throughout the generation of shoremen who still recall the events.)

The Court of Appeals in the early thirties had a far different schedule than do appellate courts today. When the arguments on the issue of the Lee trial removal were presented, the court actually retired and went to deliberate its decision the same day. The judges were intent upon causing the case to be decided by fast action. With all the things going on in the lower shore courts and on the political scene, it was becoming obvious that the odds were being stacked against the Worcester County prosecutor. In light of all these events, it was questionable whether the premature appeal would be given the short procedural shift that it deserved under the law. Indeed, the answer was not long in coming.

On December 29, 1931, the Court of Appeals issued its opinion in *Euel Lee v. State of Maryland*, found in the Maryland Reports at 161 Md. 430. It was written by Chief Judge Carroll T. Bond. It is interesting if only for the fact that it became authored at all. In fact, the chief judge's opinion was only supported by two other judges on the court, Judge Hammond Urner and Judge T. Scott Offutt. Judge William H. Adkins and Judge D. Lindsey Sloan thought the case should be dismissed and the opinion should go no further; Judge W. Mitchell Diggs would have reversed the lower court outright; and Judge Francis Neal Parke would not have tampered with the lower court's discretion. Indeed, normally the court would merely refuse to consider the case because of its improper filing. This time, however, the court issued a remarkable opinion:

The appellant, or plaintiff in error, indicted on charges of murder in Worcester County, exercised his constitutional right to have the case removed from the circuit court of that county for trial, and now, before any further proceedings have been had below, he seeks, by a petition upon a writ of error, a reversal by this court of the trial court's selection of a place for trial. But action upon that question at this stage of the cause seems clearly barred by the rule that this court cannot take up cases from the trial courts piecemeal. Its jurisdiction is limited to the reviewing of final actions of the trial court...Indeed this is the first time during the history of the court that it has definitely been asked to review a selection made by a trial court upon removal of a case…The accused has been allowed his constitutional right of removal from the court of origin, and therefore has no complaint of a denial of that right, which has been held immediately reviewable; and he seeks a review only of the subsequent discretionary selection of a new court for the case, and on that selection no appeal for proceeding as upon writ of error now lies. The proceeding upon the assignment of error must be dismissed.

The court did not stop there, however. It continued to resolve the issue even though it had already dismissed the appeal:

It cannot be the practice to do this ordinarily, but we agree that the course may well be followed in this case.

The opinion then proceeded to give an extensive and detailed review of the events that had transpired since the murders. It determined that the following was particularly significant:

The official estimate of the danger from popular feeling is illustrated by a plan which appears to have been suggested by the State's Attorney of Dorchester County to the Governor of the State, that the accused be brought to Cambridge by boat strongly guarded, and that during the period of the trial he should be housed on one of the boats, anchored in the stream at night, instead of being held in the normal manner in the county jail. And the Attorney General of the State, when requested to aid in the trial for the State, announced his conviction that a fair trial could not be had in Dorchester County, and strongly urged that a trial there should not be attempted.

The court also made mention of the fact that the allegations of mob violence advanced by Ades had not been denied by Godfrey Child, but it noted that he did attribute them to the misconduct of Ades.

The remarkable opinion concluded with these words:

In the opinion of this court, the conditions evidenced by the occurrences recited would leave no latitude for discretion, but would demonstrate that the securing of a fair unprejudiced jury from the county selected as the place for the trial of the charges against this man and any defenses he may make, is unlikely, and that to attain the object of the Constitution and statutes the cause must be removed for trial to some other portion of the state, on the one shore of the bay or the other, where it appears at least more likely that the local prejudice may be avoided. That there is, in the section of the state so far selected, such prejudice as forbids attempting a trial there, seems to this court to be manifested in the recited attacks on the jail in Snow Hill, and the entrances gained, in endeavors to get the man for lynching, the conclusion of the local authorities that he must be taken away from both Worcester and Dorchester Counties to Baltimore city for safe-keeping while awaiting trial, and that he must be brought to trial with a guard of troops, the opinion of the Attorney General, representing the state in the prosecution here, that the condition of mind of the population of the counties from which a jury would be drawn in the circuit is still such that it makes a fair trial unlikely and requires that trial be had elsewhere.

Ades, with an untimely appeal, which had been ruled premature and had been legally dismissed by the highest court in Maryland, had, nevertheless, won. It was apparent that, at the time the case would be ruled upon, he would be granted a new trial due to the improper action of the circuit court to require an effective removal of the case.

The effect of the opinion was evident to the press. The *Salisbury Times* in its December 30 edition stated:

> *ADES TO FILE MOTION FOR TRIAL REMOVAL. Jurists, Upheld By Highest Tribunal, Silent As To Next Step In Process: Although the Maryland Court of Appeals yesterday ruled that the Circuit Court acted within its constitutional authority in holding the case of Yuel Lee [sic] within the First Judicial Circuit on the lower Eastern Shore there has risen some doubt that the lower court will insist it be tried in the circuit. It is considered likely that the three jurists themselves might take voluntary action on sending the trial farther away from the scene of the quadruple crime, the commission of which the defendant has confessed…Chief Judge John R. Pattison of the first circuit, which includes Worcester, Dorchester, Wicomico and Somerset counties, indicated that he and his associates might take cognizance of the appeals court's holding that a fair trial could not be obtained in the circuit. Further than that, he would not discuss the case.*

XV

Lee Goes to the Western Shore

Faced with the opinion of the Court of Appeals, the lower shore judges met. They were not foolish men, and they were, after all, judges. On January 5, 1932, they issued an opinion. It read, in part:

> *A few days ago, the Court of Appeals rendered its decision in which it held that the orders appealed from were preliminary and not final orders from which an appeal would lie. The court, however, in its opinion did not stop with a mere dismissal of the appeal…but in addition thereto, said, "the problem before the judges when removing this cause from the Circuit Court for Worcester County, was solely that of the selection of a new jurisdiction, which, so far as could be seen, was likely to be free of the hazard of an unfair, prejudiced jury."*
>
> *In other words we are in effect told by a majority decision of the Court of Appeals in advance of the trial that, if the case is not removed to some other court other than the Circuit Court for Dorchester County, but is tried in that county, and the verdict should be against the prisoner, and an appeal then taken to the Court of Appeals, the judgment of the Dorchester County Court will be reversed. And this, it seems, would be the result, notwithstanding that, at the trial of the case, it might be shown that the prisoner had a fair and impartial trial, free and clear of all prejudices. In view of this situation, a trial of the case in Dorchester County would be not only futile, but would result in the imposition of unnecessary costs upon the taxpayers of Worcester County. And therefore we feel constrained to remove the case to a court other than the Circuit Court for Dorchester County.*

That day the judges ordered that Lee would be tried in Baltimore County, far from the First Judicial Circuit. Ades had gotten his way. Trial would be held on the Western Shore of Maryland. Godfrey Child would have to journey into the area of Ades's practice.

Godfrey Child was, however, no country bumpkin. A suave, gentle, sophisticated man, educated at Washington College in Chestertown and with a law degree from the University of Maryland, he was the epitome of a country gentleman. He was not a rabble-rouser, nor a Babbitt. His was the politics of reason, even though he had espoused the trial in his home court. He was, therefore, prepared to go forth into the urban setting of the Baltimore County circuit court.

Ades, also, had his work cut out for him. Notwithstanding the initial victory of the removal, he still had a case of formidable problems on his hands. Even though he was shed of the shore, he still had a defendant who was facing huge odds. There were the two confessions, the items found in Lee's room, the motive for the killings and, not least of all, the opportunity to commit the crime. Ades surely had gauged his adversary by now; he knew that Child would be a formidable opponent. With a reticent client facing overwhelming evidence against him, Ades knew that a tough road lay ahead. It is perhaps for that reason that another attorney soon would enter the case.

The *Sun* reported on January 17 that there were two lawyers assisting Ades: David Levinson, from Philadelphia, and Eli Schwarzblatt, of New York, who were assisting in the nationally sensational trial in Mississippi defending the "Scottsboro Boys." While radical Levinson would become prominent in the Lee trial, Schwarzblatt did not become a part of the defense team. It turned out that his duties in the Scottsboro case would require too much of his time. [During the fall and winter of 1931–32, the ILD was challenging the NAACP for dominance in the Scottsboro case, a sensationally publicized trial of several young black boys accused of raping two white women on a train near Scottsboro, Alabama. Despite the efforts of the NAACP, including retaining Clarence Darrow of the Scopes Monkey Trial as a potential defense attorney, the ILD won over the defendants with the inclusion of Samuel Lebowitz, an equally renowned defense attorney.]

Soon the circuit court for Baltimore County would set the trial date. The *Salisbury Times* of January 6, 1932, reported that the State's Attorneys for Worcester, Dorchester and Baltimore Counties were meeting with the circuit court judges for Baltimore County in a conference regarding Lee's trial. The first matter was to arrange for the transmission of the Worcester County record to Baltimore County. It was evident that the trial would be held in the month of January. Judge Frank I. Duncan stated that all other cases would be subordinated to the Lee trial, and that after certain matters were resolved, all other pending matters would be suspended until the completion of Lee's case. He, together with Judge C. Gus Grason and Chief Judge T. Scott Offutt, would jointly preside at the trial.

The case was set for Monday, January 18, 1932, and the *Salisbury Times* edition of January 11, proclaimed in banner headlines: "Lee Case Set For Trial Monday." The article also announced a significant, though little noticed statement by Ades on behalf of the defendant: "Bernard Ades, attorney for the International Labor Defense League and counsel for Lee, announced that he will seek a jury trial, and would demand that negroes be represented on the jury. It was pointed out that no jury here had ever included negroes, and opposition was expressed to Ades' demand." This offhand remark by the press had a portent that few people realized at the time.

At the same juncture, State's Attorney Child announced that the indictment of Lee alleging the murder of Green Davis would be tried first. It should be remembered that there were four separate indictments handed down, and that each charging document constituted a separate and distinct offense, which would be tried separately. Child announced that the State had summoned fifty-seven witnesses, and he believed that, although the trial would last but three days, at least one night session would be required. As the weekend approached, the stage was set for the trial to commence on Monday, January 18.

Also, on that same day in Snow Hill, the case of assault against Helen Mays was indefinitely continued, resulting in no fixed trial date being scheduled. As reported by the *Baltimore American*: "The case of Miss Helen Mays, comely, frail bodyguard of robust Bernard Ades, chief counsel for Euel Lee, was indefinitely continued in circuit court today. Miss Mays was seized on a charge of carrying a concealed weapon on November 4, when a crowd jostled her and Ades after they had come here in connection with the Lee defense. On November 6, Godfrey Child, State's Attorney for Worcester County, moved for forfeiture of Miss May's bond. It was for $500 and was signed by Ades."

Helen's case in Worcester County and the forfeiture of $500 was the least important matter in the mind of Bernard Ades. In less than seven days the trial for Lee's life would commence.

A photo purported to be Green Davis and his wife Ivy just prior to the murder. Actually the lady in the photo is his first wife; Ivy is described by a family member as "small and blonde." At the time of the murder, Green Davis was fifty-five years old and his wife was thirty-eight. Berlin-Ocean City News.

Downtown Berlin, c. 1920. Theodore Purnell's soda fountain, where young Charles Lynch took the phone call announcing the horrible murders, is in the center at the intersections of Main and Broad Streets. The magistrate's office and police station is just out of the picture to the left. *Collection of Joseph Moore, courtesy of Reese F. Cropper Jr., Calvin B. Taylor Bank.*

State police guarding the murder scene at Taylorville, two miles east of Berlin and five miles west of Ocean City, Monday October 12, 1931. *Baltimore* Sunpapers *and Photograph Collections, University of Maryland, Baltimore County.*

Local and state police at the scene of the murder. Green and Ivy Davis's second-floor bedroom is the closest to the camera; the bedroom of their daughters, Elizabeth and Mary Lee, is the far left window on the front of the house. Berlin-Ocean City News.

Scene outside the Davis home. It was first reported that the murder weapon was an ax, due to the mutilation of the faces of the victims. In the interrogation of Jones, he was asked if he used an ax as a weapon, and he denied it. *Baltimore* Sunpapers *and Photography Collections, University of Maryland Baltimore County.*

MESSENGER

ER 17, 1931 $1.50 A YEAR. $2.00 OUT OF COUNTY

Quadruple Murder Near Berlin---Negro Confesses The Crime

William Green Davis, His Wife and Two Daughters Are the Victims of Orphan Jones, Virginia Negro, Who Had Been Employed By Davis As Farm Hand—Confesses and Is Hurried to Baltimore Jail by Sheriff Purnell and State Police—Funeral of Murdered Family Attended By Hundreds of People At Berlin On Thursday—Interment At Bishopville—Grand Jury Will Take Up the Case Next Monday, Oct. 19.

William Green Davis, Mrs. Davis and their two daughters were brutally murdered in their home, near Taylorville, last Saturday night, by Orphan Jones, a Virginia negro, who is alleged to have made a confession that he shot Mr. and Mrs. Davis with a pump gun, and the two daughters with a shot-gun and pistol, his object being robbery.

Jones had been employed by Mr. Davis as a farm hand for several weeks, and it is claimed that Mr. Davis discharged the man because he had no more work for him to do. It is said Mr. Davis agreed to give the man a dollar a day, board and lodging, for his work. In settlement he deducted one dollar for a day the negro had not worked, and this was the occasion of a quarrel. The negro left, and it is said Mr. Davis discovered tracks under a window made by shoes like those worn by the negro. He reported this occurrence to an officer and asked that the negro be arrested. The officer said he could not arrest the man on such evidence. In a short while thereafter Mr. Davis and his family were murdered by Jones, who was subsequently arrested at Ocean City, carried to Berlin and from there brought to Snow Hill jail for safe keeping. The negro broke under more than 12 hours of grilling at the Snow Hill jail. To Randall Purnell, Snow Hill chief of Police, and Corporal M. D. Brubaker, State Police, Jones early Tuesday afternoon declared he would "tell all" if State's Attorney Godfrey Child were summoned.

The negro is said to have made a confession, in which he said he alone committed the crime, using a sixteen-gauge pump gun and a pistol to slay his victims before they could awaken. He declared he was drunk and wanted Davis' money. Immediately after procuring the confession, Jones was put into one of two automobiles which headed for Baltimore, escorted by six State policemen, Sheriff Purnell and two Baltimore city detectives.

When Jones finally decided to talk, all spectators and nearly a score of newspapermen and photographers loitering about the jail awaiting developments were ordered away. A cordon of State Police was then thrown about the prison. More than an hour after the prosecutor entered the jail to talk with Jones, the interrogation of the accused man continued.

Jones will be presented to the Worcester Grand Jury next week and will probably be tried before the adjournment of this Court.

State's Attorney And the Sheriff Work On Case

GODFREY CHILD
State's Attorney

WILMER S. PURNELL

The body of Davis, 52 years old, was found lying in bed beside that of his wife, Iva, 48, in the second face of their farm house. Bodies of the two girls, Elizabeth 15, and Mary Lee 10, both high school students, were found in an adjoining room.

Unless the slayer moved the bodies after committing the crime, each of the four must have been killed before being aroused from sleep. All were in night clothes and the bed clothing was only slightly disarranged.

Officers said the bedroom and kitchen floors had been sprinkled with

Funeral Services Held In Berlin

It is estimated that over a thousand people gathered in and around the Presbyterian church, in Berlin, to be present at the funeral of the Davis family, Thursday afternoon. It was a heart rending sight to see the four caskets carried into the church, as soft music by the organ greeted the funeral party. The caskets were covered with flowers

Report of the murder in the *Democratic Messenger*, Snow Hill, Maryland, October 17, 1931. The photo is of Godfrey Child, State's Attorney for Worcester County and Worcester County sheriff Wilmer S. Purnell. Democratic Messenger.

91

Orphan Jones was removed from the Worcester County jail in Snow Hill in order to protect him from possible mob violence. Notice the bandage over his left eye, surely a result of being hit during the trip from Berlin to the jail or during the interrogation. The officer escorting Jones from the jail is Snow Hill Police Chief Randolph Purnell. The person in profile in the left of the photograph is Ocean City Chief of Police Robert Allen Sr. *Baltimore* Sunpapers.

Although Jones had been removed to the Baltimore city jail for his safety, crowds of surly men congregated at the scene of the crime near Berlin and in Snow Hill, intent upon taking justice into their own hands. One group actually searched the Worcester County jail to ensure that Jones was not there. *Baltimore* Sunpapers.

The small, one-story building on the right beside the Globe Theater was the office of magistrate William J. Bratten and housed the Berlin police. It was here that Sheriff Wilmer Purnell first brought Orphan Jones after his arrest on October 12, 1931. *Collection of Joseph Moore, courtesy of Reese F. Cropper Jr., Calvin B. Taylor Bank.*

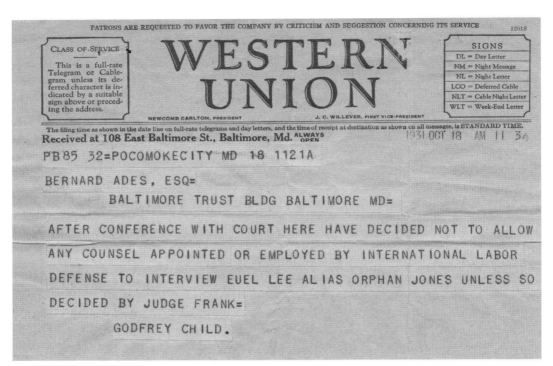

WESTERN UNION

NEWCOMB CARLTON, PRESIDENT   J. C. WILLEVER, FIRST VICE-PRESIDENT

CLASS OF SERVICE

This is a full-rate Telegram or Cablegram unless its deferred character is indicated by a suitable sign above or preceding the address.

SIGNS

DL = Day Letter
NM = Night Message
NL = Night Letter
LCO = Deferred Cable
NLT = Cable Night Letter
WLT = Week-End Letter

The filing time as shown in the date line on full-rate telegrams and day letters, and the time of receipt at destination as shown on all messages, is STANDARD TIME.

Received at 108 East Baltimore St., Baltimore, Md. ALWAYS OPEN   1931 OCT 18 AM 11 34

PB85 32=POCOMOKECITY MD 18 1121A

BERNARD ADES, ESQ=
      BALTIMORE TRUST BLDG BALTIMORE MD=

AFTER CONFERENCE WITH COURT HERE HAVE DECIDED NOT TO ALLOW
ANY COUNSEL APPOINTED OR EMPLOYED BY INTERNATIONAL LABOR
DEFENSE TO INTERVIEW EUEL LEE ALIAS ORPHAN JONES UNLESS SO
DECIDED BY JUDGE FRANK=
      GODFREY CHILD.

Western Union telegram from Godfrey Child to Bernard Ades on October 18, 1931, refusing to allow his participation in the case. *Collection of Joseph Moore.*

Old Worcester County jail (c. 1970) immediately behind the Worcester County courthouse (on right) where Bernard Ades, Helen Mays and Oscar Rabowsky were housed by Judge Joseph Bailey and Sheriff Wilmer Purnell in order to be protected from the mob on November 4, 1931. The sheriff's office is on the left and the cell block in the jail lockup is on the right. *Collection of Joseph Moore, courtesy of Harold Morris.*

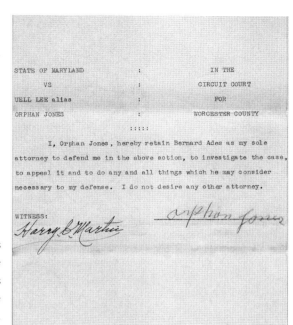

STATE OF MARYLAND   :   IN THE

       VS   :   CIRCUIT COURT

UELL LEE alias   :   FOR

ORPHAN JONES   :   WORCESTER COUNTY

               : : : : :

     I, Orphan Jones, hereby retain Bernard Ades as my sole attorney to defend me in the above action, to investigate the case, to appeal it and to do any and all things which he may consider necessary to my defense. I do not desire any other attorney.

WITNESS:

Retainer of Bernard Ades, signed by Orphan Jones and witnessed by Warden Harry G. Martin of the Baltimore city jail, filed on October 30, 1931. It was this retainer document that Ades feared would be destroyed by the Worcester County clerk's office. *Collection of Joseph Moore.*

WORCESTER COUNTY COURT HOUSE AND MARKET STREET, SNOW HILL, MD.

The restaurant where Bernard Ades, Helen Mays and Oscar Rabowsky were accosted on November 4, 1931, by the mob is on the right (Brimer's Restaurant). Ades's automobile was located to the immediate left just out of the picture, in front of Bates Methodist Church. The jail, where they were taken for refuge, is behind the courthouse to the left. Judge Joseph Bailey and Sheriff Wilmer Purnell, with three deputies, rushed out of the front door of the courthouse at the portico (in the left of the photo) in order to rescue the trio from the mob. *Collection of Joseph Moore.*

Lawyer Beaten By Shore Mob

BERNARD ADES

SNOW HILL MOB BEATS LAWYER AIDING NEGRO

Bernard Ades And Two Companions, One A Woman, Victims

3 ARE ATTACKED TWICE DURING DAY

Escorted Out Of Town, They Promise Never To Go Back

[By the Associated Press]

Snow Hill, Md., Nov. 4—A Worcester county mob, thwarted in three attempts to gain possession of Yuel Lee, Negro, accused of killing a family of four, today turned its wrath on Bernard Ades, of Baltimore, attorney for the International Labor Defense League and voluntary counsel for Lee.

Twice during the day, Ades and two companions, one a woman "protector," were attacked by the mob. After the second attack, Ades and his companions left Snow Hill for Baltimore, promising never to return.

The second and more serious demonstration came as Ades, with Miss Helen Mays and Oscar Rabowsky, attempted to leave the courthouse when Circuit Court was adjourned. The mob attacked the trio and beat them se-

Bernard Ades at the time of the mob attack in Snow Hill on November 4, 1931, together with the report of the incident in the *Sunpapers. Baltimore Sunpapers and Photography Collection, University of Maryland, Baltimore County.*

Judge Joseph Bailey, Wicomico County circuit court judge who rushed out of the Snow Hill courthouse with Sheriff Purnell and three deputies and waded into the mob to rescue Ades and his companions. (As Worcester County had no resident judge, Judge Bailey sat in cases in the county.) *Courtesy of Wicomico County circuit court.*

Interior of Worcester County circuit court clerk's office, Snow Hill, c. 1931. *From left:* Joseph Brimer, deputy clerk of court; unidentified woman; Paul Jones, register of wills; Miss Bessie Bowen, clerk of court (who, it is said, had an abiding dislike for Bernard Ades); unidentified woman. *Collection of Joseph Moore, courtesy of Stephen Hales, Worcester County clerk of circuit court.*

Crowd on Market Street in Snow Hill, November 6, 1931, after the rumor spread that Orphan Jones was to appear in court the next day. The courthouse is on the right, as identified by its front portico. A report of the event is graphically portrayed in the *Sunpapers. Baltimore* Sunpapers *and Photography Collections, University of Maryland Baltimore County.*

Peninsula General Hospital, Salisbury, c. 1925. It was from the "colored ward" in this building that Matthew Williams was dragged on December 4, 1931, to be lynched a few blocks away on the courthouse lawn. At the time of the incident the author's aunt, Virginia Cropper, was a patient in the hospital, giving birth to her first daughter, Joan. *Collection of Joseph Moore.*

Wicomico County courthouse, Salisbury, c. 1930. Matthew Williams was lynched by a mob at this site on December 4, 1931. The location of the hanging is on the right, around the corner of the courthouse along East Main Street. *Collection of Joseph Moore.*

Maryland, My Maryland!

From A Window In Fleet S

By FREDERIC N

London Bureau

GLASGOW, like any other city, is seen to best advantage in the company of a man who knows it. I am, therefore, particularly in the debt of a man who was determined that I should really see Glasgow. But first he would take it out of the legs, and we stood about in several places this morning, and had stood before handsomest churches, and delightful campanile of Street Church, and had most of the principal streets, stood outside the house in which Asquith spent her youth, admired (still standing) the Exchange Building, silent as a peak in Darien at best view of the "wan water" by the time I had done it, were pretty well worn down.

IMAGINE my feelings, then, when my friend, guide and no matter either, announced eagerness of one about to enter into unprecedented pleasures. "And now I'm taking you to a unique place for lunch where you eat standing..."

Fighting back the temptation to make some remark about finding them standing in a Russian restaurant, where standing is also the custom, I followed him.

LANG'S is. I can see now, had a couple of days well the desk, unique restaurant packed to the doors with of Glasgow's trade and of them standing so close it is miraculous that there are no collisions.

With your elbows held close to your sides and your eye on the food, bearing down in your effort to make way with a plate of pie with beans, an apple and a cup of tea. Each one of these is to be taken in turn from the luncher and borne on a favorable position obtained, warded off traffic which would, if you push your way through the crowd to where the...

Or if you want a sandwich though a sign warns you the sandwiches unnecessary make choice of a loaf always backing off in case munchers when you want a place...

AND, IF YOU want a place, may walk to the table you see for yourself. They do it in London, but it is the best people doing it. Find the cashier's desk, I crown, say, "One and" get back your change.

To my embarrassment I realize it was as simple as held up a line of customers while I made the most of it, calling the restaurateur, I even said, "What do you remember on the floor..."

LETTERS to the EDITOR

Would Repeal Smoot-Hawley Law

To the Editor of The Sun—Sir: We hear little now, after nearly ten years' operation, about the flexible tariff. It was the alibi to soothe the consumer and keep him from objecting to extortionate tariff rates. It proved to be a fake alibi. During nearly ten years' operation it accomplished nothing for the consumer.

Did it adjust the inequalities and extortions of the Smoot-Hawley law? It did not. Did it produce scientific tariff making? It did not. It is an arbitrary, guesswork process. It is a fake from beginning to end. The cost-difference formula, mixed up with advantages and disadvantages in competition, was not invented to benefit the consumer. It is based upon the absurd theory that the levy of tariff taxes is merely a contest between the domestic producer and the importer, leaving the consumer out of the picture. It leaves domestic manufacturers as well as importers upon a hot griddle of perpetual uncertainty, because under it the tariff tax affecting their business may be changed at any moment, whenever the so-called experts so desire. It la...

The Origins Of Tariff

To the Editor of The Sun—Sir: For the younger generation, and for its application to present-day practices in our own country, I retell the origin of the word tariff.

At the entrance to the Strait of Gibraltar stood Tarifa, a pirate stronghold, admirably situated for its main industry. Preying upon passing trading vessels and exacting of them toll, or tribute, was the chief business of the Tarifans.

The tariff system which we enjoy (?) today was the adoption, with refinements, of the methods of the pirates of Tarifa. The system, without refinements, adopted by the racketeering gangs of Chicago and elsewhere was identical with that of the pirate gang of Tarifa: "If you want to do business here, pay us for the privilege, or else"—

It is true that our tariff was first designed for the protection of infant industries. It is equally true that those same infants have long since grown to be rapacious giants. Today it is we, their helpless victims, who pray for protection...

Cowboys Still Riding In West

[The letter in the Nation]

The Drifter's sighs over the cowboy and his pony, whom he pictured as a "dying race," have brought a lively response from one of the last of the great open spaces—Montana. The letter is typewritten and signed "A Dude Wrangler's Wife." It runs as follows:

Dear Drifter—I like you too well to stand idly by while you are needlessly unhappy. You evidently like cowboys. So do I, and I bring you the cheering news that, contrary to your observations, they are not members of a "dying race."

True, the cowboy of today may not be the blue-jeaned, tobacco-chewing, two-gun outlaw that he once was; but where did you get the idea there are no more cattle to be driven to shipping points, no more bawling calves to be caught and branded, no more wild range horses to be wrangled and broken—time-honored occupations of every cowboy that ever lived? Come out West and see—

There are plenty of good new ranches left in this part of the country, where...

---

delegations are in nearly every intrenched at Washington than gations.

...rtionment act, which takes effect seventy-third Congress, will by representation of the metropolitan help to give the cities the national affairs for which the urban population properly calls. Impossible for the cities to take place until they and their spokesmen o a sense of their national responsibilities. The decision of the Tammany meet its responsibilities at Washington ove toward such an awakening urban centers may be grateful. steps in the same direction and it be almost as well represented as our farming regions.

...AKER, MR. GARNER

...ination of John N. Garner, of ..., as their candidate for the the Democratic members of the have selected an able parliamentarian to be their leader in a session their narrow majority will make it fighting inevitable. Mr. Garner a good account of himself in battle in which he has engaged. not always emerged victorious been due more to the slenderness forces with which he went into his own lack of foresight and

...majority of five to start with. prospect that it may be increased on of a number of contests in cratic candidates, the odds will time, be in Mr. Garner's favor, ve an opportunity to show that well in the constructive process latterly as he has done in the processes of opposition. The man he has reconciled conflicting past few weeks and arranged matters in such a way as to make caucus a thoroughly harmonious suits that he can work with a mass as with a minority and argues access in the office for which he pointed.

...prospect of a Democratic majority Mr. Garner has maintained a close as to the program which he king out in consultation with atic leaders both in and out of disclosure of that program will er and a better opportunity for capacity of the party leadership d of Mr. Garner in particular, e enlarged responsibilities which fall to the Democratic lot. In Mr. Garner, Mr. Henry T has been nominated for the post leader, and the other candidates ices will need and deserve the support which was in evidence nominations were made.

PLAN COMMISSION

the Commission on City Plan an is doing nothing more than the law. The Charter provides dy and its need is so obvious few large cities in the country create one.

...sion will consist of eight members to the Mayor. Members serve but may employ a secretary. to investigate all plans for construction of public highways and kinds of public improvements. ...ely advisory powers, but, wisely

Image of "Maryland, My Maryland," published in the December 6, 1931 Baltimore *Evening Sun*. Created by *Sunpapers* cartoonist Edmund Duffy, this graphic and compelling image won a Pulitzer Prize. *Baltimore* Sunpapers.

Henry L. Mencken, c. 1933, around the time of his *Sunpapers* editorials excoriating the events on the lower shore. *Courtesy of the H.L. Mencken Collection, Enoch Pratt Free Library, Baltimore.*

Chief Judge John Pattison, First Judicial Circuit of Maryland (Worcester, Wicomico, Somerset and Dorchester Counties), 1931. *Courtesy of the circuit court for Wicomico County.*

Bernard Ades and David Levinson (front) at the time of the Orphan Jones trial, Baltimore County, January 1932. The unidentified man in the rear is likely Louis Berger, secretary of the International Labor Defense. *Baltimore* Afro-American *newspaper.*

CONSTABLE J. W. HALL
Snow Hill, Md.

STATE POLICEMAN W. R. MAY

RANDOLPH PURNELL,
Chief of Police, Snow Hill, Md.

Eastern Shore law enforcement officials taking evidence to the Orphan Jones trial in Towson, January 1932. Constable James W. Hall was a deputy sheriff for Worcester County; W.R. May was a member of the Maryland State Police; and Randolph Purnell was chief of police for Snow Hill. Hall was accused by Bernard Ades of being the person who beat Orphan Jones on the way from Berlin to Snow Hill on the night of his arrest. *Baltimore Sunpapers and Photography Collection, University of Maryland Baltimore County.*

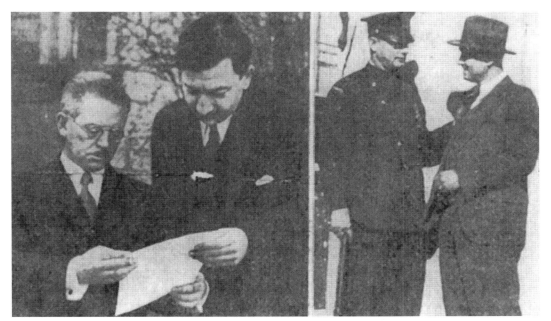

Scenes at the trial of Euel Lee (Orphan Jones), January 12, 1932. Ades and Levinson are on the left and on the right is Baltimore County policeman George Hohman determining the right of Perry Darby to enter the courthouse. Security was very tight as the court wanted no display of violence at the trial; there was none. *Baltimore* News *(later the* News-American*)*.

Chief Judge T. Scott Offutt, circuit court for Baltimore County, who participated on the Court of Appeals in the first *Lee v. State* regarding the removal of the case to Cambridge, and who later presided at the two trials of Orphan Jones in Baltimore County. *Baltimore* Sunpapers *and Photography Collection, University of Maryland Baltimore County.*

JUDGE C. GUS GRASON

Judge Gus Grason, circuit court for Baltimore County, who also presided at the Orphan Jones trials in Baltimore County. *Baltimore* Sunpapers *and Photography Collection, University of Maryland Baltimore County.*

Judge Frank Duncan, circuit court for Baltimore County, the judge who had chosen jurors in Baltimore County for twenty-five years, and who was challenged by David Levinson regarding his bias in doing so. (Judge Duncan had never chosen a black man for jury duty.) The challenge resulted in the Maryland Court of Appeals, for the first time in Maryland history, reversing a criminal conviction based on the bias of excluding African Americans from jury duty. *Baltimore* Sunpapers *photo.*

XVI

A Trial at Last

On Monday morning, January 18, 1932, at Towson, an uneasy calm prevailed. There had been extensive arrangements for police presence at the courthouse, due to the volatile nature of the case and its long history of confrontation and difficulties. But this morning, those extra measures seemed unnecessary. It seemed the opinion of the Court of Appeals had been correct on their decision of the relocation of the trial. No mobs surrounded the courthouse square; there was not the ominous portent of violence or the impending notion that the community was in turmoil. No militia was present; no special cordon of police was required to maintain order. There was a feeling that the influence of the groups of citizens who confronted the perceived threat of the Labor Defense League had dissipated. All the pervasive hue and cry of Worcester County was absent.

No longer were the jail and courthouse seen as representations of sanctuary for a man who should be delivered to the public opinion. No longer were the insipid notions of lynching and the delay of trial creating feelings of injustice. There was, rather, a sense that here, at last, the judicial system would go about its work and the process would proceed to its stated end.

The atmosphere of order and authority was also improved by the limitation of spectators at the trial. Only those persons who could be seated in the courtroom and a double row of standing spectators would be allowed entry. The capacity, therefore, was to be limited to two hundred. No milling, surging crowds of spectators would taint the proceedings; no restless groups of people would fill the halls of the Towson Courthouse. Indeed, the very fact of the great distance imposed by the removal of the trial created an effective buffer from the discontent experienced on the lower shore. In 1932, few of the many spectators who had jammed the streets of Snow Hill could even think about journeying the more than 120 miles to Baltimore County, let alone consider taking the necessary arrangements for accommodations there for the trial's duration. It was, therefore, evident that unless the citizens of the region had some intention to create an uproar over the notorious trial in their midst, the previous troubles would not surface at the trial. And, in fact, they didn't.

The morning of trial dawned clear and cool, without any inclement weather to interfere with the business at hand. It is true, of course, that an unusually large contingent of law enforcement officers was present, but their presence was a clear gauge of the seriousness with which the judicial system and the county officials considered the proceedings. Their numbers were an indication that no nonsense would be tolerated and they milled about the confines of the courthouse with the assurance that they would be able to control any situation with which they were confronted.

Early in the morning, Godfrey Child arrived, prepared to begin the most important day of the most important case of his career. Although out of his bailiwick, he was nevertheless confident that his case would be compelling to any panel of jurors, whether strangers to him or not. Besides, he was to be assisted by the State's Attorney for the county, and would therefore have the prestige of the duly elected prosecutor for the county on his side of the counsel table. He also had the weight of evidence with him. Ades, a radical attorney with only a Philadelphia Labor Defense attorney at his side, was still the odd man out.

Ades also arrived in the early hours, and must have pondered the huge burden he faced. It was true, of course, that he did not have the burden of proof, and could await the State's case before his moment would arrive, but he surely knew that the evidence was strongly arrayed against his client. He knew that Martha Miller was not going to sustain the position that he had urged upon her, and that the police had physical evidence which was very damaging to Lee. He would have assumed that the confession was going to be introduced against the defendant and, although Ades believed that it had been coerced, it would, nevertheless, be heard by this jury and would surely be considered by them.

Ades realized that he needed the assistance of David Levinson, a more experienced trial advocate, in the worst kind of way. Here he was, an inexperienced young attorney, in one of the most high-profile cases in the history of Maryland, facing three experienced prosecutors (James McAllister of Dorchester was also at the trial table) and with a client who was confronted with substantial and damning evidence shortly to be presented by no less than fifty-seven witnesses. It was not a situation that made Bernard Ades feel all that comfortable with his circumstances.

In addition, Ades's trial tactics required an even more perilous issue: he was going to have to confront the judges of the circuit with their refusal to empanel any black men on the jury. Therefore, from the outset, Ades could not expect that he would receive any consideration from the bench during the process of the trial. While it is true that in jury trials, judges routinely instruct jury panels that the judges' demeanor during the course of the trial is not to be construed against either side, there is a subtle and distinct message sent from the bench to the jury box about what is going through the minds of the judges. It is an unmistakable vibration that only the most doltish of jurors fail to perceive. To take on the court from the outset was a risky but necessary tactic that Ades would have to pursue. One can only speculate whether he discussed this matter with his client, but it is certain that if he did, Lee acquiesced in the decision. After all, Ades was the man who had faced the Snow Hill mobs and been beaten and threatened with serious harm, all in the course of representing this indigent black man. Ades had not received a penny for his efforts and had gone to the limit and beyond all reasonable expectations in his defense of Lee. No other lawyer would have done what he had done, and certainly no other lawyer who had represented Lee, no matter how fleetingly, had even come close to the dedication and advocacy that Ades had exhibited to his client. If Ades chose to embark on a course calculated to offend the court, so be it. He had gone to such extremes in Worcester County that his actions caused the lower shore court to try to ban his participation in the case and that effort had been to no avail, so, in Lee's thinking, whatever he thought was the proper course in the trial would be okay.

The saga was set: Godfrey Child, unable to thrust the case to a speedy conclusion in his home county, would now be called upon to produce the evidence necessary to convict before an alien jury panel; Ades, who had sought tenaciously to get the case to this venue, would now have to face the substantive evidence of his client's guilt.

A Trial at Last

Jury selection under the procedure employed in Maryland at the time consisted of summoning qualified "veniremen" (the entire panel from which a jury is selected) and, from their total, choosing a jury to sit in the case. The selection of a jury has been an art in which various State's Attorneys have excelled throughout the state of Maryland. One prosecutor, it is said, would urge various supporters of his to congregate on the green of the courthouse; then, by various means, he would exhaust the panel that had been summoned, whereupon the sheriff would venture out at the courts' order to find more veniremen on the streets of the town. The supporters on the green would then be summoned to the courtroom and the prosecutor would have his handpicked panel. It is said that with such a jury, he was invariably successful.

There is no indication that such maneuvering went on in the Towson court, but here there was a very different strategy at hand. Bernard Ades had determined to challenge the implicit veto of any African Americans being eligible for service on any panel in Baltimore County. He had determined that Lee, a black man, was entitled to a jury of his "peers," which, to Ades, meant men of the same color, the same economic background and the same culture. Those men would at least have the perspective to determine whether Lee should be convicted for the crime, without experiencing the conflict of cultures implied by the normally all-white jury panel.

In order to balance the jury, however, Ades would be required to directly confront the judges who were presiding in the trial. In 1932, the judges of the circuit court determined who would be summoned as veniremen in cases in their county. The selection of juries was a time-honored tradition of the judges that had been in place without challenge for as long as anyone could remember. (In fact, as a young attorney in Worcester County working in the Land Records of the Clerk's Office in Snow Hill in the early 1970s, I observed Judge Daniel T. Prettyman, together with the sheriff and the clerk of court, spinning a wheel full of numbered balls representing registered voters who would then be placed on the venire rolls to later be summoned for jury duty.)

Such tradition held no esteem in Ades's mind. He did not care that this was the way it had always been done; neither did he care that the judges would defend their right to determine such matters. He was intent upon allowing Lee to be judged by his fellow African Americans, whether or not they had ever enjoyed the privilege of sitting in judgment of their fellow citizens.

Ades would, therefore, make the jury selection process the keystone of his defense in this trial. It is interesting to note that his efforts, laudable though they may be, focused on a collateral issue: rather than stating that Lee was not guilty, Ades sought to have someone accede to his position that black jurymen were required to be available to judge a black defendant. Did this show an inclination of Ades to attempt to deviate from the salient issue at hand—the guilt of his client? Probably so, but it is an effective tactic given the overwhelming evidence amassed by Godfrey Child against Lee in the case.

Early on Monday, the officers arrayed throughout the courthouse began letting the spectators enter the courtroom. There were no security devices at that time, nor are there reports of searches or interrogations as the citizens passed under the scrutiny of the officers and into the gallery of the circuit courtroom. There would be a strict limitation of observers to two hundred. It was of no importance to the judges that there was a huge public interest in the trial; they were intent upon seeing to it that the trial proceeded in an orderly fashion, without the aura of the previous proceedings on the shore.

The protagonists then took their places in the courtroom. There is no contemporary account of the interaction, if any, between Child and Ades. One must guess that, by this time, they could not abide each other. Child was certainly offended that Ades had been successful, thus far, in thwarting Child's efforts to achieve a speedy trial on the lower shore. Ades, for his part, must have resented Child's efforts to exclude him from the entire process of defending Lee. As to Lee, one can only speculate his innermost thoughts as to his very serious predicament.

One thing is certain—by the time the three judges ascended the bench, tensions were at a high level. The trial was to shortly commence resume with all the various emotions, ready or not.

One of the challenges in recreating historical events is the loss, over time, of important documents that could aid research into the accurate portrayal of events. The trial transcript from Towson is now, apparently, lost to antiquity. Therefore, the record of the trial in Towson must come from the not entirely satisfactory source of contemporary news articles. It should be noted, though, in fairness, that the news media of the day were extraordinarily thorough in their reporting.

The newspapers of the day devoted considerable coverage to the trial because, of course, it was a major story of the time. The account of the trial that follows comes primarily from a compilation of articles in the *Sunpapers*, the *Baltimore American* and the *Salisbury Times*. There are also excerpts included from the *Afro-American*, in which one can observe its markedly different view on the events.

XVII

A Jury is Chosen

The first matter at hand was choosing a panel of jurors. Ades's request to have the case removed from the shore had been granted, but there was another essential facet of his trial strategy now at hand. He had to convince the court to allow black veniremen. This portion of the defense of the case would prove to be problematic, as jury selection normally proceeded with a complete disregard for any black person being on the list of eligible jurors. Ades, however, was not going to acquiesce to this long-standing practice.

The *Sunpapers* reported:

> *Lee, a short stocky Negro of 64, entered the courtroom about 10:00 A.M. and took his place on the defendant's elevated bench at the center. Later he was moved, at his counsel's request to a chair directly behind them.*
>
> *He wore a rumpled blue serge sack coat, a blue denim shirt without a tie and dark gray trousers.*
>
> *Approximately 200 persons, including a dozen Negroes, four of them women, crowded into the courtroom. The spectators included more than a dozen white women.*
>
> *At the outset, defense counsel filed a motion with the court challenging "the array of jurors" upon the ground that the panel of 200 had not been selected "fairly and impartially, with special reference to their intelligence, sobriety and integrity"; that all Negroes had been excluded from the panel "by reason of their race or color and without reference to their intelligence, sobriety and integrity," and that the method of the panel's selection deprived the defendant of a fair and impartial trial.*
>
> *Chief Judge T. Scott Offutt, who is sitting with Judge Duncan and Judge C. Gus Grason, gave the prosecution time to prepare a formal answer. He also denied the request of the defense to be provided a transcript of the testimony "free of cost."*
>
> *When the prosecution filed its answer, the court overruled the defense motion challenging the panel, and defense counsel began an investigation of how the panel had been selected, summoning John R. Haut, chief clerk, Baltimore County Board of Commissioners, and Louis McL. Merryman, clerk of the court. Both denied having anything to do with selecting the panel.*
>
> *Judge Offutt volunteered the information that Judge Duncan had been selecting talesmen for the court for many years and suggested he be asked for an explanation.*
>
> *Judge Duncan said that he had been drawing the panels for nearly twenty-six years, that he had before him a list of voters presented to him once a year by the supervisors of elections, and a tax list, and from the two he made his selections. He added that he selected men from any part of the county, that when he came into contact at church affairs and on similar occasions with men whom he thought*

were good jury material, he noted their names and followed this up by making inquiries about them as to their responsibilities and other qualities.

"The very objection you are making now was made some years ago," Judge Duncan said. "I told the Court of Appeals just what I am telling you now and the Court of Appeals said all I did was sufficient and gratified the law."

Judge Duncan said he had never selected a Negro, neither had he excluded Negroes from consideration, that he "hadn't considered them at all."

Under questioning by Judge Offutt, Judge Duncan said he did not consider Negroes any more than he considered "any other race, sect or religion," that he proceeded "on about the same line that the President of the United States when he selects his cabinet."

He added that there was "nothing in the Constitution or the law of this state that says I must select Negroes or Chinamen or any other particular race."

Defense counsel then had Judge Duncan sworn and the explanation he had given entered in the record as testimony. A few minutes later the selection of the jury was begun. It was then a few minutes after 11:00 A.M. and a 12:35 o'clock, the panel had been exhausted and there were only ten jurors in the box. Judge Offutt told Sheriff Bremen A. Trail to summon "ten or twelve" additional talesmen.

Defense counsel objected to the procedure and had the Sheriff put on the stand when he reported ten talesman had been summoned. He was asked why he had not summoned any Negroes when there were Negroes in the Courtroom. He denied that he had excluded Negroes and said, "I aimed to get the best men I could find," and, "I didn't see any reason why I should pass through a crowd of men to go over to that corner" where the Negroes were seated.

Half an hour later the second panel was exhausted and the Sheriff was instructed to summon ten more talesman. Defense counsel asked the court to instruct the Sheriff to summon them "irrespective of race or color." Judge Offutt sent for Sheriff Trail and told him he was "to summon no man on account of his race or exclude any."

When Sheriff Trail reported he had found ten more talesmen he again was put on the stand by the defense and asked why the list included no Negroes. He replied that he had "found ten before I got to them; if I had to get a greater number of talesmen I might have got over to that corner."

The new panel was soon exhausted and the Sheriff was sent out to get ten more talesmen. When he reported he had found them he was again put on the stand by the defense and was asked:

"Isn't it a fact that you didn't intend to summon any colored men?"

The State objected, but the objection was overruled.

The *Sunpapers* reported that the jury selection proceeded slowly because of the repeated challenges of the defense. The paper reported that all the questioning of the prospective jurors was conducted by David Levinson, noted as "Mr. Levinson of Philadelphia, chief counsel of the defense. Mr. Ades, of Baltimore, Lee's original counsel of record," the *Sun* reported, was "taking little active part in the case." However, both lawyers were reported to consult Lee frequently while questioning the talesmen. The defense had used all its twenty peremptory challenges (used to strike a juror without having to state any cause) before the State had used even one. One prospective juror was excused when he admitted that he had a conscientious objection to the death penalty, and another left when he stated that he had already formulated an opinion of the case. Two members originally chosen were dismissed when they admitted to having a hearing impairment. One juror was ordered to step down when he emphatically acknowledged that he would not believe a black man as quickly as he would a white man.

There was, though, some levity even in the midst of the seriousness. Mr. Richard Sparks, who was empaneled, was asked how he happened to be in the courtroom (he was one of the talesmen selected by Sheriff Trail). He replied, "Well, I'll tell you. You see, business has been awfully slow, and I came here expecting to see a lot of my customers. I came here hunting business." When asked about his opinion regarding the statements of a black man, he said, "If a colored gentleman was telling me something, and a white man was telling me something, I'd believe the one who could look me in the eye the longest." He was promptly seated in the jury box.

When　full jury was finally empaneled, defense counsel repeated their challenge regarding the lack of black jury members, were overruled and took an exception. Ades and Levinson had laid carefully their groundwork for an appeal, but the judges were confident that there would be no basis that the Court of Appeals would find compelling; after all the Court of Appeals had previously ruled on the identical issue in previous cases from Baltimore County. The tactic was simply the desperate effort of two liberal lawyers grasping at straws in a case that had strong evidence about to be presented against their client.

The final jury panel, all white, all male, consisted of the following: Howard H. Stocksdale, a carpenter from Glyndon, was named foreman; E. Stabler Maxwell, a bus line operator from Overlea; Harry C. Stillwell, a building superintendent from Dundalk; Norman J. Wagner, a hauling contractor from Riderwood; Leo W. Fauth, a farmer from Bradshaw; Joseph M. Crowther, a farmer from Cockeysville; John McMahon, a quarryman from Mount Washington; John A Ensor, a Sparks farmer; William Winow, a steelworker from Dundalk; Ernest W. Schoelkopf, a contractor from Sunnybrook; Riggs A. Leishear, retired, from Woodlawn; and Richard R. Sparks, a Monkton salesman.

These twelve men would determine whether Euel Lee would live or die.

XVIII

Evidence is Heard

It was now time for the defendant to enter his plea to the charge of murdering Green Davis. The court ordered Lee to stand.

"How do you plead to the charge before the Court?" intoned the judge.

"Not guilty," replied Lee, facing the bench.

"And how will you be tried?" asked the judge.

"By God and my country," Lee stated.

"He means 'by a jury,'" Levinson interpreted for the defendant.

After the grueling efforts at seating a jury and taking Lee's pleas, the court ordered a recess, and the courtroom cleared quietly, with the spectators going out into the hallways and corridors of the courthouse. During the near hour of recess, Godfrey Child retired to a quiet room to go over his opening statement that would soon be forthcoming. The time was at hand at last—after the delays, the maneuvering, the incessant tactical moves by Ades—this was the hour Child had sought for these many months. At last, his moment to present the overwhelming evidence he had amassed against Lee would begin.

After the recess passed, the court reconvened and the jury and spectators settled into their seats. It was approximately 2:45 p.m. when Child stood and slowly approached the jury box. He began by explaining to the jurors that in Worcester County the defendant was also known as Orphan Jones, and that most of the State's witnesses would refer to him by that alias. He advised that the evidence would show that Lee had been discharged for some reason by Mr. Davis and that Lee (Jones) had told several people that Mr. Davis owed him a dollar, and that he would get even with him. Child also said the State would present several witnesses to show that Lee was in the area of the Davis house on the Berlin-Ocean City Road on Sunday morning, the day of the murder.

Warming up, the State's Attorney told how the bodies were found by Charles Johnson and Sebie Howe, the Davises' neighbors, and then proceeded to describe in graphic detail the condition of the bodies and the house, which Child said had been thoroughly ransacked and that there was coal oil "nearly ankle deep" on the first floor of the home. Child then detailed the items of clothing belonging to the Davises that had been found in Lee's room, which included Mr. Davis's best shirt, his initialed cuffbuttons and a large quantity of women's stockings. Child also related for the first time that Lee had intended a getaway to Baltimore the next morning. He concluded that the State would ask for "a verdict—an unqualified verdict—of murder in the first degree." He then turned and walked solemnly to the counsel table.

Not one word had he spoken about the much-publicized confession. [Indeed, the document did not surface in Maryland court records or in any files I was able to locate seventy-odd years after the crime until unearthed by James Platt in the National Archives in 2004 in the unlikely locale of the disbarment proceedings against Bernard Ades.] It is so obvious from the exclusion of the confession from evidence, that Ades's assertion was surely true: the admission had been coerced. Child would not mention a single hint of the statement during the entire trial, although a provocation from another member of the prosecution would bring it to light.

That did not mean that there was not extensive evidence to be presented by the State, however. Child was about to begin the parade of fact witnesses in the case. Late in the afternoon, Child put on the "motive" and "opportunity" witnesses, beginning with Robert J. Lewis, an elderly farmer who lived near the Davis home. Mr. Lewis, together with three other witnesses, testified that Lee had threatened to "get even" with Mr. Davis. The witnesses each testified that the statements were made on the seventh and eighth of October, just before the killings occurred. A hushed, crowded courtroom heard Mr. Lewis quote Lee as saying, "Friend Davis ain't the man I thought him to be. His damn wenches have 'nigger' and 'coon' in their mouths all the time. I showed them there ain't no such thing in the Bible. I worked for Davis for twelve days and only got paid for eleven. I'll get even with him."

Levinson, who would be the sole verbal defense counsel, tried to put his spin on the statement by asking Lewis whether it wasn't a fact that Lee had said, "I'll get even with him, I'll not cut his corn." Lewis, not moved, said flatly, "No, sir, he didn't say that." Lewis also damaged the defense by testifying that he had seen Lee walking toward Berlin in the area of the Davis house on Sunday evening after dusk, and later, Lee was walking toward Ocean City with a satchel in his hand.

The next witness for the State was eleven-year-old Jack Fisher, who lived in a farmhouse east of Taylorville on the way to Ocean City. Unlike most of the structures of the time, the Fisher house is still in existence, sitting in a field just east of the new Wal-Mart and near the woods of Holly Grove. Route 50 now cuts across what were then farm fields and obscures the lengthy farm road that extended from the main road to the house. Little Jack said that he had seen Lee on the road on Wednesday the seventh of October, and then again on Sunday, at which time Lee had a satchel and was headed toward Ocean City, near Holly Grove woods.

Harry Bradford was next to the stand, and he testified that Green Davis had told him that he had discharged Lee, and that Lee claimed he owed him a dollar. Bradford also advised that Davis showed him Lee's tennis shoe tracks around the Davis house. The fact that Lee had been stalking the house sent a chill through the spectators who had heard Child describe the mutilated bodies in the same location. Bradford said Davis asserted that he was not afraid of Lee. After the testimony of Charles Clark that he had seen Lee carrying the satchel as well, the court recessed for the dinner hour.

The State next called Dr. Fred S. Waesche, who had performed the autopsy on Mr. Davis's body the day after it was found. He was followed to the stand by Dr. C.M. Lowe and Dr. Charles Holland who had aided Waesche in the duty.

The session of court went into the night. It became evident that the State was beginning to concentrate on the physical evidence. Child painstakingly established that nothing had been disturbed in the house after the bodies were found. (It should be recalled that the defense's strategy was to establish a "frame-up" of Lee.) Charles Johnson, the neighbor who found the bodies; Fred Culver, the first policeman on the scene; and Harry Haines, a state policeman, all testified in detail to that effect. Mr. Johnson, a small, timid man, was obviously very nervous on the stand, with his testimony barely audible. He had to be admonished repeatedly by the court to speak up so as to be heard. He was coaxed into repeating the vivid and grisly scene that had confronted him on the discovery of the bodies. He finally raised his voice in order to be heard. [Mr. Johnson is now deceased, but his reticence did not run in the family—his grandson, Everett "Kip" Johnson, is a prominent Washington Attorney who has successfully argued a case in the Supreme Court of the United States.]

Mr. Johnson was followed to the stand by the police officers who had traveled from Baltimore to aid in the investigation; they identified the graphic photographs of the house and the bodies. The repeated testimony of each of the police investigators caused the court to become impatient with the process, but the State prevailed on the patience of the judges in order to continue the painstaking process.

Sebie Howe then added to Johnson's testimony of the discovery of the bodies, and added details on the nature of Lee's employment. He advised that Lee had actually slept in the Davises' kitchen while employed there, and that he had observed Mr. Davis's cousin and aunt stop at the house the day of the murders, knock on the door, then go away. Howe identified articles of Davis's belongings that had been found in Lee's possession. He also advised, under cross examination, that he had become suspicious on Sunday, but had not done anything about his feelings until Monday afternoon at four o'clock.

The *Sun* reported that eighteen witnesses were called on the first day of trial and that the proceedings had extended into the night. After adjournment, at about 9:30 p.m., the jurors were shown to a makeshift dormitory on the third floor of the courthouse where they spent the night.

The report of the first day's events in the *Afro-American* are starkly different. Under a byline by Ralph Matthews, the following was described:

> *Monday night at 9:30, the first day of the trial of the* State of Maryland vs. Euel Lee, alias Orphan Jones, *charged with the murder of Green Davis and his family, was brought to a close.*
>
> *Up to that time, except for the statement of States Attorney Godfrey Childs [sic] there has been little or no evidence to directly connect the defendant with the crime. Bernard Ades, the bushy-haired attorney for the keen-eyed bald-headed little black man of 60 years, put the situation most aptly to reporters when he answered their inquiry as to what sort of case the defense had up its sleeve by saying, "Unless the State gets Lee off of that road and closer to the Green Davis house, we won't need any case."*
>
> *To all intents and purposes, it appears that nothing short of a meeting of the Maryland Grange, the Eastern Shore Agricultural League, or the Delmarva Association for the Promotion of Produce Sales on the Peninsula could have been holding a meeting near the Green K. Davis home for at least three days prior to the murders because every farmer in the vicinity seems to have seen Lee snooping in or about the property sometime prior to the tragedy.*
>
> *Lee, it seems, must have been a most loquacious and accommodating criminal who not only planned the murder for several days, but tramped about the neighborhood for several days informing the rustics of his nefarious intentions. That Lee either stuck to one stereotyped line of chatter to the effect that he worked for Mr. Davis and he did not get paid and that "he was going to get even," or else the witnesses were well rehearsed on this particular point, was likewise very apparent.*
>
> *None of the witnesses seemed to recall, however, the additional assertion that Mr. Levinson, the assistant defense attorney, tried to jog into their memories when he contended that Lee said: "I am*

going to get even by not helping him cut his corn." While I designate Mr. Levinson as the assistant to Mr. Ades, it would really be more fitting to call him the hero of at least today's proceedings. It is he, a diminutive gray-haired man not more than four feet tall with a heavy Bing Crosby voice and a pair of double strength glasses, that is really tearing the State's case to shreds.

A stubborn little Napoleon, he is fighting every inch of the way. In a maneuver of no mean discernment, he appears at times to retreat a trench or two in the suavest manner graciously admitting a deference to the court only to turn with the agility of a rattler and place a stinging blow under which even the bench seems to smart.

Such was his action in the case of the empaneling of the jury early this morning. After challenging the panel as unconstitutional and questioning a number of county officials as to whose duty by law it was to select the panel and they all pleaded "not guilty," Mr. Levinson in a desperate attempt to learn who committed this apparent misdemeanor in violation of the statutes, learned to his amazement that Judge Duncan himself had selected the jury. Silence reigned for several moments before the little man realized he had put his foot in an embarrassing keg of pickles, decided to fight his way out. He challenged the judge.

A trial as serious as that of a quadruple murder is not without its ludicrous moments and the humor of this occasion was furnished by the towering, tousle-headed sheriff who found it impossible to reach the colored section in selecting the jurors after three attempts. After being instructed by the bench not to exclude prospective jurors on account of color, he brought back three bunches of ten talesmen at different intervals, but "Just couldn't get over as far as where the colored gentlemen were seated." His excuses for this failure were so amateurish and nonsensical that gales of laughter greeted his remarks.

Up to the close of the first day, the prosecution, through the testimony of sundry witnesses, has placed Lee (or Jones) in the woods, on bridges, in fields and in various places, but at all times at least a mile, and often more, from the Davis home.

Others, however, by the same testimony, have been much closer. Cousins, aunts, next friends and kinsmen have been seen in the yard trying doorknobs and performing other suspicious acts about the murder house about the time that the crime could have been committed.

At a cursory glance, one might imagine that this commentator was running afoul of the machinery of law and justice and attempting to favor only the accused. While I am only going to the evidence thus far produced, the intention mentioned above would not be at variance with the function of the courts, if we are to believe that every man is presumed to be innocent until proven guilty and that the court wants every defendant to have every benefit of the doubt. Of course, if hanging Euel Lee whether or no, is the object, and only such an outcome will satisfy, and appease the wrath of the Eastern Shore, this will hardly be appreciated in the light in which it was given.

The next morning, according to news reports, the courthouse was a very different scene from that of the first day. "The crowd in the courthouse corridors today was nowhere near so large as yesterday's," reported the *Sun*.

There were no "early birds" trying the doors at sunrise and the police guard in and around the courthouse was not so imposing as it had been. There was no overflow crowd to turn away from the trial room doors, although the room itself was crowded to just about its capacity. The two tiers of spectators' benches on either side of the room were filled. Colored persons occupied the topmost bench on one side. A semi-circle of standees three or four deep lined the curved rail that separated the bench from the spectators' part of the courtroom.

Wearing the same dark blue coat, blue denim shirt and faded and worn gray trousers that he wore yesterday, the short and stocky defendant arrived at the courthouse with the same strongly-armed escort of Baltimore detectives that brought him to Towson from the Baltimore City jail yesterday.

The prisoner arrived some time before the opening of his trial and very few persons were curious enough to be on hand. Yesterday, several hundred persons lingered in the courthouse corridors to see Lee.

The prisoner was locked up in a barred cage a few feet to the right of the bench to await the opening of court. After the jurors had filed in and the court had been called to order, Lee was led by a detective to his seat in front of the bench. He does not sit in the prisoners' chair but, at the request of his counsel, occupies a chair directly behind theirs. Behind him a half dozen Baltimore detectives sit in a semi-circle. Lee sits most of the time in an attitude of easy attention. He and his counsel hold brief conferences.

According to the *Sunpapers* report, the jury seemed fresh and rested, notwithstanding the fact that they had been sequestered to sleep all night on cots borrowed from the Baltimore County Fire Department. Their meals had been sent in from a nearby hotel.

On the morning of the second day, the first witness was Maurice Timmons, a nearby neighbor of the Davis farm. He and two other witnesses were called to the stand to place the defendant near the scene of the crime. William Duncan, "a colored youth," and Mattie Johnson, "also colored," related their sightings of Lee near the Davis home. Mattie, a washerwoman, testified that she not only had seen Lee, but also has washed some clothes for him. She related that she had seen him on Sunday, the day of the murders, heading toward Ocean City away from the Davis home, with a suitcase in his hand.

"How was he traveling?" asked State's Attorney Child.

"He was going fast." Mattie replied. Under cross examination by Mr. Levinson, she acknowledged that Lee had not been running but, she said, "He was just going a little faster than usual."

Elijah Shockley, of Whaleyville, and Edward Vickers, both employees of the Samuel Riddle Horse Farm, located nearby on the Ocean City Road, testified that they had been going to work on Sunday morning, October 11, so that they could arrive by 5:00 a.m. and that their automobile had passed within four feet of Lee and he was headed in the direction of the Davis farm.

They were followed to the stand by perhaps the most important witness in the State's case: Martha Miller. She was described in newspaper accounts as "a somewhat infirm colored woman," who was addressed by Godfrey Child as "Aunt Martha." Under prodding by Child, she recounted the activities of Lee during the few days prior to the murder. She said that he had breakfast and lunch with her and her husband on Saturday, and left before supper. At that time, she said, he was carrying a little brown satchel. She was asked to identify the satchel, which she did, pointing out the case that several other witnesses had identified as being in Lee's hands as he walked toward Ocean City after the time of the murder.

Martha testified that Lee returned to the rooming house about half past seven or eight in the morning and had the brown satchel. She said that when he left on Sunday, he did not return until

Monday morning. And when he returned at that time, he had a gun with him. She recalled that he had sat on her porch and cleaned the gun. She said that he had cleaned the gun with coal oil, which he said he had bought at a store across the street from the rooming house. (Everyone certainly recalled that the Davis kitchen had been saturated with coal oil when observed by Johnson and Howe.)

Child asked Martha to describe Lee's appearance when he arrived on Monday morning. She replied that he was wearing a clean shirt with a "beautiful pin" on his coat lapel. He also had with him a watch and chain. She identified both items when they were held up by the prosecutor. She also advised that Lee had emptied his pockets of a large amount of change and that he had also shown her paper money. Later, while they were sitting on the porch, a bus came by. Lee asked Martha's husband what time the bus would put him in Baltimore, and advised the couple that he was going there the next day for the purpose of purchasing "two corduroy suits and a pair of calfskin shoes."

The State led Martha carefully through her testimony, drawing out that no one but Lee had gone into his room from the time he left it on Thursday night until the officers were let into the room by her on Tuesday night after the crime. On that night, Martha said, she went with the officers and they found the shotgun, the satchel, a pistol, twenty-five or thirty pairs of women's hose, several scarves, a collection of handkerchiefs, women's lingerie, some rings, necklaces and other odds and ends of jewelry.

Mr. Child then asked her to relate Lee's reaction when Chief of Police Robert Allen called at the rooming house for him and informed him that the Davis family had been murdered. She said that Lee threw up his hands and said, "God Almighty!" and staggered backward a few steps.

In an obvious effort to indicate that her testimony was coached, Mr. Levinson, on cross-examination, asked her how many times she had talked to the police. She was unable to remember how many times she had spoken to them, recalling only once specifically, and Levinson kept at it until admonished by the court to stop.

In retaliation, Child on re-direct asked Martha to recount for the jury how Helen Mays had spirited her off to Baltimore to meet Ades in his office. She identified Ades at his seat, began to recount the conversation with him but was cut off by Chief Judge Offutt who interrupted with, "Don't go into that."

After Martha Miller came Chief Allen, who spent an extensive amount of time identifying the numerous items of evidence taken from Lee's room. He pointed out Green Davis's coat and vest and his watch and holster, which were then given to the jury to examine.

Levinson pounced on the chief when it came time for cross-examination. Now was the time that the defense's theory of a vulnerable black man being "tortured" by law enforcement officers could be introduced. Levinson began by having Allen testify to the arrest in some detail. He stated that he had told Lee only that "the captain wants you to come and go with me," and that he had not told Lee of the Davis murders.

Levinson asked Allen if Lee had been beaten on the trip from Berlin to the Snow Hill jail after his arrest. "I wouldn't say no," replied Allen. In answer to another question, he replied, "He was hit." Allen advised that he had no idea who it was that had struck Lee, nor how he had been hit.

"Then how do you know he was even hit?" asked Levinson.

"I heard him when he was hit, and he said 'I'm hit,'" said Allen. Allen stated that he had been driving the car in which Lee was riding, and that State Trooper M.D. Brubaker was in the front seat with him. Sheriff Wilmer Purnell and Constable William Hall were in the back seat with Lee.

Levinson asked, "Isn't it true that you handed Hall a blackjack and that it was with your blackjack that Lee was hit?"

"No sir." replied Allen, although he did admit that he always carried a blackjack. Sheriff Wilmer Purnell followed Allen to the stand, for the purpose of further identification of the seized items of evidence.

Finally that morning, Harold Scarborough, the principal of Buckingham High School, took the stand. His testimony must have been the most poignant, as he carefully identified a ring that had been found in the defendant's room. He said that it was a "standard school ring" and it had been purchased by Elizabeth Gertrude Davis, the oldest daughter of Green and Ivy Davis. It had the initials E.G.D. inside and had been bought on September 24, 1931, a mere sixteen days before she was murdered.

The first witness called by the State on afternoon of the second day of trial was somewhat unexpected; Mrs. Howard Bryant was the widow of the former president of the Baltimore City Council. The purpose of her testimony soon became clear. She advised that she spent her summers in Ocean City and that she had given several pairs of stockings to the Davis girls to use as material for rag rugs. Those were the very same stockings found in Lee's room.

Green Davis's sister also identified articles found in the room and matched a green belt found there with an oil-soaked dress belonging to Ivy Davis.

After all the items were in evidence, Mr. Child recalled Chief Allen and Sheriff Purnell to the stand in an effort to relate the details of the arrest. Allen testified that when he went to Lee's room, he was sitting with his chin drooped on his chest. Scarcely looking up, Lee asked, "You want me?" and upon being advised that he was wanted, he said "All right, sir." When he picked up his coat, according to Allen, he volunteered, "I haven't killed nobody; I haven't murdered anybody. Where are we going?" Allen replied that they were going for a ride. "I guess it will be a long ride, too." Lee said. On the way to the jail Allen testified that Lee asked a lot of questions and also was swearing; "To hell with Green Davis. He wasn't no account nohow. Whoever says I killed Green Davis is a liar."

Sheriff Purnell testified on his recall to the stand that no one had offered Lee any promises nor had anyone threatened him during the time he was in custody. The sheriff said that Lee had told him that his head was clear, that he wasn't drunk and that he hadn't taken any drugs. At this time Levinson got his chance at Purnell:

"You don't know whether he was kept under a spotlight for sixteen hours, beaten and had his toes stamped on until one toenail came out?" Levinson asked, incredulously.

"No sir." replied the sheriff, coolly. He also denied that it was he who hit Lee in the car, thus leaving Constable Hall as the unspoken, but obvious perpetrator of the act.

After the physical evidence was admitted, the State called the doctors who performed the autopsy to testify as to the cause of death. The medical evidence was concluded in a short time and then Godfrey Child paused. He looked at his notes and conferred quietly with the other State's Attorneys at the trial table. He rose and faced the court.

"Your Honors," said Child, "The State rests." It was five o'clock on the second day. There would be no confession of the defendant presented to the jury. After all the banner headlines and all the reported details in the press back in October and November, nothing that Lee had said that day in the Worcester County jail—or later in the Baltimore city jail—would be introduced. Child rightly opted to forego the confessions in view of the extensive physical evidence and the movements of the defendant, so extensively observed by the numerous witnesses.

XIX

The Defense Has its Turn

L evinson stood. He had reserved his opening statement until the close of the State's case. He now asked permission to approach the jury. The court granted it.

The Philadelphia lawyer stood before the panel. He began to speak in a very soft voice, almost inaudible to the members of the press. He stressed the importance of the decision that the jury would soon be called upon to make. He then said that it was fortunate that the case was being tried in Baltimore County, and not on the Eastern Shore. The court, alert to the tactics of the defense, ordered the remark stricken from the record and admonished the jury to disregard it. The judge cautioned Levinson, who thereupon withdrew the remark. He could see that he was not going to be allowed to cast aspersions on the lower shore folk.

His tactics then shifted to a review of the State's case, which he chided as being purely circumstantial. Once again, Judge Offutt intervened. He reminded the jurors that under Maryland procedure, the purpose of an opening statement is to advise what the attorney proposed to prove and not to remark upon the State's case. Levinson, for the second time in his brief presentation, withdrew the remark. Apparently defeated, he then said, "The defendant here says that he did not commit this crime. The best possible way to try this case is not by speeches of counsel, but by the evidence itself. I close." He had spoken for less than five minutes.

T he defense of any case is purely a device of the attorney for the accused. The law casts no burden upon the defendant to prove anything. The entire burden of proving the guilt of a person is with the prosecution. In many instances, the defense, believing that the State has failed in its burden, will simply not present a case. Lawyers and judges understand that the accused has every right to remain silent; indeed it is a Constitutional privilege. One wonders, though, do laymen, not trained in the law, really appreciate this nicety? Many people think, "If he is innocent, why doesn't he just take the stand and say so? What has he got to hide?"

This was certainly on the mind of David Levinson that day in the Baltimore County court. Accordingly, he began his defense with a build-up toward Lee's taking the stand in his own defense. His first witness was Assistant Attorney General Willis R. Jones, who testified to the Baltimore City Code regarding the registration of firearms. The second witness was Martha Miller, who was again asked about the statements of the law enforcement officers to Lee regarding the murders of the family. Their testimonies took only a brief time—everything was building toward the climax of the trial.

After Martha's brief testimony was concluded, Levinson conferred briefly with the defendant. He stood. "The defense calls Orphan Jones," he said.

The courtroom, as if in unanimous anticipation, was deathly quiet.

Slowly, Lee rose. He looked tentatively at Ades, who gestured toward the witness stand. Stoically, he walked across the courtroom from the trial table with every eye in the room intent upon his movement. He paused at the witness box and a bailiff instructed him to raise his right hand and gave him the oath. As he entered the witness box, Lee did not seat himself, but stood, fervently twisting a folded paper in his hands.

Levinson began by having Lee recount his background. Lee testified that he had been born in Lynchburg, Virginia, in 1872. He said his mother had died when he was about six years old and his father had died so long before that that he had no recollection of him. He related that he had been "adopted by some white people" by the name of Jones. To this "adoption" and the death of his parents at the early time in his life, he attributed the alias "Orphan Jones" (it is interesting to note that all the witnesses and every attorney throughout the case invariably referred to him by this name).

He related that he had worked for Green Davis about four days in May of 1931, and went to work for him again on August 18, continuing his employment until October 7, at which time, Lee related, "I didn't quit—not for anything occurring between Mr. Davis and me. I just quit because I could make more money otherwise."

Lee claimed that he had last seen Mr. Davis the Thursday before his death. He related a conversation between himself and Davis: "Mr. Davis said, 'Hello, Jones, we've had some words about a day's work. Here's two dollars.' I said, 'No, you only owe me one dollar,' and I laid the other dollar back on the seat of his truck and Mr. Davis said, 'Orphan, I've got some corn I want you to cut, and I want you to help me get in my potatoes.'" Lee testified that that was the last time he ever saw Davis and that he was to return to work on the following Wednesday, but was arrested on Sunday.

Prompted by Levinson, Lee testified that the Davises were fine people. "No finer people ever I meet than the Davises. They treated me just like one of their own. 'Course, I didn't eat with them. Anybody says I ever said anything about Mrs. Davis is wrong. They were just like the white people who raised me. Mr. Davis give me anything I wanted."

Then came the inevitable question from Levinson: "Nobody saw this crime committed, but you were charged with the murder of Green Davis. I want to ask you, are you guilty of the charge?"

Lee looked straight at the attorney. "If they would only let me tell what I wanted, you would believe me, but they made me say what they wanted me to say. If Mr. Davis was to rise from the dead he would tell you I didn't kill him."

At this point, Levinson asked Lee to relate to the jury his defense in his own words. This is a tactic which is sometimes used to try and get the jury to relate to the defendant by having him tell the story "his way," without the dry, back and forth of the normal question and answer of a trial examination. This was an opportunity that Lee had pleaded for; he clearly wanted to tell his own story in his own words. The desire prompted frequent admonishments by Levinson, who urged Lee to curb the flow of words coming out. In some of those encounters, Lee spoke sharply to his attorney for his efforts. In many instances, he had to be cautioned to speak more loudly and less rapidly.

Lee's story began to develop. He had quit, he said, in order to engage in bootlegging, an occupation that paid much better than farming. "If I get twenty pints of whiskey, see, that makes me ten dollars. If I can catch a sucker, my profits increase. I couldn't sell no whiskey at Mr. Davis's house, he didn't drink any, and I don't think he'd stand for it"

He made efforts to explain the testimonies of the State's witnesses by putting his own view on the statements he had made. He said, for instance, that his threats toward the Davis family had not actually taken place. His statement regarding getting even with Mr. Davis had meant merely that if Davis had wanted him to cut some corn, he would "get even" by not cutting the corn for him.

After Lee had said all he wished, Levinson paused, looked at some papers in front of him on the counsel table, and sat down. He turned to the State's Attorneys. "Witness with you," he said.

State's Attorney James Anderson began the cross-examination. He asked if Lee had spent time in Pittsburgh and Lee replied that he had lived there from 1901 until 1918. Then he blurted, "Just come out with it and say I was in prison. Yes, I was. I know you got it all there [pointing to papers in front of the lawyer], for killing people named Davis, same as here. But I was acquitted." He advised that he had left Pittsburgh last year and worked in Baltimore for a while, then worked his way down the Eastern Shore toward Salisbury. Lee said he had met Mr. Davis when Davis picked him up in his car and offered him a job. He had worked there until he quit the Wednesday before the killings.

"Where were you on Thursday…Friday…Saturday?" Anderson asked in rapid succession.

"At Martha Miller's," Lee responded.

"Did you leave there Sunday morning?" Anderson asked.

"No—Oh, I did go around to another house on the beach, but I never crossed the bridge," Lee responded. "I went to the boardwalk, and returned to the house about 9:30 p.m., and then I sat on the porch until daybreak." Then he said, "Oh, are you talking about Sunday?" I thought you were saying 'Saturday.' On Sunday, I just went to bed." After being pressed on the issue, Lee said he didn't know whether he had gone to bed at all on Sunday evening.

"Well, what did you do Monday morning?" Anderson asked.

"I went off with Will Miller to get a hunting license."

"When was that?

"About 10:30."

"What did you do before that?"

"I just got up, dressed and washed."

"And then you cleaned your gun?"

"Yes."

"Why did you clean your gun?"

"Because it was rusty. I had not cleaned it for six months."

"But you were in prison before."

"Oh, the man I bought it from said it had not been cleaned for six months."

"Had you fired the gun?"

"Yes, I shot it off near Mr. Davis's house in a grove of trees."

"Did you own a pistol?"

"Yes, I bought the gun in the morning and the pistol in the afternoon."

"Did you clean the pistol on Friday night?"

"Yes, I did."

"Why did you clean it also?"

"I go deer hunting with the pistol."

Anderson changed the subject. "How much were you paid by Mr. Davis?"

"I was paid $63.00, which was for six weeks and three days. I was paid a dollar a day."

"Are you saying that Mr. Davis didn't pay you at all during that time?"

"I didn't need the money before."

"And did you get all that was coming to you?"

"I was owed $1 more. He owed me $64.00."

"Do you remember your arrest?"

"Yes, Mr. Allen told me that all the Davises had been found dead in bed."

"How do you account for all the nickels and dimes you had at that time?"

"Didn't you hear me say that sometimes a man wanted me to have a drink with him, and I had to have change?"

"What about the pouch belonging to Mr. Davis that they found in your room?"

"A white man gave it to me."

"And who gave you the shirt that was found in your room?"

"I don't know who put that up there!" Lee interrupted, "Just the same as I don't know who put all that other stuff up there in my room!"

Anderson again abruptly changed the line of questioning. "Isn't it true that you made a statement contrary to your denial of guilt here today?"

Before the defense could object, Lee replied, "Under punishment, I have." The belated objection from Levinson was sustained by the court and the jury was told to disregard the question and the answer. (This admonishment, frequently given by judges in trials to jurors, is said by attorneys to resemble "unringing a bell.")

"Mr. Anderson," said Judge Offutt, "You know you are not to ask any questions as to any statements in the nature of a confession."

"I am sorry, Your Honor," replied Anderson.

At this point in the questioning, the trial stood in recess until 7:15 p.m. At the appointed time, Lee re-entered the courtroom and stoically climbed onto the witness stand, again. However, the remaining time of his occupancy of the stand was taken up by arguments over the legality of Anderson's questioning.

After the court disposed of the legal issues, Anderson paused, looked at his notes and whispered something to Godfrey Child. Child shook his head. Anderson turned to the court: "No further questions, Your Honors." He sat down. Lee had been on the stand for an hour and a half.

"The witness may step down," said Judge Offutt.

Lee looked at his attorneys, who indicated for him to return to the table. He looked at the jurors, then at the judges, and slowly departed from the stand. His effort at saving his own life had come to its anticlimactic conclusion.

"Mr. Levinson, you may call your next witness," said Judge Offutt. Levinson did not hesitate. "Your Honor, the defense rests." Lee's defense was over.

The State was, however, not quite finished. In rapid succession, three rebuttal witnesses were called to the stand: Henry Hornstein, the pawnbroker Lee claimed had sold him the gun, denied that the transaction had ever occurred. Mr. and Mrs. Frank Weisman, owners of the Fullerton Hotel, verified that Lee had worked there for six weeks up to September 1, 1931. Finally, all the evidence had been presented. The case was winding down. Without fanfare, the court adjourned for the night. It was 8:00 p.m., Tuesday, January 19, 1932.

Lawyers in the midst of a trial, especially a capital case, often get caught up in the emotions of the moment. The slightest deviation from the planned sequence of events can cause an advocate to second-guess himself and wonder if the trial was going in the manner he had planned. One can only speculate as to what was going through the minds of the lawyers who had just completed the evidence on that late January evening. Surely there were strategy sessions in the hotel room of Godfrey Child and in the living room of Bernard Ades. Just as surely, time was spent in polishing up the closing arguments, which would begin at 9:45 the next morning. The closing arguments in a criminal trial are the last (and normally the lasting) impression the jurors have of the evidence, the attorneys and the case itself. An effective closing can sometimes sway certain jurors' thinking in a case, and where unanimity is required, it may be the key to the finding of guilt or may create enough doubt so as to hang up a jury. If a jury cannot reach a verdict, a new trial is required; if a new trial can be accomplished, anything can happen—witnesses die, memories fade, evidence may be stricken, a new twist taken. Therefore the effective closing is very often essential.

XX

The Moment of Truth

Promptly at 10:00 a.m. on Wednesday, January 20, in the courtroom packed full of spectators, Godfrey Child stood at the prosecution table. "May it please the court," Child said.

"You may go to the jury," replied Judge Offutt.

Child walked slowly across the room, and stood for a moment. He thanked the jurors for the courtesy extended to him and the law enforcement officers from Worcester County, and then started:

"Orphan Jones is charged with murder, and there are five possible verdicts you can bring in. You can call him guilty of murder in the first degree, which carries the death penalty, or life imprisonment; you can bring in a verdict of murder in the first degree without capital punishment; or, you can return a verdict of guilty to murder in the second degree; a verdict of manslaughter; or a verdict of not guilty."

Child pulled forth a photograph of the Green Davis bedroom soon after the murder. He leaned forward, close to the jurors: "We say the man who committed this crime is guilty of murder in the first degree. There is no other verdict which can be given." Child then proceeded to review the provisions of the criminal code of Maryland related to homicide:

> We say Orphan Jones killed Green Davis for one purpose or both. He did it to satisfy a grudge against Mr. Davis or to rob him of the few possessions he had, or he did for both. Whether he did it for one or the other or for both reasons, it is murder in the first degree.
>
> What can you say about premeditation in a crime like this, when you find a man dead lying at the side of his faithful wife in bedclothes—murdered! The defense will tell you that there were no eyewitnesses to the crime. Of course there were no eyewitnesses! A man who commits a crime like this doesn't go out in daylight or get a lot of newspaper reporters to photograph him. He planned this. Jones planned this crime. The State has proved it. We can show you a picture much clearer that any eyewitness could have seen it. We can make the things that happened in that house almost clearer than if you had seen it.
>
> We say that Jones went to that house about twelve days prior to October 7. He lived there. He worked there and he slept there. He admits that he was discharged, or stopped work on October 7, which was Wednesday. And he tells you that because he wants to account for the money he had when he was arrested.
>
> Mr. Howe, the nearest neighbor, tells you that Jones worked there for twelve days. Mr. Peter Davis and Mr. Coon Cooper, who saw him while they were fishing on the Ocean City bridge on Wednesday,

saw Jones coming from the Davis home. Jones told them he had worked for Mr. Davis for twelve days and had only been paid for eleven. Those witnesses prove our case.

You are going to hear about a "reasonable doubt." But we will show you there can be no doubt. We have told you about the threats made by Jones against Davis. These same two gentlemen, Mr. Cooper and Mr. Davis, saw him soon after he left the Davis home on Wednesday. He had come away so boiling mad that he couldn't get any further than the bridge without stopping and talking to strangers and telling them about how Davis owed him money, and how Mrs. Davis and her daughters always had "nigger and coon" in their mouths. He told all these strangers that he had had trouble with Mr. Davis and that "damn him, he'd get him."

He was discharged Wednesday after a dispute over $1 and anger took possession of him and he couldn't see anybody without telling them about it. On both Wednesday and Thursday, gentlemen.

And there, gentlemen, is the anger taking possession of the man. And what did he do on Friday? Why, gentlemen, a very significant thing happened on Friday. He told his old colored landlady that "you needn't fix anything in my room and you needn't go into my room anymore." Why did he say this, gentlemen? Because there was something coming into his room that he didn't want anyone to see. Late that evening, he was seen walking near the Davis property, but not by the state highway, by the back way. It was dark. He was walking toward the Davis home. That has not been disputed. That has not been denied. Why? Why was he there? Why, he tells you, "I was bootlegging!"

In tones of derision, Child continued:

He was leaving Ocean City, a community of several hundred people, and going out into a sparsely settled country district to sell liquor! Now what manner of man are we dealing with? The prosecution did not say anything about his character, but he did. He told you he was in the Penitentiary. Blurted it out. Proud of it! He listed some of his aliases: Slim Jim, Major Lee, James Majors and Pittsburgh. He tells you he worked six weeks for Mr. Davis cutting corn before he learned he could make more money bootlegging. Six weeks for a man of his type to learn he could make an easy living bootlegging! He told you that he spent Saturday night on his porch with a man named Sam. Where is Sam? Why wasn't he here to testify as to that fact?

Autopsy reports fixed the time of the crime between midnight Saturday and daylight Sunday morning. Now, what did Euel Lee tell you? He said, "Oh, I was out all night, but I did not go near the Davis Farm." But Roger Vickers and Elijah Shockley have told you they saw him about 4:30 Sunday morning going toward the farm and little 11-year-old Jack Fisher saw him coming back. We have put him there! We have proved by not one witness, but four, that he did go near the Davis farm on the night of the murder and the night after it.

Child was getting wound up. His voice rose in a shout: "He was mad on Wednesday, he was madder on Thursday, he planned this crime on Friday, and on Saturday night he went out and committed it! The night after the murder he made a second trip to the house to rob! When the crime was discovered the place was drenched with coal oil and Euel Lee intended to make a third trip and the Davis house would have gone up in smoke!"

Levinson was on his feet instantly. "Objection!"

"What's the objection?" Judge Offutt asked.

"I make a motion that the jury be dismissed, and that a mistral be declared," said the diminutive, gray-haired attorney.

"On what grounds? What's your objection?" The judge pressed.

"On the grounds that Mr. Childs has told the jury what the defendant intended to do and has prejudiced the defendant's case." Levinson replied.

"Motion overruled," snapped Judge Offutt. "Take your exception." Levinson did.

Child, who had turned from the jury to observe the exchange, once again resumed his task. "You have heard Lee's statement, 'You framed me, you planted that Davis stuff in my room.' But who planted the Davis possessions on Lee's person?" cried Child, "Who planted the little Davis girl's brooch on Lee's coat? Who planted Green Davis's watch and chain in Lee's pocket? Who planted the key to Green Davis's automobile in Lee's pocket?"

Child turned and picked up the coat of Green Davis that had been offered into evidence. It had been identified as Davis's best suit coat, and had been worn by Lee when arrested. In his other hand Child held the photograph of the bloody bedroom that depicted the bloody bodies of Davis and his wife lying in the bed. He turned to the jury; speaking slowly and with a rising crescendo: "There are Green Davis's socks hanging on a chair. There is his underwear. There are his trousers…but where is his coat?" Holding up the coat worn by Lee when arrested, Child stormed: "There is his coat! There is his coat! All this crime is plain to me, gentlemen, it's plain to me! The man who committed it is guilty of murder in the first degree! He showed no mercy to Green Davis and his wife. He did not give them any moment for a farewell to each other. He did not give them any chance to utter a brief prayer before he sent them into eternity. He showed them no mercy."

His voice lowered to a whisper: "He deserves no mercy. The State asks you for a verdict of guilt in the first degree."

Child stood before the jury, drained. He looked at each one of the twelve men in the box. He turned and strode back to the trial table. He sat down heavily and stared at the floor Anderson grasped his arm, as if to say, "Way to go." The courtroom was silent.

After a perceptible pause, Judge Offutt looked at the defense lawyers. "You may address the jury." Bernard Ades, who had remained silent to this point, rose. Carrying his notes, he approached the jury.

Each witness here from the Eastern Shore has been trying to play his part in this exciting drama. Each is trying to remember whether or not he didn't see somebody. You must remember, however, that all the people who are telling you that they remember seeing Lee going to, or coming from the crime scene at certain times, had no reason to recall having seen anyone, because the crime had not yet been discovered. You must remember that many of the State's witnesses had never seen Lee before the time they said they saw him coming or going from the crime scene, and they have not seen him until this trial. I suggest to you that their imaginations have been inflamed by the prosecution.

You have heard Everett Jones say on the witness stand that he does not like colored people. He is anxious to pin this crime on the defendant, just as everyone in Worcester County is anxious to pin it on the defendant—

"Just a minute," retorted Judge Offutt, from the bench, "if you've got to make a remark like that—"

"—all witnesses," amended Ades.

"I refer to your remarks as you made them," replied the judge. Turning to the jury the judge snapped, "Disregard that remark."

"I withdraw the remark. I beg Your Honor's pardon." Ades apologized. He turned once again to the jury.

Most of the witnesses who saw Lee coming to or from the house said they saw a brown satchel. But the crucial witness whom the State hopes to pin the murder on Lee says he saw nothing in his hand.

Jones has no scheduled alibi, he had admitted his actions and has even told things which were against his interest. But what were his actions on Sunday and on the Monday after the crime supposedly was committed? He let a bus go by and he did not get on it. He cleaned a gun in public and applied for a shooting license publicly. That shows no evidence of a guilty conscience. The State would have you believe worse things than that. They would have you believe that he took a young girl's stockings and some underwear. Gentlemen, these stockings were old. It has been proved that they were given to the girls to make a rag rug. Why would Jones have taken those stockings? What would he do with them? Jones, we all know, was seen around his home in Ocean City after the crime. That does not show any consciousness of guilt.

What motive has the State proven? They say he was mad because Davis owed him $1. But no person would commit a crime like this one because of a thing like that. The State also says that he was mad because he had been called "nigger" and "coon."

But this is an old man. How many times do you suppose has he been called "nigger" and "coon"? Thousands of times, probably. But he has never committed murder because of that and, surely, he would not commit murder because of a thing like that.

Furthermore, I remind you that Jones got another colored man named James Fassitt to work for Davis, and said, "These are fine people to work for."

The State says that Jones knew that the murder had been committed when he was arrested. But Martha Miller, a very careful witness for the State, says Chief Allen, himself, told Jones of the crime and, she says, Jones started back in surprise. She tells the truth, and she was careful. Chief Allen says he did not tell Jones because he wanted to build up the State's case. Allen, himself, testified that a man in his custody, whom he was supposed to protect, got beaten in his automobile. He violates his duty, and he testifies to it here, and then he tries to tell you that he did not tell Lee about the murder.

The State's case is based entirely on that pile of stuff, supposedly found in Jones's room. But Martha Miller says that some of the things brought here in court as having been found in Jones's room were never there. She was asked whether there were stockings on the chair in the room and she says "yes." Then they show her the stockings here in court and she says they were not the ones. They were not even the same color. Who took the stockings—men's stockings, probably—from Jones's room and who brought in these other stockings to be identified? Who led the frame-up except Chief Allen?

Ades turned and gazed at Chief Allen, who sat in the audience of the courtroom. Allen steadily returned the look. Neither man flinched. After a moment, Ades turned once again to the jury. "Gentlemen, consider the fact that every single piece of evidence identified here has been brought by the police. No outside witness says it was found in Jones's room."

Then, Ades embarked on what was one of the more inflammatory aspects of his defense. Stepping close to the jury box, he began an explanation of how the State could have built a circumstantial case against Sebie Howe, the neighbor who, together with Charles Johnson, had found the Davis family bodies. He related that considerable evidence could have been amassed against Howe, and while he explained that he was not accusing Howe, the evidence against Howe would have been stronger than that against Jones.

Concluding, Ades said, "This case is nothing less than a brazen frame-up. They have let the police do most of the identifying. It is the law of this state and of every state that if we break down enough evidence to create a reasonable doubt in the minds of the jury, we have done enough. And we have done that, gentlemen, by showing the falseness of most of the State's evidence. We say that the State is not in good faith. We ask for a verdict of 'not guilty.'"

As he turned from the jury, Ades must have realized that Child's barnburner of a closing eclipsed his own rather plodding recitation. Yet, he had done what he could. He had lived with this case for over three months and had, indeed, been the best friend that Lee had had in the state. He had given it his all, including bringing in Levinson, a much more experienced trial lawyer, to assist in the defense. As he returned to the trial table, his eyes met those of Lee. They looked upon each other as if to say silently to the other, "Well, here we are at last and now we'll know if the plan worked."

Levinson rose. His task was to follow Ades and sum up for the defense. The small man walked across the courtroom and stood before the twelve men. His remarks were brief:

There is a responsibility on you gentlemen. It is a matter for your conscience. It is a matter of life and death. None of us here were in that room. I don't know what happened and you don't know what happened, but there have been many discrepancies and these discrepancies have been brought forward by the State's own witnesses.

You remember the Miller woman's testimony. She was very careful and particular. But her testimony conflicts with that of Chief Allen. And I want you to remember that Chief Allen modified one of his own statements considerably when he took the stand the second time. There is a life at stake here. This is not a mass meeting. We are here on serious business and if, after having heard the testimony, you feel beyond a reasonable doubt that it has not implicated Lee, you should acquit him. There have been a good many discrepancies in the stories told by both white and colored witnesses. Weigh them carefully. Let us examine some of the testimony. If this murder was committed with a shotgun, as the State says it was, there should have been some noise. It is almost inconceivable that four people in different rooms should not be aroused by the noise and put up a fight. The State has done one thing to make its case a little too good. One of the items found in Lee's room was a key to a car. That car meant safety and freedom. Would any murderer remain around the scene of a crime for many days and wait for a bus to take him away? Of course not. He would take all things and get away safely and quickly. Would a murderer take evidence of the crime to his room that had no lock on it, and keep it there for several days? No. I say no. I ask you to consider this case most carefully. Don't do something that you would regret when it is too late. Rather let ten guilty men escape than let one innocent man suffer. I will not ask you for freedom for this man unless you think—honestly and sincerely—that we have demonstrated a reasonable doubt. We cannot create a human life and we should consider very carefully before we send a man to his death.

Levinson also surely realized that Child's address scored heavily, while his was tepid by comparison. He had, nevertheless, done his duty to his client, and he walked across the courtroom and sat, without flourish, beside Lee and Ades. It was over for the defense, as only the closing remarks of State's Attorney Anderson remained before the jury would deliberate the fate of Euel Lee.

The court, once again, announced a one-hour recess.

After the hour had passed, the spectators and personnel filed once again into the courtroom, with the certain knowledge that the trial was about to come to its conclusion.

"All rise!" intoned the bailiff, as the judges entered the courtroom. "You may be seated," said Judge Offutt. The court settled down as the judges once again regained their chairs. Judge Offutt turned to State's Attorney Anderson. "You may go to the jury, sir."

Anderson rose. He walked across the silent room. It was precisely 1:30 p.m. He stood for a moment, secure in the knowledge that this was his county and his jury. He began speaking quietly and in measured phrases. Most of the time, he looked directly into the faces of the twelve men he addressed. At times, the *Sun* reported, his voice sank to a whisper, then at times, his summation rose to emotional peaks, and he "spoke through gritted teeth."

He attacked the defense's contention that the case against Lee was purely circumstantial, and that no one had seen him commit the crime. "The perpetrator of the crime made it certain that there would be no witnesses to remain. He wiped out a whole family of decent, law-abiding citizens of the Eastern Shore of Maryland. He has had his chance today, but they had none," he said. He reminded the jurors that the murderer had to be familiar with the Davis house so that, "in the space of fifteen seconds he could wipe them all out."

He ridiculed Ades's notion that Sebie Howe could have, likewise, been charged with the crime. "Defense counsel have endeavored to pull the old time-worn trick of dragging a herring across the trail in order to get into the minds of the jury the impression that Mr. Howe, a decent, upright, law-abiding citizen of Worcester County, had stepped in and committed this crime because Mr. Davis had a roadside stand. I am surprised at the defense for its attempt to sully the reputation of such a white gentlemen by such an insinuation. To balance the State's testimony, we have from the defense—what? A simple denial of practically everything the State has produced. The defense has only produced one witness—the defendant himself!"

Anderson turned and pointed at Lee. "Can you put any credence whatsoever in the testimony of that man in the light of contradiction after the contradiction in his testimony?"

Lee gazed stoically back at the prosecutor.

Anderson then pointed out the story of the shotgun found in Lee's room, identified as Davis's gun. "Is there any doubt in your mind that the gun was Mr. Davis's? Lee said he bought it from a pawnshop, but Mr. Hornstein, the pawnbroker, has denied selling it to him! The State's witnesses time and time again identified it as that of Mr. Davis, pointing out specific marks on the gun. And what about the testimony of Martha Miller? She said she saw Lee cleaning the gun the day after the murder! Lee said he cleaned it the day before! Out of their own mouths do I condemn them!"

He paused, took a drink of water; "The defense charges that the witnesses are able to give detailed testimony because their imaginations are inflamed and they are determined to convict this man. If it were not so serious it would be laughable! Mr. Ades would have you men of Baltimore County believe that reputable people whose character cannot be assailed would come up here and for the sake of a conviction would perjure themselves! Why, they would be guilty not only of perjury, but also of murder!

"The defense would have you believe that the police planted the items of clothing found in the defendant's room. Again, I condemn them out of their own mouths!" Holding up the brooch identified by witnesses as the property of one of the teen girls, Anderson spat: "Lee had this on his clothing when he was arrested! How did it get there? Frame up? Oh, no! Out of his own mouth he said he found it on the road to Pocomoke!"

He turned to retrieve the tobacco pouch witnesses had identified as that of Mr. Davis: "How did this happen to be in his pocket when he was arrested? Frame up? No! It was given to him, he says, by a man at the Fullerton Hotel. Can there by any doubt, any reasonable doubt, any suspicion of a doubt about that?"

Once again, from the evidence table, he picked up the roll of money containing eighty dollars, found on Lee when he was arrested. "I say to you that this money was the receipts from Mr. Davis's fruit stand for the week. He wants you to believe that it came from the sale of whiskey."

His voice dropped to a whisper. Speaking very slowly, he continued, "We have proven to you that Lee worked at the Fullerton Hotel until almost September 1. Lee has said that he was paid $63, and that Davis owed him an additional dollar. He would have had to work for Davis since sometime in August. Witnesses, however, said that he told them that Davis owed him $12 and only paid him $11. Is there any doubt—not reasonable doubt, a doubt—that as of September 1, he was working right here in our county at Fullerton? Men lie and witnesses forget, but facts stand out beyond any possible contradiction."

Anderson paused for a long moment. "If there is any framing up in this case, let me call your attention to it. The defendant told you on the stand himself—I didn't ask him; he just blurted it out—that he was in prison in Pennsylvania. Murder will out. There comes a time when the small voice of conscience begins to speak. The murderer begins to fear. Can't you see it in this case?

"Jones begins to fear. So, he tells poor old Jim Fassitt where these people—the Davises—are cutting corn. This was at two o'clock Monday. The Davises are lying dead in their beds and Jones wants to put Jim Fassitt there where these dead people are so that the crime will be pinned on poor old Jim. There's the frame up, if there's any frame up! There's the story! He had never seen this man but told him where there was work for him!"

Anderson was now shouting. "He wanted to get away from any possible suspicion! Where's the motive? The motive was revenge and robbery! The defendant said he quit Mr. Davis so he could make more money bootlegging! Isn't it remarkable that he should work hard at the Davis place for six weeks before discovering it was so much easier to make money bootlegging?

"The defendant's story does not make sense. He does not have a good story. That's because he is guilty of murdering the Davis family. Remember, he worked here in Fullerton. This crime could have occurred right here in Baltimore County, but it happened in Worcester County, not here, it's not close to home."

His voice dropped to a whisper. "It happened in Worcester County. Put yourself in the place of the Davises' neighbors and bring it home. On the mosaic tables, it is written, 'Thou shalt commit no murder.' In the name of the State, I ask you gentlemen—not because I want it but in the name of decency, law and the protection of lives and property of the citizens of this state—to show by your verdict that Baltimore County will not countenance the commission of a crime of this kind."

The Moment of Truth

He stood before the jury, and looked intently at them. He turned and looked at the clock on the wall of the courtroom. It was 2:40 p.m. His role in the trial had ended. He turned, and, as had the others before him, he returned to the counsel table and sat, heavily.

Chief Judge Offutt began the charge to the jury: "Gentlemen of the jury. You may return any one of five verdicts in this case: First, guilty of murder in the first degree; second, guilty of murder in the first degree without capital punishment; third, not guilty of murder in the first degree, guilty of murder in the second degree; fourth, not guilty of murder, guilty of manslaughter; fifth, not guilty."

At just after 2:45 p.m., the jury filed out of the courtroom to deliberate. The judges left the bench and retired into their chambers behind the courtroom.

There was a rustling in the courtroom, as some spectators left the room to smoke cigarettes and attend other matters. The lawyers sat in their chairs and said very little. Godfrey Child walked over to speak to Sheriff Purnell, and stood near the rail separating the spectators from the trial area. Anderson shuffled his papers and tidied a file. Lee sat and looked at the empty witness box. Ades and Levinson conferred about some matter they thought important. Time passed.

XXI

The Jury Returns

At 3:15, just thirty minutes later, there was a knock on the door from inside the jury room. The bailiff responded, and then hurried out of the rear of the courtroom to the area of the judges' chambers. A verdict had been reached.

A sheriff's deputy went into the hall to advise the public of the turn of events. The lawyers spoke to each other in muted tones; as experienced trial counsel, they each knew a quick verdict surely indicated the jury had found Lee guilty. In a matter of a few minutes, the stage was set. The spectators filed back into the room, some bewildered by the quick unfolding of the finale. The police officers from Worcester County and those witnesses who had remained to see the final results of the case, more than fifty of them, all of whom had ignored the announcement that their buses were leaving, spoke to each other in guarded tones, and there was a definite buzz in the crowded courtroom as more than two hundred people crammed in to hear the expected verdict. The newspaper reporters were busily scratching at their notepads, trying to portray the atmosphere of the moment. The room fell silent as the three judges once again resumed their seats on the bench.

As the judges settled into their chairs, Judge Offutt addressed the crowd. "We are shortly going to receive the jury's verdict. There will be no comments, noise or disorder of any kind." He turned to Marshal C.E. Stansbury. "Mr. Marshal, if there is any one who violates the court's order, you are to arrest that person forthwith." Stansbury nodded his understanding.

"Mr. Bailiff, see to it that the jury returns to the box," said Judge Offutt. The bailiff moved toward the jury room door. With a quick movement, he opened it.

"Gentlemen, you may return to your seats," As he stood aside, the grim-faced jurors solemnly filed into their appointed places in the jury box.

All eyes in the crowded room gazed upon the twelve men. None of them looked back. The silence was palpable.

"Mr. Clerk, you may call the roll," said Judge Offutt. The clerk read over each juror's name. Each man replied, "Here."

Upon the completion of the roll, the clerk advised the judge, "All present." He then turned to the panel: "Have you reached a verdict?"

"We have," replied the twelve, in chorus.

"Who shall say it?" queried the clerk.

"Our foreman," they answered.

"The defendant shall rise and face the jury," said Judge Offutt. Lee, Ades and Levinson got to their feet in unison.

The foreman, Howard H. Stocksdale, the carpenter from Glyndon, also stood, a small piece of paper clutched in his hand. He looked at Euel Lee.

"What is the verdict?" asked the clerk.

"Guilty of murder in the first degree," replied Mr. Stocksdale. The marshal looked intently at the crowd of spectators. There was not the slightest stir. Lee's face betrayed not the slightest emotion. He gazed without expression at Mr. Stocksdale.

David Levinson, experienced in such matters, requested that the judge poll the jury, individually for the purpose of verifying that the vote was unanimous. Judge Offutt said, "Mr. Clerk, poll the jury." In accordance with Maryland trial procedure, the clerk began questioning each jury member.

He said, "Each juror will answer when his name is called." Beginning with Stocksdale, the clerk inquired, "How do you find the defendant?" Each of the twelve, as his name was called, responded, "Guilty of murder in the first degree."

"So say you all?" asked the clerk.

"Yes," was the reply in unison.

The jury had been out less than thirty minutes. And it was done.

Levinson requested a bench conference, which was granted. While at the bench, the judges gave instructions as to how they would receive motions for a new trial. Levinson advised that one would be promptly filed, and the judges immediately set a date for the hearing.

Judge Offutt now once again turned to the crowded room. "Mr. Sheriff, no one will leave or enter the courtroom until the defendant has left with his escort." In a moment's time, the sheriff and his deputies whisked Lee out of the room and into waiting cars in order to deliver him back to the Baltimore city jail. A quiet murmur went through the courtroom, but no one, in anticipation of Judge Offutt's ire, moved from their appointed seats.

The judge then turned his attention to the jury: "Gentlemen, the court thanks you for your service in this case. You are now excused." As the twelve men filed from the box, through the room and out the door, none of the spectators stirred. The judges sat impassively on the bench. The sheriff and the marshal stood, poised and ready to pounce on the first miscreant who would dare to interrupt the procession. No one did.

Once Lee had departed and the jurors had cleared the door, Judge Offutt glanced around his courtroom. He paused; "The Court is adjourned," he announced. After the slightest hesitation, people began to move. With increasing intensity, the realization that it was over began to dawn on those present. As if a tide were rising, people began to talk, move and head for the exits.

The newspaper reporters hastened to meet their deadlines for the evening editions. They had not far to go. But there was also a similar notification taking place, as from the nearest available telephone locations the word began to be flashed back to the Eastern Shore.

Chief Randolph Purnell of Snow Hill, who had defused the threat of mob violence on the evening of November 4, telephoned the verdict to the Worcester County courthouse, where, he said, crowds of people were awaiting the news. Various other methods were used to send the eagerly awaited news throughout the Eastern Shore. At last, the long delayed verdict would be received by all those people who had clamored for the quick disposition of the determination of guilt of Euel Lee.

Meanwhile, in the courtroom, Godfrey Child received the accolades of his peers. State's Attorney Anderson, Sheriff Purnell and several law enforcement officers from Worcester County surrounded him and gave him their congratulations. He stood and received his due in modest, but relieved mien. At last, the goal that had eluded him had been achieved. The murderer had been convicted. His job in the most difficult case of his career had been successfully accomplished. The infernal Communists had been brought to bay. It was over…at least for the moment.

Nearby, however, at the same counsel table where Child was being lauded, Ades and Levinson were conferring. Theirs were not the accolades of the hour, but they were even now planning for tomorrow, and they believed that they had the issue that would reverse the determination of the jury in this emotional case. They would let the passions of the facts stand but would call upon cooler heads of the appellate court to chastise the judges of Baltimore County for ignoring the right of a black man to have the judgment of his peers—other black men—determine his fate at the bar of criminal justice. They felt, confidently, that they had preserved the essential issue of the case, the exclusion (although perhaps considered benign by the judges) of blacks from the jury panels of Baltimore County.

Levinson and Ades agreed that their work, far from being finished, had, in fact, just begun. Tomorrow, although they had to fashion a motion for a new trial, they would focus on the salient issue of the case: the exclusion of black men from Baltimore County juries.

In the meantime, Godfrey Child and the other prosecutors in the trial allowed themselves some time for celebration. They enjoyed a good dinner in Towson, with Mr. Child certainly relishing his upcoming triumphant return to Worcester County, assured of the accolades that would surely follow his long sought, yet long delayed victory. He had been frustrated by the inability to get the trial in motion, but now the sentencing, which would surely be the most severe allowed, was all that remained of the process (except of course for the inevitable appeal). It was, surely, a sweet victory.

The feeling of relief, however, was to be short-lived, indeed.

XXII

Ades Maneuvers

In 1933, any motion for a new trial had, under Maryland Rules of Procedure, to be filed within three days. Therefore it was expected that the motion from Ades would be forthcoming. And it was. On Friday, January 22, shortly before noon, Bernard Ades delivered the defense's motion for a new trial to the clerk's office in the Towson courthouse.

As promised, the motion cited several alleged irregularities in the trial, foremost among them being the exclusion of black jurors on the panel. The motion, however, left nothing out. It contained eight grounds for error which were noted in order:

> *1. The names of the veniremen were not taken from the lists of the male, taxable inhabitants or residents of the county;*
> *2. That the selection of the special panels by the Sheriff were not fairly and impartially selected from the general population of the county;*
> *3. Negroes were excluded from the drawing of the regular panel of veniremen and from the special panels chosen by the Sheriff, thus depriving the defendant of the equal protection of the laws contrary to the Constitution of the United States;*
> *4. Because the court sustained the state's objection to the question of the foreman of the jury as to whether he had any case pending in court;*
> *5. Because the court refused to allow the defense the opportunity to show that Green Davis had fired a shot at his neighbor sometime before he was killed;*
> *6. Because the court refused to allow the defense to explain why they had been unable to produce "Sam," a witness referred to in the testimony;*
> *7. Because James C.L. Anderson, counsel for the State, had stated to the jury that the defendant had intended to set fire to the Green Davis house, and the statement was made intentionally and with great prejudice to the defendant;* [actually the statement had been made by Godfrey Child]
> *8. Because the court overruled various objections by the defense which are unable to be stated because the court refused to allow the testimony to be transcribed and furnished to the defendant without charge;*
> *For such other and further reasons which will be advanced at the hearing on defendant's motion.*

The motion was not the only thing in the news surrounding the trial, however.

The local police were busy investigating a bomb threat that was received scribbled on the edge of a newspaper. Although police stated that they believed the threat to be a prank, they nevertheless posted guards at the homes of all three judges, and additional security was provided at the courthouse.

One very good reason for the extra precaution was the fact that it was discovered that fifty sticks of dynamite had been stolen from a quarry at nearby Loch Raven. It was also revealed at this time that, during the trial, threats had been made against Ades and Levinson, and that police had guarded their automobiles. The judges and the defense attorneys were apparently not perturbed about the threats. So, an uneasy weekend arrived and the events paused, but not for long. It became known that the argument on the new trial motion would be scheduled for Thursday, January 28, 1932.

It is certain that there was little rest for the defense lawyers that weekend. They knew that as soon as the new trial motion was disposed of, unless the court granted the request, sentencing would follow. There was no doubt that the sentence would be severe, and most likely would include the imposition of capital punishment.

On Monday, January 25, Ades announced that there would also be a brief filed for the defense, and that he would not rely on oral arguments alone. He stated to the press that he was "hard at work" on the brief, and that, unexpectedly, Levinson would not journey from his office in Philadelphia to participate in the hearing, presumably due to the press of other cases. Meanwhile, the guard of police officers at the courthouse and at the judges' homes was continued.

On the same day, a letter to the editor of the *Evening Sun* appeared. It stated:

> *I think the taxpayers and the reading public generally are quite weary of the long-drawn-out Euel Lee or Orphan Jones case.*
>
> *Can you enlighten us as to the estimated cost of this case to the taxpayers of Maryland? It must be large.*
>
> *And would it be legally possible for the State of Maryland to enter suit against this Labor Defense League, whose agent here seems to be the man Bernard Ades, to recover the difference between the cost of the case as handled by Ades and the probable cost if this league, through Ades, had not he interfered?*

The letter was signed "Anxious."

On Wednesday, the *Sun* reported that the attorneys were working hard preparing the arguments that would be presented to the court on the next day. Bernard Ades was quoted as saying that he was ready to make his argument when the hearing convened. The report also said that Mr. Child would be assisted in his argument by Mr. Anderson.

Thursday morning was a clear, cold day as the spectators—once again in large numbers, due to the substantial likelihood that the day would bring the sentencing of the defendant—descended on the court at Towson. The crowd was orderly and the policemen assembled showed no noticeable air of urgency about their actions in monitoring the entrance of the public into the courtroom.

Prior to the scheduled hour of the hearing, the lawyers entered the now familiar room; at the prosecution table were Godfrey Child, James L. Anderson, James McAllister and a new face, J. Howard Murray, assistant State's Attorney for Baltimore County.

As always, Lee arrived under guard by Baltimore County policemen. Ades, without the presence of Levinson, was there to greet him. Ades shuffled in his seat and studied his copious notes as he contemplated his task: the burden was on him to convince the judges to find that there had been an error in the conduct of the trial which would warrant the retrial of the convicted murderer. In other words, the judges were being urged to find that they themselves had erred and that as a result of that, they should give Lee another chance as a free agent in society.

The crowd exuded a low murmur as the spectators shifted and sought out their seats among the entering throng. There were still a scattering of people from Worcester County, and there was a large contingent of press present. The deputies gazed over the crowd and made the judgment that there was little chance that any disturbance would be forthcoming on this day. Precisely at the appointed hour, the door opened and the three judges filed into their seats at the bench.

As they settled into their seats, Judge Offutt, once again presiding, asked the clerk to bring forth the new trial motion. A copy was handed to him, and he read the motion aloud for the benefit of the two other judges. After he finished, he looked at Bernard Ades. "All right," he said.

Ades began. "If Your Honors please, among the reasons for a new trial are two dealing with the selection of the jury. One is that the panel of veniremen was improperly drawn, and the second is the Negroes were excluded from the jury." He had led with his most oft-stated position: the exclusion of African American men from the panel had deprived Lee of his Constitutional privilege of due process. Ades continued, stating that the manner of selecting juries in the state of Maryland was governed by the general provisions of Maryland law; no local law regarding the selection of juries existed for Baltimore County.

Judge Offutt interrupted: "Have you examined the recent Acts of Legislature?"

"As to Baltimore County? No sir, I have not," replied Ades. "Would Your Honor indulge me while I examine the public local laws of Baltimore County?"

"Don't you think you should have done so before coming into court?" sniffed the judge.

Nevertheless, Ades was permitted to send for the requisite code book. Continuing, he sought to make his point: "I am not alleging that the local law of Baltimore County contains a discrimination statute, but when such exclusion occurs through the conduct of county officers, that exclusion becomes the act of the State." He then cited a Supreme Court ruling regarding jury service for blacks. He argued that the Fourteenth Amendment to the U.S. Constitution had been violated because "Negroes had been excluded from the panels from which jurors were chosen."

Chief Judge Offutt was having none of it. He promptly interrupted Ades and said, "The burden lies upon you, Mr. Ades, to show that Negroes were excluded. I realize that you assume Negroes were excluded because none were on the jury, but you must go further than that." Offutt: "No traverser has the right to have Negroes on the jury, nor Chinese, nor members of any other race, simply because of their race."

"Your Honor," replied Ades, "No Negro has been picked for jury duty in Baltimore County in the last twenty-four years. If Negroes are being excluded by the jury clerks who consider them unfit to serve, that prejudice works against a Negro defendant just a strongly as though it is an act of the legislature."

"But," Judge Offutt snapped, "the law does not permit jury clerks to pick a man for jury service because he is colored or because he is white. The burden lies on you, Mr. Ades, to show that in this particular case the law has been violated."

Ades was unfazed: "Your Honor," he inquired, "if I show that over a period of twenty-five years there has not been a Negro on a jury in Baltimore County and that during that time there were eligible Negroes in Baltimore County, haven't I made out a prima facie case?"

"But in this case," the judge retorted, "it isn't a prima facie argument that you want to present; it isn't a prima facie case you are dealing with. You have the statement of Judge Duncan who has been selecting jurors here for twenty-five years. He says he has been selecting jurors without consideration to race or color, but only to honesty and sobriety. You see, Judge Duncan was a witness in this case, and you have his testimony. He said, under oath, that he selected jurors without using unfair discrimination. It is the duty of the judge to select men who are intelligent and sober and Judge Duncan has said that he did that. The burden is on you to prove that this statement is erroneous. It is not a prima facie affair and you must meet his testimony to show that there was a prejudice against Negroes."

"In response, Your Honor, allow me to explain my concept of the Fourteenth Amendment," retorted Ades. "The purpose of the amendment was to keep juries from feeling that white men are superior to Negroes. When no Negro jurors are chosen over a long period of time, that creates an impression among the jurors which is damaging to a Negro defendant."

"But, sir, to carry out your notion of how to select a jury would require that Negroes would have to be selected, at some time, regardless of their qualifications. That is not the law."

"I acknowledge that your interpretation is substantially correct, Your Honor, but Negroes should be considered at some time or other when they are otherwise qualified," Ades stated.

"Move on to your next point," said the judge.

"I believe that Mr. Anderson's statement regarding the kerosene in the Davis house was prejudicial to the fair determination of the case by the jury," said Ades. "It was an unwarranted statement. In making that statement the State was simply trying to introduce evidence that they could not otherwise enter into consideration by the jury legitimately."

"I recall the evidence," replied Judge Offutt. "I believe that Mr. Anderson's statement reflected a legitimate inference to be drawn from the known facts."

"I disagree, Your Honor," said Ades. "The State was clearly trying to get the jury to consider the evidence they could not explain legitimately. That is wrong." Ades insisted that this point mandated a new trial. He then began his third line of attack. He brought up the point that he had not been allowed to inquire as to a shot that Davis had supposedly fired at a witness's son, indicating that this event allowed the inference of a motive imputed to someone other than the defendant.

Finally, Ades returned to his first argument as to the jury selection process. He asserted that Judge Duncan, in selecting the grand jury and the panel from which the petit jury was chosen, had not selected them from a list of two hundred picked from the county registration books. Judge Offutt again demurred, stating that he did not recall that Judge Duncan had made such a statement, and in fact, recalled that the judge had stated otherwise. Sharply, he stated that the court records would show conclusively that the group of two hundred had, in fact, been chosen first.

Ades hesitated, fearing that he had gone too far in his rhetoric regarding the jury selection process. It was, however, too late. Angrily, Judge Offutt called upon the clerk to hand him the list of two hundred people from whom the grand jury and petit jury panels were chosen. "Hand this to Mr. Ades for his perusal," snapped the judge.

The courtroom was silent as Ades sat and examined the list for what seemed to be an interminable span of time. Surely his thoughts were whirling, for it soon became evident that he had misstated the testimony of not only a witness in the case, but, indeed, a presiding judge. During the interlude, Lee sat before him staring directly forward, not moving a muscle. If dread was still a part of his makeup, it must have been particularly evident at this moment.

After a pause, Ades rose and handed the list back to the clerk. "Your Honor, I will withdraw the position that the jury panel had not been chosen from the prescribed list."

"Is there anything else you wish the court to consider related to your motion?" Judge Offutt asked, glancing at the motion that had been presented to him.

Ades paused, looked at his notes, and after his review, said "No, sir." He recognized that the judge was intent upon disposing of this matter as quickly as possible and he clearly saw the futility of prolonging the effort. At that moment, however, he must have thought, perhaps fleetingly, of his motion for removal, rejected out of hand by the First Judicial Circuit, whose decision had been chastised by the Court of Appeals. He would again have his chance before that body. He would bide his time.

Judge Offutt looked at the two other judges. It was evident that they had nothing to add in the way of inquiry. "Does the State wish to reply?" inquired Judge Offutt. Child, Anderson and McAllister conferred for a brief moment.

Child rose. "No, Your Honor," he stated. The prosecutors could surely take a hint from the tenor of the exchange between Ades and the court that there was no need, on this morning, to gild the lily. Much against the grain of a trial lawyer, Child decided to keep quiet.

Judge Offutt announced that the judges would retire to consider the motion. After they disappeared into the chambers behind the bench, the courtroom once again came alive. Spectators rose, stretched and talked among themselves. The members of the press chatted also, certainly grading the effectiveness of Ades's effort. Although the result was, from the nature of the judge's inquiry, a foregone conclusion, there was the realization among some that Ades had struck a nerve—he had articulated for perhaps the first time that there was a pervasive scheme in the county, among the perceived most liberal in the state, to systematically exclude all black citizens from participation in the judicial process.

Now, like the ugly aunt in the basement, the issue had been exposed to the light of day. Anyone who reflected for more than the most fleeting of moments that morning must have realized that there was a new slant on things. A man who had taken on the most unpopular of causes had, likewise, dared to fling the fact of discrimination into the faces of the judges of Baltimore County. It had never been done before. It was yet another of the events that this trial would expose for consideration of thinking men around the state.

The judges, however, did not lend their deliberations this morning to such notions of philosophical reflection. In less than five minutes, they returned to the bench. Anticipation now reached a heightened level, as it became obvious that the judges were going to state their decision for the record and then proceed to sentencing. (As perhaps a footnote to history, an observer would have seen that in the crowd of people there that morning, other than the defendant, there was only one African American man in the courtroom, a reporter from the *Afro-American* newspaper of Baltimore.)

Police stood at the doors and a semi-circle of detectives stood behind the defense table. As the murmur died away and silence became prevalent, Judge Offutt spoke: "In the opinion of the court, the motion for a new trial in this case should be overruled." It was that simple.

He looked around sternly. "Before proceeding, the court wants to warn the persons standing in this room that there must be no demonstrations and no disorder. Marshal Carroll Stansbury and his officers have orders to take into custody anyone who violates the court order. No one will leave the courtroom until the defendant has been taken out." Once again Judge Offutt's eyes scanned the courtroom. No one stirred.

His attention focused on Lee: "The defendant will rise." Lee compiled, Ades at his side. "Have you anything to say before the judgment and the sentence of the court is imposed?"

Lee hesitated only a moment. "Well, I'll say that I have not had a fair trial, that's all," he declared.

Judge Offutt did not pause. "Mr. Lee," said the judge, "You have been indicted in the regular course of proceeding, you have been defended by a counsel of your own choosing at a fair and impartial trial. You have been found guilty of a horrible crime. The sentence and judgment of the court is, therefore, that you Euel Lee, alias Orphan Jones, be remanded to the County of Worcester in the custody of the sheriff of the County of Worcester, in the state of Maryland, who shall deliver you to the warden of the Maryland Penitentiary to be held by said warden in solitary confinement until such time as his excellency, the governor of the state of Maryland, by his warrant appoint the time, when at the death chamber of said Maryland Penitentiary you shall be hanged by the neck until you are dead, and may God have mercy upon your soul."

When Lee heard the sentence, he smiled.

The courtroom was as silent as death. Following the judges' departure once more from the bench and after a moment's delay, the officers who had escorted Lee into the court surrounded him and after handcuffing him, led him from the court. He never spoke a word. Ades, left behind at the trial table, sat and stared at the floor.

The State's Attorneys, without outward visible sign of exaltation, silently shook hands, gathered their papers and left the courtroom, without any acknowledgment of Ades.

The entire proceeding had lasted just one hour and five minutes.

Slowly, the spectators cleared the room. Still, Ades remained seated, until he was the only one in the room and was requested to leave so that the courtroom doors could be locked. If there was to be any redemption for his client, it would await the next step in the legal process.

XXIII

The Condemned Man

As Ades left the courthouse, reporters surrounded him. By this time, he had regained his composure. "This case will be taken to the Court of Appeals," he said. "It is a violation of the Constitution to exclude Negroes from the jury, and we will acquire a new trial. That's all I have to say." He trudged to his automobile, and drove out of the Towson area, back to his office in the Baltimore Trust Building in downtown Baltimore City. He had a lot of work to do.

The process following a death sentence, however, was proceeding. On the very day of the sentencing, in accordance with Maryland law, the certified copies of the docket entries were mailed to the governor in Annapolis, the clerk of the circuit court for Worcester County, the warden of the penitentiary and the sheriff of Worcester County. Lee was being made ready for his hanging.

Ades, it can be presumed, conferred with Lee later that day to inform him of the plans for the appeal and to attempt to reassure him of the chances that the matter was not finished. As he sat in his cell in the new surroundings of the Maryland Penitentiary, Lee must have pondered his future. Although Ades had defended him tenaciously, Lee had now been convicted by the very same Baltimore County jury that Ades had fought to acquire. This was no crowd of inflamed Worcester County men; here was the relative quiet of the Western Shore. But, as Ades repeatedly reminded him, they were all white men. Therefore, the issue of being tried by a true panel of his peers, said Ades, would await the reflection of the Court of Appeals once again.

Also, though there is no report of the event, Ades most certainly reported to the Labor Defense the events of the day. There must have been lights burning late into the night in Ades's office as the strategy unfolded for the days ahead.

Likewise, Godfrey Child surely reported back to the Worcester County citizens and officials of the final culmination of the victory: the death penalty. He could now resume the duties of both his position as State's Attorney in Snow Hill and the additional responsibility of his successful private law practice in Pocomoke City. His ordeal of the extended trial of Orphan Jones was finally concluded.

Or was it?

The inevitable appeal process was a foregone conclusion. It was not mandated by statute, but a capital case was certain to be reviewed by the Court of Appeals. Even the most mundane and clear-cut trial that resulted in a sentence of death would surely be reviewed. This case, however was very different. Ades had raised numerous challenges to the prosecution of his client. There were several pitfalls that he had created in the procedural record of the case. At each juncture, he had objected, quarreled, obstructed and simply dug in his heels.

He had created such a lengthy record of procedural problems that at least one or two would catch the attention of the reviewing panel of judges. The problem with a notorious case is that it is examined with great care and the tenacity of the defense in bringing to light even the most apparently insignificant missteps could torpedo the best of prosecutions. One must not forget that in the present case, a man's life hung in the balance. If Ades was not successful in his advocacy, Euel Lee would be killed.

So the days and weeks following the initial trial were not times of relaxation for Bernard Ades. His position was a tenuous one, indeed. As Judge Offutt had stated during the trial, the method of jury selection in Baltimore County had withstood appellate challenge before. The idea of requiring black men to be on a panel of prospective jurors in 1932 in the state of Maryland was a foreign and abstract notion, indeed.

Nevertheless, Bernard Ades was not dissuaded from his goal. An avowed Communist, Ades had an additional agenda. The simple fact was that he believed strongly in the then-obscure fact that black men deserved the same consideration under the law as did whites.

One must recall that Maryland in 1932 was essentially a Southern venue. It was conservative, and it was definitely a segregated society. The Eastern Shore was not the only area of the Free State that had this established leaning toward the separation of the races. The areas around Baltimore City, had, since the Civil War, only seventy years in the past, been a hotbed of Southern philosophy.

It is apparent from the published law in Maryland at the time, that there was not yet a willingness of the judiciary to confront the equity of race. It was because of this status of precedent in law that made Judge Offutt comfortable with his stated notion that Lee had received that degree of justice to which he was entitled. Ades, it can be readily discerned, did not agree, nor did he give a damn. He had confronted the system before in this case and he was prepared to do it again. Thus, he began to fashion the basis of his appeal.

On February 19, Ades, good to his word, filed an order for appeal on behalf of the defendant, "to the Court of Appeals of Maryland from the action, judgment and sentence of the circuit court for Baltimore County." The issue, once again, was joined.

Meanwhile, another point of view was put forth. In an editorial in the issue of the week of January 30, the *Afro-American* newspaper put a new light on the trial:

> *A drama was staged in Towson, Maryland, last week. Two Jewish lawyers, backed by the Communist Party, defended an humble black man accused of murdering four people.*
>
> *No one conceded them a chance to save their man, but they battled heroically against public sentiment, against an admittedly unlawful method of selecting jurors and against the known race prejudice of Baltimore County which expresses itself in inferior schools, economic, social and political exclusion of persons of color there.*
>
> *The Red lawyers towered like a church spire above the four county prosecutors and some of those who looked into the Jim Crow courtroom with its all-white judges, jury, police, bailiffs, and court clerks and colored spectators herded in a rear seat, wondered whether the ends of justice would not better have been served with Red judges on the bench.*
>
> *Here was a legal battle in which, in our judgment, Messrs. Bernard Ades and David Levinson won a brilliant victory.*

The alleged unlawfully picked jury voted against them, but the Court of Appeals and the U.S. Supreme Court may not agree with those hand picked boys up in Baltimore County.

Also, in its February 6 edition, the *Afro-American* stated in a headline: "I.D.L. To Carry Case To Court Of Appeals." In the article, which stated that the motion for a new trial was a mere sham because the judges had already made up their minds, Louis Berger, local organizer of the International Defense League (who threatened to storm Snow Hill back in November) reported to the *Afro* that the whole procedure at Towson "was a legal lynching in which the machinery of the court was operated to prevent the defense from introducing evidence to point to the possibly guilty parties."

Berger was not finished there, however. "The judges and all the officers of the court displayed openly their racial antipathy, which of itself prevented the accused from getting a fair and impartial trial. The national office in New York has instructed us to carry on the fight and has pledged more funds and additional lawyers to assist Mr. Ades if they are needed."

Ades was also quoted by reporters as stating that he would file a petition for stay of execution of the sentence and that his appeal would concentrate on the position that "the exclusion of colored jurors was the result of deliberate acts of discrimination."

XXIV

A Chapter is Closed

Meanwhile, back in Worcester County, the relief of finishing the trial that everyone said should have been concluded long ago was showing in the everyday life of the area. The *Sun* reported in its January 21, 1932 issue that in Snow Hill on January 20, word had been received about 3:30 p.m. by telephone form the Towson courthouse. The news was then passed around the county seat by word of mouth. Within two hours thereafter, special editions of Baltimore newspapers were on sale, carrying accounts of the day's court proceedings. The paper reported that, aside from the general interest in the outcome, no unusual excitement was evident in the town.

In Salisbury, however, the newspaper office of the *Salisbury Times* reportedly received hundreds of phone calls from all over the shore. The *Times* posted bulletins of the trial's conclusions in its windows, and thousands of copies of the Baltimore papers were seen on sale in the city.

While all this was taking place, Lee was beginning his routine as a prisoner of the penitentiary. Up to this point, he had been merely an accused criminal, and had been housed in the Baltimore city jail. Now, however, he had been sentenced to the custody of the warden of the penitentiary and therefore, while awaiting the determination of his sentence, he was processed accordingly.

He was given the number 28-735. His record index card showed that he was 5 feet 6¾ inches tall, 181½ pounds, brown eyes, "wooly hair," dark complexion. His birthplace was given as Virginia, and his residence as Berlin, Maryland. His occupation was listed as laborer; education, none, "left an orphan when eleven years old." He was single, a Baptist and "not addicted to alcohol or drugs." He was housed on death row, away from the ordinary prison population. There were at the time no other men awaiting execution, so Lee was the only prisoner on the isolated tier that made up the death row section. Although he was allowed visitors, as the months passed, no one came to visit him except the faithful Bernard Ades.

Delegation of Eastern Shoremen at the Towson trial of Orphan Jones. *Baltimore* Sunpapers *and Photography Collection, University of Maryland Baltimore County.*

Captain Edward McKim Johnson, commander of the Maryland State Police, was involved in most of the events surrounding the case of Orphan Jones, and was also injured trying to protect George Armwood at the Somerset County jail. It was upon his orders that his troopers did not fire upon the mob at the jail. *Baltimore* Sunpapers *and Photography Collection, University of Maryland Baltimore County.*

The Somerset County jail where the mob in Princess Anne broke in to take George Armwood and lynch him on the night of October 18, 1933. The jail, still standing, was in 2005 the headquarters of Princess Anne police. *Baltimore* Sunpapers *photo.*

Judge Robert Duer, circuit court for Somerset County, who bravely confronted the Princess Anne mob at the jail in a futile effort to keep it from harming George Armwood. It was, however, Judge Duer who had previously ordered Armwood removed from the safety of the Baltimore city jail to be returned to Somerset County. *Baltimore Sunpapers photo.*

The door at the Somerset county jail was battered by a battering ram by the mob in seeking George Armwood, several state policeman, including Private Carroll Serman were severely injured by the battering ram. *Baltimore Sunpapers* *photo.*

SOMERSET COUNTY COURT HOUSE. PRINCESS ANNE, MD.

Somerset County courthouse, Princess Anne, c. 1931. This was the site of the lynching and immolation of George Armwood on the night of October 18, 1933. It is virtually identical in 2005. *Collection of Joseph Moore.*

A photograph of Sheriff Luther Daugherty of Somerset County with other law enforcement officers, after the Armwood lynching in Princess Anne. Notice Lieutenant Joseph Itzel (on the left) of the Baltimore City police, who investigated the Green Davis family murder and took the confession of Orphan Jones in Baltimore, and Sergeant William Flynn, also an investigator in the Orphan Jones case and interrogator of Jones in Baltimore. *Baltimore* Sunpapers *and Photography Collection, University of Maryland Baltimore County.*

Communist protest meeting at Baltimore's City Hall Plaza, October 21, 1933. Notice the signs "SAVE EUEL LEE!!!" and "PROTEST LYNCHING of Armwood." The crowd appears to number in the hundreds. *Baltimore Sunpapers photo.*

J. Green speaking in front of a makeshift gallows at the Communist protest meeting on October 21, 1933. Signs reading "Save Euel Lee" are visible. *Baltimore* Sunpapers *photo.*

Police officials in Baltimore keeping watch at the Communist protest meeting, City Hall Plaza, October 21, 1933. *Baltimore* Sunpapers *photo.*

The gallows chamber located in a wing of 'C' dormitory of the Maryland penitentiary. It was in this foreboding room that Euel Lee was executed on October 27, 1933, the seventeenth man to be hanged in the penitentiary. (Prior to 1923, executions had been held in the county where the crime occurred.) By 1955, when the state mandated that the gas chamber replace the gallows, seventy-five hangings had taken place here. The building has since been demolished. *Courtesy of Maryland Division of Correction.*

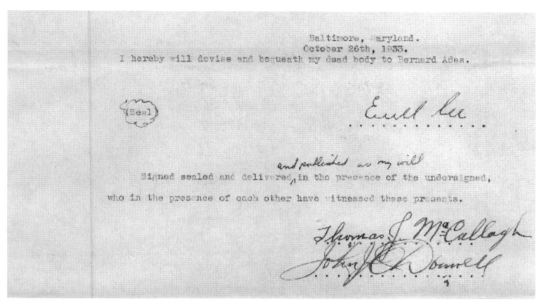

Baltimore, Maryland.
October 26th, 1933.
I hereby will devise and bequeath my dead body to Bernard Ades.

(Seal)

Euel Lee

and published as my will

Signed sealed and delivered, in the presence of the undersigned,
who in the presence of each other have witnessed these presents.

Thomas J. McCullough
John J. O'Donnell

Euel Lee's will bequeathing his body to Bernard Ades. *Courtesy of Hall of Records, Maryland State Archives.*

Maryland penitentiary warden Patrick J. Brady, who had custody of Lee for well over a year after his first conviction in Towson, January 1932, and who supervised his execution on October 27, 1933. Brady also refused to accede to Bernard Ades's demand for Lee's body, thus causing Ades's ill-conceived lawsuit to secure the body and subsequent restraining order. *Baltimore* Sunpapers *and Photography Collection, University of Maryland Baltimore County.*

Law enforcement officers at the site of Euel Lee's burial at Mt. Calvary Cemetery, Brooklyn, Maryland, on the night of his burial. It may be presumed that the men in civilian clothes in the center of the photograph are Sheriff Joseph C. Deegan of Baltimore City and Sheriff Glenn Prout of Anne Arundel County. The Baltimore *Afro-American* noted disdainfully that more officers guarded the grave than had been posted to guard George Armwood at the Somerset County jail in Princess Anne. *Baltimore* Sunpapers *photo.*

Opposite top: Maryland militia troops sent by Governor Albert C. Ritchie on November 28, 1933, to Salisbury to secure the arrest and removal to Baltimore of four accused mob leaders in the lynching of George Armwood, at Princess Anne. The site of the photo is on South Division Street at the intersection of Circle Avenue at the Armory (since demolished), which is the present location of the Wicomico County Public Library. *Baltimore* Sunpapers *photo.*

Opposite bottom: Maryland militia troops using tear gas to attempt to control the crowd protesting the detention of the Armwood lynch mob leaders. *Baltimore* Sunpapers *photo.*

157

The Armwood lynching leaders are escorted out of the Salisbury Armory on the way to buses that will take them to Baltimore. On the left, in full uniform, is Adjutant General Milton A. Reckord of the Maryland militia. General Reckord has a star denoting his rank on his shoulder and is wearing boots with spurs. Maryland State Policemen are leading the accused, who cannot be identified from the photo, but who can be seen, respectively, second from right in fedora and boots; fifth from right, hiding his face with a coat; immediately behind General Reckord with his hat pulled down; and finally, between two policeman on the left with just his hat visible. Judge Robert Duer soon would issue a writ of habeas corpus in order to have the four men returned to Somerset County where State's Attorney John Robins would assert that he had no charges to file against them. They were summarily released. *Baltimore* Sunpapers *photo.*

Bernard Ades (center) at the scene of his disbarment proceedings in 1934 in the U.S. district court for the district of Maryland. To Ades's right is Charles Houston, dean of Howard University Law School in the District of Columbia. To Ades's left is a very young Thurgood Marshall, later justice of the United States Supreme Court, whom Bernard Ades would always refer to as "young Thurgood." [The men's coat lapels and trousers have been enhanced to make the photo more distinct for publication.] *Baltimore* Afro-American *photo.*

The unmarked gravesite of Euel Lee (Orphan Jones), Mt. Calvary Cemetery, Brooklyn, Maryland (c. 2000).
Collection of Joseph Moore.

XXV

Once Again to Annapolis

A des was, however, doing more than keeping Lee company on visiting days. Work continued apace on his upcoming brief to the Court of Appeals. He found several Supreme Court cases that he believed supported his argument as to the make-up of the jury. He fashioned them into a compelling proposition for the Maryland court to consider. Within the allotted time for filing, he sent his brief down to Annapolis.

In it, he spared no one; least of all Judge Duncan. Portions of his brief clearly reveal his disdain:

Juries in Baltimore County have been picked for the last quarter century by Judge Duncan. There is no question that Judge Duncan firmly believes in his own mind that he has no prejudice against Negroes. He states so clearly and emphatically. He never consciously excluded them from jury service and, as he himself states, he never considered them just as he never considered Chinamen or other races. Of Negroes as jurors Judge Duncan was as unconscious as he was of the religion of strangers whom he had met.

But the existence of prejudice in a man's mind cannot be ascertained by questioning the man. The very idea of prejudice is that the holder of it is unable to realize his bias…To him his distorted view seems to be the correct one and he cannot understand why he is accused of prejudice. Bearing the real nature of prejudice in mind it is manifestly absurd to investigate the matter through the statement of the very person who allegedly harbors the prejudice; it is necessary to examine his actions and from them to draw a conclusion as to his prejudice, if any.

There are in Baltimore County 11,764 Negroes out of the total population of 124,565. From among these Negroes, Judge Duncan has never selected a single one for jury services. Is this failure an accidental one?….No other conclusion is possible except that Judge Duncan unconsciously excluded from consideration all black men that he saw. The prejudice of which he is unaware displays itself in his action.

The bare statement of Judge Duncan and Sheriff Trail that in selecting jurors they did not discriminate against Negroes must give way to the positive testimony of Judge Duncan that in twenty-six years he had never summoned a Negro as a juror although there were, to his knowledge, Negroes fully qualified for jury service in his county…Judge Duncan's statement that he did not consider Negroes because the Constitution did not require him to select Negroes as jurors is specious in the light of his statement that he had selected jurors from among those whom he had met at church or social gatherings; for it is proper for this court to infer that Judge Duncan did not associate with Negroes socially or at church gatherings.

The proof in this case establishes the fact that the absence of Negro jurors in the case at bar was not fortuitous. It resulted from the fact that the officials empowered and designed by law to summon, select, and empanel a jury, willfully and arbitrarily excluded Negroes from their consideration despite the fact that they were eligible and available and that this was the consistent policy and practice of these officials for twenty-six years.

Ades's brief was finished. Now he would await the reply brief from the State.

It was not long in arriving. The State, as could be expected, came to the aid of Judge Duncan and his method of selecting jurors. Assistant attorney general William L. Henderson prepared the brief. (At that time, as now, the attorney general's office, rather than the State's Attorney, represented the State in appeals.) In it, he took a swipe at Ades, who, either inadvertently or because of his inexperience, had failed to timely file a "bill of exceptions," bringing to the appellate court's attention the specific errors alleged in the selection of the jury. Henderson claimed that Ades's failure necessitated a dismissal of the appeal.

At the time the record was filed with the Court of Appeals in Annapolis on April 23, 1932, the Baltimore County judges explained that the bill of exceptions had not been signed within the term of the court in which the case had been heard, and was therefore technically flawed, because no extension of time for filing had been requested or granted until after the expiration of the term. The judges noted, however, that they had signed the bill for the purpose of allowing Lee's counsel to present any contentions he had with regard to the validity or propriety of the exceptions. Thus the issue was thrust squarely in the judicial lap of the Court of Appeals. The issue of whether to even allow the appeal would, presumably, be considered by the high court when it convened on Tuesday, April 26.

Henderson also had a fallback position. In his brief, he stated that, although Judge Duncan had violated the provisions of the statute on jury selection, his method had, indeed, been approved by the Court of Appeals. In the case of *Hollars v. State* (125 Md. 367), the Court of Appeals had stated that the procedure was in "substantial compliance" with the law. [In Hollars, a 1915 case, there are several interesting sidelines; first, the attorney general of Maryland at that time was man named Edgar Allan Poe (a relation of the famous poet); secondly, the charge against Mr. Hollars was a violation of the liquor laws of Baltimore County by virtue of his "sale of alcoholic beverages on Sunday"; and, finally that the Court of Appeals held that Judge Duncan's list of potential jurors "was exactly the kind of list set out [in the statute] as a proper source from which to make a selection of names to be placed in the jury selection box."]

On May 10, the court announced that it would advance the argument of the case from the October term, as it had been originally scheduled, to the April term and indicated that arguments may be heard as soon as the following week. The case was advanced at the request of Attorney General William Preston Lane. The argument before the Court of Appeals was scheduled for Thursday, May 19, 1932.

On Saturday, May 14, a group of Communists, representing the International Labor Defense, the Trades Unity Council and the Unemployed Council, described by the *Sunpapers* as "both men and women, white and Negro," picketed the home of Chief Judge Carroll Bond, located at 1125 North Calvert Street in Baltimore, for about a half-hour, carrying banners demanding the liberation of

Euel Lee. At the conclusion of the demonstration, Louis Berger mounted the steps and rang the bell. He was armed with a petition demanding Lee's freedom. He was greeted by the judge's butler, who informed the group that the judge was away for the weekend. He declined to accept the petition, which Berger then announced he would mail to the attention of the judge.

The day before the scheduled court argument, the Communists were at it again. On May 18, about thirty-four demonstrators headed out from Baltimore by bus for the stated purpose of calling upon Governor Ritchie and Chief Judge Carroll Bond of the Court of Appeals. Apparently the group was under the impression that this was the day scheduled for argument in the court. Armed with large placards demanding justice, they marched to the statehouse from nearby Church Circle.

Surrounding the governor's mansion just across the street from the statehouse was a cordon of twenty-five state policemen, under the command of Captain Edward McKim Johnson. Also present were Annapolis policemen in plain clothes and armed with tear gas. The delegation of protesters, with their placards pronouncing, "Down With Lynch Justice," "We Demand a New Trial for Orphan Jones," "We Demand Freedom for Orphan Jones" and "We Demand Justice for the Scottsboro Nine," marched silently past the formidable police line and headed for the Court of Appeals building just in the next block.

At the court building, a delegation headed by W.C. McCuistion and the ever-present Louis Berger, and also including George Woodall and Clifford Berton, was met by the chief deputy, clerk of court, R. Lee Waller, in his office. At that time Waller informed the representatives that their timetable was a bit off, and that the case was scheduled for the next day. He stated further that Chief Judge Bond would be unable to see them as he was on the bench hearing appeals at that very moment. However, he invited them to come back the next day to observe the proceedings, or, if they wished, they were welcome to observe the arguments then ongoing in the courtroom. As they departed and arrived back outside, they also were informed that the governor was not in residence at the mansion, as he had remained in Baltimore overnight. There seemed to be little to do but render a few speeches on the steps of the statehouse, which drew a crowd of about one hundred spectators. While there, they received a telegram from International Labor Defense lawyers in Baltimore, certainly somewhat belatedly, stating that the argument was set for the following day. The *Sun* reported that "after a stay of about two hours, the bus left for Baltimore, but only after it had been delayed by the quarter-hour tardiness of two comrades who had taken leave to see Annapolis while in town. State policemen escorted the bus to the city limits."

The next morning, in the ornate Court of Appeals building across from the statehouse, the lawyers would once again be heard regarding their respective positions in the case. The *Sun* reported the event this way:

> *Annapolis, May 19—Only two spectators were present in the courtroom today when the Court of Appeals took up Yuel Lee's appeal from his conviction of murder and sentence of death. None of the delegation from the International Labor Defense which yesterday picketed the State House and the Court of Appeals Building in behalf of the colored farmhand accused of the murder of an entire Worcester County family, was on hand when the hearing began. Judge T. Scott Offutt, who presided at the Towson trial, and Judge John R. Pattison, from whose jurisdiction the trial was removed, were absent from the court.*

Lee was represented by Bernard Ades, Joseph R. Brodsky who delivered the first argument today, and David Levinson. The State was represented by Assistant Attorney General William L. Henderson and State's Attorney Godfrey Child of Worcester County.

Even though the intended show of support by the Communists had fizzled, the arguments proceeded to take the case to its next phase, and all the parties awaited the decision of the court. It would, by virtue of the previous opinion regarding the question of removal, be the second visit by Maryland's highest judicial panel as to the issues related to the events of October 11, 1931, in the far-off reaches of Worcester County. The court had been asked once again to determine the issues related to this murder and now the lawyers, as lawyers always do, surely speculated as to the results of their best efforts on behalf of their respective positions.

XXVI.
New Law in the Free State

On July 5, 1932, the Maryland Court of Appeals handed down its decision in *Lee v. State*, 163 Md. 56. Written by Chief Judge Bond, it was a shocking statement and wove new law into the fabric of Maryland jurisprudence. It held that the practice in Baltimore County as to the selection of jurors, although previously sanctioned by the court, now constituted a denial of equal protection and, therefore, violated the Fourteenth Amendment to the U.S. Constitution. The State's motion to dismiss was also rejected by the judges.

Although Attorney General Henderson may have been technically right in his stated position filed with his brief regarding the bill of particulars, the Court of Appeals, once again, as it had in Ades's premature appeal from the Cambridge removal issue, let the young lawyer off the hook. It held that a bill of exceptions was not the sole method of preserving the record, and that, in any event, this was a unique case in that the basis of appeal was the action of the judge presiding at trial. Therefore, the court reasoned, there was no need to follow the strict requirements of the rules of the court.

As to the merits of the case, the court also held forth. Ades had put in his brief interesting facts regarding the demographics of Baltimore County in 1932. It seems that the black population accounted for just under 10 percent of the total population of the county. Therefore, since no black had been placed on a panel of eligible jurors, the conclusion urged upon the court was that there was de facto discrimination. Although the Court of Appeals of Maryland had, in 1915, approved the method utilized by Judge Duncan in the case of *Hollars v. State*, the U.S. Supreme Court had handed down a series of decisions related to the exclusion of blacks from juries. It had held that "There is no legal right in the accused to a jury composed in part of his own race. All that he could rightfully demand was a jury from which his race was not excluded."

Judge Bond's decision also noted that the Supreme Court had previously spoken on the issue: "The principles which control are derived from the decisions of the Supreme Court of the United States, and are thus summed up in the case of *Carter v. Texas*, 177 U.S. 442, 20 S. Ct. 687 (1900): 'Whenever by any action of a state, whether through its legislature, through its courts, or through its executive or administrative officers, all persons of the African race are excluded, solely because of their race or color, from serving as grand jurors in the criminal prosecution of a person of the African race, the equal protection of the laws is denied to him, contrary to the Fourteenth Amendment of the Constitution of the United States.'" (*Carter v. Texas*, although decided before *Hollars*, had apparently never been cited in a case before the Maryland court.)

With this principle in mind, the Court of Appeals reviewed the action of Judge Duncan in detail. Then, somewhat surprisingly, the court said, "This evidence, with the long, unbroken absence of

Negroes from the juries selected, seems to show an established practice, confining selections to white men as effectually as if such a restriction were prescribed by statute. And the court has concluded that this, under the authorities, amounts to unconstitutional exclusion of Negroes…The overruling of the challenge must be held erroneous, and the judgment must, for the error, be reversed, and a new trial ordered." For the first time in Maryland, the judicial system recognized implicit racial exclusion practiced by a trial court of the state.

The International Labor Defense had a field day. The establishment had been challenged by one of their own, and he had won!

However, on the shore, the news was taken in a very different vein. The prevailing feeling among the citizens was that now that a Western Shore jury—where Ades had insisted the trial occur—had convicted Lee fair and square, a group of uninvolved men in Annapolis had reversed the conviction and had ordered that the murderer get yet another trial. And on what grounds? Of all things, the makeup of the jury. Residents of the Eastern Shore could see nothing in the opinion that indicated that the evidence had not been sufficient; nothing which said that the witnesses had not given testimony which was truthful and compelling; nothing which indicated that the State's Attorney had done anything wrong. The people's frustration escalated. How much more delay, expense and legal shenanigans would the citizens who bore the memory of this awful murder have to take?

The feeling prevailed that the judges in the highest court in the state had deferred to this upstart Communist who had pushed his way into a case where it was evident all along that he had no business. Lee would not hang before he got yet another trial—the third opportunity for Ades to pull some more of his tricks, delaying and denying justice to the Worcester County citizens. Sentiment began to indicate that Godfrey Child had not done what he should have in order to convict this confessed killer and hasten his trip to the death house. Such sentiments, however, as far as they went, were patently unfair.

The entire system of justice on the lower shore had created its own problems. The necessity of removing the trial in light of the prevailing and evident local belief in the rule of the rope lynching should have been realized. When the case was finally removed, the judicial exclusion of black jurors in far-off Baltimore County was certainly no fault of the State's Attorney from Worcester County. Nevertheless, Godfrey Child would be called upon to try the case of Euel Lee yet again. It should be said that there is no evidence whatsoever that indicates that he was not up to the task—indeed, anxious to get into the fray. He had an abiding faith in the guilt of the defendant and would prosecute the case to its final conclusion. He was, however, painfully cognizant of the problem that the case had created for him: he was being scrutinized by the very voters who had elected him. They had had enough. This Communist and his organization had to be stopped. Lee had to hang.

That final desired result was not, however, quite yet to come. Since the beginning of the trial, as had been earlier observed by Godfrey Child in the motion hearing in Snow Hill, it became more and more evident that Euel Lee was a convenient cause célèbre for the American Communists who adopted his cause. There were, at that time, cases in other parts of the United States that would also garner extensive publicity because of their racial overtones. The most notorious was the aforementioned case of the "Scottsboro Boys," a group of young African Americans who were accused of raping Ruby Bates and a female companion on the railroad tracks of rural Alabama.

Even though that case received much more national press than did the Orphan Jones case, Lee's case was truly a magnet for the Communist Party, desiring to showcase the downtrodden black men who could not get a fair shake in American society. Indeed, each new victory, even though temporary, was a great moment in the ranks of the Communists. Each new headline provided yet another forum for the party philosophy of exposing corruption and elitism in society.

So far, not one effort of the judicial system to convict Euel Lee had succeeded. Every effort to convict and sentence the man had been overruled by the highest court in Maryland. The evils of the establishment had been exposed and publicized by the attorneys for this indigent black man, and in the bargain, had served to further the cause of the Communist party—primarily due to the untiring efforts of a young, inexperienced attorney who had shown that he would stop at nothing to help his client and the Party.

In fact, after the decision, it took Ades no time at all to go to work for Lee. On July 7, a mere two days from the court's decision, he telegrammed a request to Governor Ritchie to have Lee removed from the death house in the penitentiary. The warden stated to the *Sunpapers* that he had received no orders from anyone for such removal. Therefore, on Wednesday, July 13, Louis Berger again attempted to get Lee transferred. According to the *Sun*,

> *Louis Berger, secretary of the International Labor Defense, and four Negro members of the organization, failed in an attempt to secure the removal of Euel Lee, alias Orphan Jones, from a cell in the death house of the Penitentiary this morning.*
>
> *The Secretary of the group, accompanied by three colored men and a colored woman, made their formal demand for Lee's removal in the office of Warden Patrick J. Brady, at the penal institution shortly before noon today.*

Berger declared that Lee was being held illegally because of the appellate court's decision. Brady replied that, as far as he was concerned, Lee was still a convicted prisoner awaiting the setting of an execution date and until advised to the contrary by a court, Lee would stay put, and that was that. However, at some time subsequent to the warden's statement, the judges did allow Lee to be removed from the penitentiary and relocated him to the Baltimore city jail.

XXVII

To Towson Once Again

Back on the Shore, Godfrey Child had to go back to work. He knew that he had tried a good, effective case. He had convinced the jury in Baltimore County, without difficulty, of Lee's guilt. But now that the time-honored system of prejudice in that county had now been chastised by Maryland's highest court, it was necessary to start over and get ready to face his nemesis, Ades, once again. Child was, nevertheless, up to the task. It would be a challenge that he would gladly face, given the fact that the importance of the result was all encompassing.

Without delay, he set about to request a trial date. Before long it was granted: the second Lee trial would take place in Towson on Monday, September 26, 1932. Godfrey Child would be prepared this time, as he was before.

Ades, also, would be ready for the second round of trial. He surely discussed the circumstances with his client, as well as various members of the Labor Defense Fund. He would seek to derive the maximum amount of press out of the next confrontation with the legal system, just as he had done in the first. In addition, he just might prove another error to be made in the judicial system's adjudication of the case this time around.

The judges in Towson were also well aware of the mandate that had issued from Annapolis. They were now required to do something new and unique in the county: they had to place black men on the panel of prospective jurors in the circuit court. Therefore, the order went out to garner a list of eligible African Americans for the empaneling of the prospective jury for the next Euel Lee trial. The sheriff was now being required to tally certain names of eligible black citizens who would be placed upon the jury rolls for the first time in Baltimore County history. This time, the judges determined, there would be no loopholes for the defense to put forth with regard to the procedures of the selection of the jury. The sheriff found black men to be placed on the lists in anticipation of the next round of legal maneuvering by Ades and his compatriots. The defendant would be tried without the technical irregularity of the jury composition, fair and square.

There is little or no reporting in the public press regarding the preparation for the second Towson trial, but preparations were, indeed, necessary. The witnesses had to be re-summoned; conferences and trial tactics discussed; preparations for accommodations completed and all the other preliminary preparations for a high-profile capital case taken care of. Thus, through the spring and summer months, both parties worked.

As the second trial date approached, a stir was created among the citizens of the lower shore when the *Sunpapers* reported that David Levinson would arrive in order to gather "evidence for trial." It was very clear also that Governor Ritchie was having no more of the threats and physical abuse that had accompanied Ades's visits to the area before the first trial. On September 12, he offered Levinson an escort of police, should he wish to have such protection. Levinson wrote the governor that he did, indeed, believe that a police or military escort would be required when he visited the scene of the murders near Berlin.

Therefore, on September 21, a squad of state policemen led by Lieutenant Ruxton M. Ridgely arrived on the shore and assembled at Selbyville, Delaware, just north of the state line, to escort Levinson into Worcester County. The state police commander, Captain Johnson, said that there were a total of fifteen state policemen on the shore, although not all were in the escort. In fact, Levinson was escorted by twelve officers, and visited Berlin, the murder scene nearby, Snow Hill and the areas between, taking photographs and "rechecking evidence of witnesses."

On the same day, Bernard Ades announced that he would seek to quash the indictment under which Lee was charged, on the ground that the grand jury that indicted Lee was chosen from a panel that had excluded blacks. Ades also stated that he intended to request yet another removal of the case, seeking a change of venue from Baltimore County, notwithstanding his previous request to have the trial there. His stated reason was that the county had a Jim Crow attitude toward blacks. He pointed out that Negroes attending court in Baltimore County were obligated to sit in a special section reserved for them and stated that he would point out other vestiges of segregation also. This would all take place in court on Monday.

On Monday, September 16, 1932, at 10:00 a.m., the second trial of Euel Lee began. For the first time in the history of Baltimore County, black men were seated in the jury panel array. Lee arrived in the custody of six detectives headed by Charles H. Burns and Sheriff Trail. During the morning session of court, the defense offered several petitions regarding the makeup of the grand jury in Worcester County. The lawyers contended that, just like the previous Towson jury panel, no blacks had been allowed on the jury array from which the Worcester grand jurors had been chosen. Chief Judge Offutt, who in this case was joined by judges Walter W. Preston and C. Gus Grason (Judge Duncan apparently having been banished from the panel this time), ruled that the challenge to the grand jury array came too late. The judge pointed out that any such challenge should have come when Lee first offered his plea in the first trial or, indeed, when he first offered his pleas in Worcester County after the crime. Levinson countered that at that time, the lawyers had no reason to know of the exclusion practice, but the judge was having none of it. He reiterated his ruling, which was sustained by the full bench.

Levinson then moved for a change of venue from Baltimore County, citing the allegation that "the people of Baltimore County were antagonistic to Negroes." He alleged that Jim Crow laws were prevalent in the county and that in the very chamber in which the proceedings were happening, African Americans were segregated by seating. Judge Offutt summarily dismissed that petition citing the law that a defendant was only entitled to one change of venue. Next, the defense moved for a continuance of the case stating that, "in view of the feeling toward Negroes in the county, a postponement of the entire case was warranted." This, not surprisingly, was disposed of by the court without comment.

Finally, the legality of the present jury panel was challenged, on the ground that "many of the present panel members had been considered for service on previous panels which had disregarded the availability of Negroes, therefore limiting possible service by Negroes." Upon this motion, the judges recessed for a conference in chambers, which lasted nearly an hour. Upon their return, Judge Offutt announced that it was the collective opinion of the court that the members of the jury panel had been chosen in accordance with the law and with due regard for the appellate court's opinion in the Euel Lee case.

Jury selection then began. A regular panel of twenty-five men had been selected, with no black men among them, but this time black men had been considered in the panel selection. In addition, twenty-six men were selected at random in the courtroom. Of the total men examined by the lawyers, twenty-one were challenged by the defense and six by the State. The court also excused an additional nine.

An additional twenty men were selected in the courtroom. In this group were two black men. They were John Pinkney of Towson and Roy Nolan of Glen Arm, who both listed their occupations as laborers. Upon questioning, each said he knew nothing of the case or the events surrounding it. Each advised that he had no scruples against the death penalty and could reach a fair and impartial verdict. The defense immediately stated its satisfaction with both men, and the State promptly struck both of them from the panel under its right of preemptory challenge.

The second panel exhausted, yet a third was called. In this panel, a third African American, George Evans, a laborer from Turner Station, was called. As it had previously, the State challenged Mr. Evans and he was therefore excused. This round resulted in a shortage of members being seated in the jury box, and five more men were called. Among them also was a black man but, the defense having exhausted its challenges, the jury was complete prior to him being questioned.

This historic event, therefore, availed the defense nothing, as the defense exhausted its peremptory challenges prior to the State, and the State was successful in exercising its strikes to exclude all the black members of the panel. In his second trial, as in his first, Euel Lee, would be judged by an all-white jury. It consisted of: Elmer B. Kemp, a carpenter from Reisterstown, as the foreman; Otto J. Braun, an Essex millwright; John B. Lancaster, a carpenter from Glen Arm; Bernard C. Ostendorf, a sheet molder from St. Helena; Henry H. Grimes, retired, from Catonsville; Henry Smith, a real estate salesman from Towson; Thomas Sutton, a Phoenix farmer; Perry B. Darby, a coal dealer from Dundalk; Israel I. Berlin, a merchant from Texas; Edgar Keifer, a real estate salesman from Woodlawn; John C. Dei, a Parkville well digger; and John W. Hessian, a Timonium blacksmith.

XXVIII

The Green Davis Murder Redux

At 8:45 p.m., Godfrey Child approached the jury once again. He had gone through all this before, but repeated the content of his first opening statement. He painted the same picture of the Davis house, and described how the bodies of the family had been found. He then asserted how Lee had gone to the house and shot all the members of the family as they lay in their beds.

Bernard Ades opened for the defense. In a brief, four-minute statement he advised the jurors that the State's case could not be substantiated. Then he sat down.

Dr. Charles A. Holland of Berlin and Dr. Fred S. Waesche both testified to the condition of Mr. Davis's body during the autopsy conducted by them. Levinson sought to discredit Dr. Holland's testimony:

> Q: Doctor Holland, I understood you to say that Doctor Waesche performed the autopsy or was with you?
> A: I guess we all three were connected with the autopsy. Doctor Waesche was the surgeon in chief.
> Q: How many autopsies have you personally performed?
> A: About three or four.
> Q: When?
> A: I can't give you dates, but in the course of my practice.
> Q: You have been practicing, I understand, for twenty-seven or twenty-eight years?
> A: Yes.
> Q: And in all that time you have made three or four autopsies?
> A: Yes.
> Q: That is outside of the one which you now speak of?
> A: Yes.
> Q: When was the last time that you personally performed an autopsy?
> A: About a year previous to this.
> Q: Was that on the body of a person who had suddenly died?
> A: Yes.
> Q: Altogether you performed three before?
> A: I said three or four.
> Q: In all the twenty-eight years?
> A: Yes.

Levinson then proffered to the court that Dr. Holland was not qualified to be an expert in performing an autopsy. The judge however, then questioned Dr. Holland himself, and determined that he had graduated from the Southern Homeopathic Institute in Baltimore, had a degree of medicine and was licensed to practice medicine in the state of Maryland. He was, therefore, according to the judge, qualified.

Doctor Waesche's testimony as to the condition of Green Davis's body was much more detailed and gruesome than was Doctor Holland's. Dr. Waesche testified that he had examined the body of Mr. Davis in the company of Drs. Holland and Lowe in the Davis home on the afternoon of Tuesday, October 13, 1931. He said that in his opinion the body had been dead for about sixty hours, that it was bloated, discolored and disheveled and the skin was peeling off and there was dried blood all over it; that rigor mortis had set in and the body was then removed to a small garage in Berlin, where the detailed examination took place. He found a jagged wound in the right side of the head, triangular in shape, starting about half an inch from the lips, up to about the middle of the ear, that half the ear had been blown away, and then the wound extended down across the cheek and neck and upward under the skull in the right half of the brain, which had been destroyed and was issuing out of the wound. He stated that he had removed some shot from a shotgun shell and some gun wads from the wound and that there were no bruises or marks of violence on the breast, chest, legs or hands of the deceased, and the only wound on Green Davis was as he had described, and that it was his opinion that the cause of death was a gunshot fired close enough to the body to force the gun wadding into the depth of the wound.

Confronted by this gruesome testimony, Levinson veered away from probing Dr. Waesche's description of the body, and instead attacked the doctor's ability to discern the length of time the body had been dead, but to no avail.

Also testifying on that first night were Mrs. Zilly Long and her daughter, Laura, who were Mr. Davis's aunt and cousin. They testified that they had gone to the Davis home on Sunday, October 12, but left after finding the house locked and no one apparently at home. The State contended that at the time of their visit, the bodies were inside the house. Late that first night, the court was finally adjourned until the next morning.

Promptly at 10:00 a.m. on Tuesday, September 27, the second day of trial began. As it had been in the previous trial, the courtroom was filled to capacity. All the seats were taken and a crowd numbering between forty to seventy persons leaned against the walls and railing separating the audience from the attorneys.

The first witness of the day was Sebie Howe, one of the neighbors who had found the bodies. As he had at the first trial, he described the discovery of the bodies. He also identified several items taken from Lee's room as belonging to the Davis family. The *Sunpapers* reported that it was "a lively session on the stand when the defense found out that Howe had a key which opened the door of the Davis home and that he was in a way a business competitor of Green Davis. Both operated roadside stands about 150 feet apart on the Ocean City road.

"He remained unperturbed under pointed defense cross-examination and went on to identify a tobacco pouch, a girl's dress and scarf, a man's suit and a pistol holster as the property of members of the Davis family."

Lieutenant Joseph Itzel of the Baltimore Detective Bureau testified to Lee's possession of Davis's clothes when he arrived at the Baltimore city jail. Also called to the stand were patrolman Fred A. Culver, Constable James William Hall, Sheriff Wilmer Purnell and Sergeant William J. Flynn of the Bureau of Identification of the Baltimore City police department.

The prosecutors also introduced into evidence a bloodstained pillowcase, bloody sheets and a bed covering with a hole the size of a man's head burned into it. It was indicated that the burn resulted from the shotgun blast that tore away most of Mr. Davis's head.

The *Sunpapers* injected a bit of personal pathos into its report of the second day's trial:

> *Two sisters of Green K. Davis, for whose murder Euel Lee is on trial in the Baltimore County Circuit Court at Towson, wept today as the State offered blood-stained clothing in evidence. Mrs. A.W. Hudson (Ethel), Delmar, Md., and Mrs. Oscar Timmons (Margaret), Ocean City, were sitting in the front row as the musty year-old exhibits were held aloft.*
>
> *Their sobs, though half-repressed, were heard clearly in the quiet courtroom, filled with spectators from the Eastern Shore. Lieut. Joseph H. Itzel of the Baltimore city police testified that he had taken from Lee, while the defendant was lodged in the city jail a year ago, a coat and vest which have been identified as the property of Davis.*
>
> *Sergt. William Flynn identified a yellow blood-stained bed spread and bolster cover, and a woman's undergarment as having come from the room in the Davis house in Taylorsville where Davis and his wife were found murdered. All smelled of kerosene and in the spread had been burned a hole as big as a dinner plate.*
>
> *A single titter as Lee's counsel was checked in a dispute with the bench on a legal technicality was the only demonstration from the well-dressed crowd of spectators that sat with concentrated attention in the courtroom. Plain-clothed police were distributed about the court but there was no need for policing.*

On this day, also, two important witnesses would testify: Chief Robert Allen of Ocean City, and Martha Miller, called throughout the reporting of the trial by the *Sunpapers* "Aunt Martha." Allen testified, once again, how he had placed Lee under arrest, and described the incident in much the same manner as the first trial. At one point however, Allen stated (describing his return to the murder scene with Lee), "I got out of the car with Orphan Jones and walked up nearly to the Green Davis house, Orphan Jones and myself, and there I met the State's Attorney, Mr. Godfrey Child, the sheriff, Mr. Wilmer Purnell, and Mr. Bill Hall who is the constable. I told them that I had the man who did the job. There never has been a minute since I got the first telephone call that the Green Davis family had been murdered but what I was sure I had the right man when I got Orphan Jones."

Levinson was on his feet instantly. He demanded a mistrial on the ground that the statement was damaging to the defense. Judge Offutt denied the motion, but granted the defense's request for an exception to the ruling, and ordered the chief's statement stricken from the record. He then turned to Chief Allen: "I must warn you that if you repeat a statement like that one from that witness stand, the court will be ready to deal with you. You answer the questions that are asked you." Allen allowed he understood, replying, "All right Judge, Your Honor."

Next to the witness stand came Martha Miller, described by the *Sunpapers* as an "aged woman." As she had been in the first trial, she was the star witness for the State, describing in detail the events of Lee's return in the evening of the murders with a satchel and shotgun that had both been identified as belonging to Green Davis. She also described the return of the police to Lee's room where numerous items of the Davises' possessions were seized in her presence. Her testimony effectively placed Lee in possession of the Davis property, and created the time frame for the events surrounding the coming and going of her boarder during the night following the killings.

On this day in total there were twenty witnesses, according to the *Sun*, all of them from Worcester County and most all neighbors or family members. One witness who had not testified at the first trial was Harvey Baker, who lived near Ocean City, and who testified that he had seen Lee right at the Davis fruit stand on the critical day.

Other additional witnesses included Peter L. Davis, who lived near Willards in neighboring Wicomico County, and who testified that he had been fishing from the Ocean City bridge when Lee had stopped to talk to him, and at that time, Green Davis drove his automobile across the bridge. "He said something to me about he had worked for Mr. Davis for twelve days and only got paid for eleven." Davis said, "It was something about it raining one day, but I didn't pay attention to it until he said, 'That little girl is a mean one, too, and I'm going to even up with them.'"

Also Mattie Johnson, "a Negro washerwoman," said that she had heard a similar complaint from Lee. Everett James of Ocean City said that he encountered Lee while selling fruit and that Lee had expressed the wage grievance to him.

At 10:00 p.m., twelve hours after it convened, the court adjourned for the night.

An incident marred the evening. As she left the courthouse, Martha Miller was cursed and threatened by two black youths. The verbal assault was observed by patrolman Thomas Callahan of the Baltimore County police. He quickly advanced toward them and they fled, with his pursuit of them being unsuccessful. He brought the matter to the attention of Carroll E. Stansbury, marshal of the county police, who thereupon assigned two patrolmen to guard the vicinity of the home of a black minister where Martha was staying. It is evident that in this trial, as in the first, Martha's testimony had no regard for the race issue, in spite of the efforts of the defense to portray the State's case as being racially motivated. Indeed, the defense lawyers continued to maintain the fact the courtroom was segregated. It was noted in the *Sunpapers* report that several prominent "Negroes" were in attendance at the trial, including the Reverend C.Y. Trigg of Metropolitan M.E. Church; the Reverend J.E. Lee of the African Methodist Episcopal Conference; Dr. James E. White, former candidate for city council; and Dr. Edward J. Wheatley, who was the president of the Colored Parent-Teacher Association, and his wife. At the conclusion of the evening's session, all remained and discussed the proceedings with Ades and Levinson, although Lee had been removed in the custody of the officers.

The next day, Wednesday, September 28, Martha Miller was provided a police escort to trial from the clergyman's home. Also accompanying her was her husband, Will Miller, who had certainly taken a back seat to the unwanted notoriety of his elderly wife. The State wound up its side of the case at 2:30 p.m. It was now the defense's turn. Many in the courtroom, particularly Godfrey Child, recalled the exchange between the State and Lee the first time around. No doubt he relished having another shot at cross-examining his long-time quarry.

Levinson called three witnesses in an attempt to damage the credibility of Martha Miller, and called attention to the inconsistencies between her current testimony and that in the first trial. He also attacked the testimony of Sebie Howe by calling Henry D. Hornstein, the owner of a pawnshop at 1637 Pennsylvania Avenue in Baltimore, who identified the holster said by Howe to be the property of Green Davis as one which he had sold Lee on September 2, 1931.

Then, as Lee slumped in his chair behind his lawyers, the defense rested. A stir went through the courtroom, as the realization dawned that Lee would not take the witness stand. The testimony was over. Godfrey Child looked over at the defense table. He had been expecting to take a long time in his cross-examination of the defendant. Now, the only matters left in the trial were the closing arguments, the jury instructions and the deliberation of the jury. It was a bit after three o'clock. The court took a recess before the jury instructions began.

At about four o'clock, the summations began. Both Child and James Anderson spoke for the State. Bernard Ades and Levinson spoke on behalf of the defendant. Anderson spoke first and told the jury that nothing but a verdict of guilt of murder in the first degree was possible in light of the evidence in the case. Indeed, he was so confident in his position that he told the jurors that if a verdict of first-degree murder was not possible, they should acquit the defendant.

Child presented his closing in the inflamed style of his remarks at the first trial. At one point in his oration he said, "The aged parents of Green Davis are waiting your verdict. They are now past their three score years and ten and their eyes are turned toward the sunset. They have been spared so that they may know your verdict!" Good stuff, indeed, from a prosecutor who was intent upon a guilty verdict, but Levinson was having none of it. Up on his feet, he demanded yet another mistrial and stated that Child's remarks contained matters not in evidence before the court and certainly were intended to play upon the sympathies of the jurors. Indeed this was so, but the court once again overruled the objection, the propriety of which would be left to the appellate court.

There is no account of the defense attorneys' closing remarks, but it must be presumed that the continuing allegations of a frame-up were included, together with the innuendo of falsity by Martha Miller, Sebie Howe and the assorted cops who were involved in the investigation. In any event, at about 10:15 p.m., the judges instructed the jury to retire and make up its verdict. At the first trial, the jury had deliberated for only twenty-three minutes. So it was somewhat unsettling to the prosecution when the clock dragged past one hour and fifteen minutes. Many in the courtroom knew of the old attorney's adage that the longer the deliberations, the better for the defense. Indeed, there was speculation that the jury may be deadlocked.

At 11:30, Judge Offutt told the bailiff, William Eger, to inquire as to whether a verdict was forthcoming. He was advised that the jury wanted another half-hour to consider the case. Then, at midnight, the jury asked to see the articles of bed clothing that figured in the case. A conference was held at the bench, and the lawyers agreed that the jury could see the items. The court had Mr. Eger inquire at 12:20 a.m. as to whether progress was being made. The jury advised that they needed another ten minutes. At 12:30, the court held another bench conference and it was decided to give the jury another half-hour. Still, no word from the jury room. The judges decided to sequester the jury for the night and lock it up in accommodations provided by the court.

Lee was handcuffed and removed from the courtroom by the officers. He was on his way back to the city jail when, at 1:10 a.m., there was a rap on the door of the jury room. The jury had a verdict. All activity was suspended while a messenger was dispatched to retrieve the defendant.

Upon the news that a verdict had been reached, the courtroom again filled to capacity and beyond. Spectators filled all the available space and the room was chockablock with spectators. Before too long, Lee was returned to the area of the defendant's trial table and all were ready for the entrance of the jury. He seemed, according to the *Sun*, to be half-asleep, "an attitude he had displayed during most of the trial."

Soon, the twelve men filed into the room. They sat, as if drained, and Judge Offutt asked if they had reached a verdict. Mr. Kemp, the foreman, replied, "We have, Your Honor."

The judge had Lee stand. As he waited to hear for the second time a jury foreman read his verdict, the *Sun* said he stood "stolidly, naturally, and, by now a veteran of murder-case proceedings, Lee showed not the slightest trace of emotion to the verdict. He stood with his shoulders hunched in his normal posture."

"What say you, is the defendant guilty or not guilty?" inquired Judge Offutt in the time-honored fashion.

"Guilty of murder in the first degree," replied foreman Kemp. At the verdict, Lee turned to his attorneys as if to say, what do I do now? At once, Levinson asked that the jurors be polled. Each answered, in his turn, that the verdict was, indeed, his and that Lee was guilty. Lee, for his part, continued to gaze around at the proceedings.

So, once again, it was done. Euel Lee, alias Orphan Jones, was found guilty of murder in the first degree. No one had much doubt as to the impending sentence. Judge Offutt again ordered that the doors of the courtroom be guarded and that no one was entitled to leave until the defendant was removed. The six detectives moved toward Lee. He was handcuffed to Detective Sergeant William Feehley and was taken out of the courtroom to the waiting automobiles, to return to the city jail.

Once again, the prosecutors stood and shook hands at the verdict. Another trial had once again been completed with success. Lee had been found guilty yet a second time. Surely this time it would end.

In the parking area of the Towson Court, the defense attorneys piled into an automobile, and headed, according to news reports, to Philadelphia.

XXIX

Events Continue

The second trial of Euel Lee was over. It can be speculated that Godfrey Child enjoyed a restful night those early hours of Wednesday morning after the trial, if in fact, he didn't go somewhere in Towson to celebrate his victory. Soon, for Child, it was back to Worcester County, and his Pocomoke City law practice.

Bernard Ades, however, was not about to let Child resume his normal routine. Early in the morning of September 30, he announced that he would file a motion for new trial, the basis for which had been discussed in Philadelphia upon the attorney's arrival there immediately after the conclusion of the trial. The stated reason for the request was the inflammatory statement by Godfrey Child referring to the desire of Green Davis's aged parents to hear a guilty verdict from the jury.

Sure enough, on Saturday October 1, 1932, the motion was filed in the circuit court. At that time, Ades also announced that in the event the new trial request was denied, yet another appeal to the Court of Appeals would surely follow. A hearing on the motion, tentatively scheduled for Wednesday, October 5, was postponed because of a crowded docket. On October 21, the court directed the warden of the Baltimore city jail to deliver the defendant over to the sheriff of Baltimore County so that he could be present in court for the arguments on a motion for new trial.

The next morning, once again in the custody of several officers, Lee was delivered to the Towson courthouse. At that time, Ades again argued the points which he urged upon the court in order to declare that a new trial was in order: first, that the second jury, just like the first, had been improperly selected; second, "that Negroes were segregated in the courtroom, in the courthouse and on the courthouse grounds"; and third, that the court improperly overruled a defense objection at trial. From the bench, Judges Offutt, Grason and Preston conferred and then Judge Offutt summarily denied the motion. At that time Judge Offutt again asked Lee if he had anything to say before sentence was pronounced.

Showing more animation than ever before in this second trial, Lee jumped to his feet and said, "Yes, I have not had a fair trial from the very first. Everything was a frame-up. Mr. Davis's sister couldn't say this time all the jewelry found in my room belonged to the family. I don't deny that the stuff was in my room, but who put it there? I was framed from the very start."

Judge Offutt asked if he wished to say anything else and Lee returned to his feet and repeated his assertion of being framed. Judge Offutt waited for him to finish and then, as Lee remained standing, condemned him again to death by hanging. Once again, in the now familiar routine, Lee was handcuffed and led from the room under heavy guard. He was taken back to the penitentiary to yet again be incarcerated on death row.

Two days later, on October 24, certified copies of the trial record were delivered to the governor, and to the clerk of court in Worcester County. Three weeks and three days later, on November 17, the third appeal to the Court of Appeals was filed. Also, on November 28, Ades, mindful of the procedural bullet he had dodged before, filed and was granted a motion to extend the time for filing a bill of particulars. The stage was once again set for the appellate court to review Lee's case.

In Snow Hill, back in Worcester County, a meeting of the Committee of Thirty-six on Legislation and Taxation of the Snow Hill-Worcester County Chamber of Commerce was held on December 15. At its meeting the committee recommended that the Worcester County delegation in the legislature seek assistance from the State of Maryland in paying the costs of the Euel Lee trial, which, the committee stated, would likely exceed $10,000. Copies of the resolution were sent to all county officials and to the governor's office. Members of the committee were some of the most influential citizens in the county: William D. Corddry, chairman, B. Herman Adkins, secretary, R.H. Robertson, W.T. Bunting, James M. Crockett, A.H. Stevens, C. Raymond Dryden, Eugene M. Mathews and Quince Ashburn of Pocomoke City; F.W. Truitt, John Lynch, C.W. Purnell, J. Edgar Ijams, John M. Mumford and Clifford Cropper of Ocean City; John D. Henry, C.D. Powell, A.H. Hardesty, Horace Davis, J. Richard Phillips and Theodore Purnell, of Berlin; M.T. Hargis, Montgomery Stagg, C.F. Chandler, J.H. Perdue and John W. Mumford of Snow Hill; John H. Dickerson, E.H. Taylor and C.C. Pilchard of Stockton; A.S. Pollitt and W.T. Onley of Girdletree; O.M. Shockley of Showell; H.R. Ringler of Bishopville; C.W. Timmons and W.H. Holloway of Newark; R.E. Shockley of Whiton; and R. McGrath of Eden. These citizens of the county were determined that the State be at least partly responsible for the extraordinary costs of this truly extraordinary case. It was universally thought in the county that the trial had gotten totally out of control only because of the interference of others than Worcester County officials and therefore there should lay the acceptance of a large measure of responsibility for the events. Thus the resolution was passed. There is no contemporary record of the efforts of the Worcester County delegation as to the request, but it is evident that no State funding of the cost was forthcoming. Worcester County and its citizens would have to go it alone. Their taxes would have to pay for the expense engendered by the ongoing legal exercise.

Events proceeded as they had before, with the International Labor Defense moving forward with the process of the appeal and Godfrey Child continuing his attempts to thwart their efforts, while juggling his obligations to his private clients in the small town of Pocomoke City. [It should be noted that the part-time nature of the State's Attorney position in Worcester County continued into the late years of the twentieth century—an effort to render the job full-time was passed by the legislature at the insistence of John L. Sanford in 1974, and then was overturned by the Maryland legislature, at my request, upon my election to the office in 1978. It remained a part-time job until 1994, when Joel Todd ascended to the office.]

XXX.
Annapolis Refuses

On January 9, 1933, after having received extensions of time in accordance with the Maryland Rules of Procedure, Ades filed his required bills of exceptions. The case was ready for the appeal process.

The *Sunpapers* reported that the arguments before the Court of Appeals were unlikely to occur until late February or early March 1933. It reported in its January 21, 1933 edition that the record would be filed in the court on the week of February 19. Soon, Ades filed yet another brief in the Court of Appeals, his third in the case. Many of the points revisited previous issues raised in the earlier cases, particularly with respect to the empaneling of the jurors. Question one was the allegation that an old invalid list was used in the selection of the jury and "that the names of Negroes" had been merely added to the tainted list; question two was regarding the inclusion of a juror's name who was not on the original list of veniremen; question three was related to the alleged abuse of the court's discretion in limiting questions of jurors by the defense; question four was whether the defendant could obtain a fair and impartial trial "in a court room where Negroes were discriminated against"; and question five was whether the court had erred in determining that the doctors who performed the autopsies were qualified in expressing an opinion as to how long a body had been dead.

The State responded with its own brief contending that all matters of the trial had been conducted in a proper and fair manner, and that no reversible error had occurred. Thus, the issues were joined.

Arguments took place before Judges Hammond Urner, William Adkins, F. Neal Park, D. Lindsey Sloan and Chief Judge Carroll Bond. Once again, Bernard Ades and David Levinson were in court for Lee, and Godfrey Child, James Anderson, James McAllister and Assistant Attorney General William L. Henderson were on the brief for the State.

On April 6, 1933, the court rendered its decision, the third of *Lee v. State*. It was authored by Judge Sloan and is found in the Maryland Reports in 164 Md. 550. It held that the issue of discrimination regarding African Americans was without authority, and that the issue of denying the continuance rested within the discretion of the trial court. As to the Jim Crow allegation, the court ruled in a manner that is discordant in the time of this writing, but was, indeed, the law in 1933:

> *If the defendant's contention is sound or logical, then so long as this State has separate schools for white and colored children, he could not be brought to trial, for nowhere is the separation more marked than there. Yet it has been frequently held that separate schools do not violate the provisions of the Fourteenth Amendment.*

"Separate but equal" was still the law of the land in 1933—*Brown v. Board of Education* was still two decades away.

The court summarily dismissed the argument that the jury panel was tainted, and did away also with the dispute over juror Edgar Keifer not being eligible as alleged in Question II, stating that the issue had been abandoned in argument before the court. Finally, the quarrel over the limiting of voir dire questions was disposed of when the court stated, "So far as this record discloses, the appellant was furnished a jury ascertained from their examination to be qualified to give him a fair trial, which is all he had the right to ask."

The court then concluded: "Finding no error in the rulings of the trial court on the challenge to the panel of two hundred from which the petit jury was drawn, on the motion for a continuance, and on the examination of the jurors on their voir dire, the judgment appealed from should be affirmed."

This time Ades would receive no consideration from the high court. The judicial errors committed in the past had been rectified, and there were no other loopholes to skirt through. After a myriad of motions and petitions, public demonstrations, barrels of printer's ink, one lynching, two trials, two appellate decisions and a year and a half of legal wrangling, it was over. Lee's guilt had been affirmed.

All the legal avenues in the state of Maryland had been exhausted. It seemed that now Ades would surely quit. It was abundantly clear that he had gone above and beyond the call in defending his client. He had almost single-handedly (although not without the aid of Louis Berger and David Levinson) taken on the combined legal and political establishment of the state and had effectively and aggressively fought for his client, an indigent and friendless black man, without compensation and against all conventional standards.

At the same time that the Court of Appeals upheld the decision of the lower court, Worcester County got the bill for Lee's stay in the Maryland Penitentiary. The *Sunpapers* reported:

> *Worcester county is indebted to the Maryland Penitentiary for $3,000 for board and guard service for Euel Lee, convicted of slaying Green K. Davis, near Berlin, Md., according to Warden Patrick J. Brady. The service given by the Penitentiary will be charged to the County Commissioners of Worcester county, it was said. Warden Brady explained that Lee had been one of the most expensive prisoners ever held in prison here.*
>
> *The salaries of three guards, Warden Brady said, are estimated at $375 a month and the board is an additional charge. Lee's conviction has been upheld by the Court of Appeals and the next step will be taken by Governor Ritchie when the chief executive sets a date for Lee's execution.*
>
> *Warden Brady asserted that Lee apparently is indifferent to his fate. He is the sole occupant of the death house and spends his time reading magazines and listening to the radio.*

In the meantime, on May 11, the governor of Maryland issued Lee's death warrant. Lee would hang on June 2, 1933. In announcing his determination, Governor Ritchie said: "I am now informed that Mr. Ades can apply to the Supreme Court for a writ of certiorari before the 25th of this month, and that he will apply for such a writ during that period. Accordingly, I am now fixing Friday, June 2, as the date of execution. If Mr. Ades takes his full time, then this will leave a week for the Supreme Court to decide on the application for certiorari. If the writ is denied, then June 2 will stand as the date of execution. If by June 2, the Supreme Court either has not decided the question or has granted the writ, then I will take whatever steps are necessary to give Euel Lee full protection in every right he has under the law."

As the governor suspected, Ades was not yet done.

XXXI

Higher Authority is Beseeched

On May 24, 1933, Bernard Ades announced that he would seek a writ of certiorari from the United States Supreme Court. (The writ is a plea for the court to order a review of the case, which the Supreme Court has the discretion, but is not required, to do.) It was not until June 8, however, that the request was filed and Lee thereby received yet another stay of execution. He would have still more time to reflect upon events, as it was announced that the Supreme Court would not consider the merits of the case until it convened in October. It was, therefore, necessary for Governor Ritchie to stand by his word, and delay the scheduled execution. Accordingly, he did so.

When the Supreme Court convened in October, it was not exempt from the continued assailing that had become commonplace from the Communists. On October 9, a demonstration on behalf of Lee took place in front of the Supreme Court building as the court denied the petition for writ of certiorari. The demonstration was turned back by police on the Capitol grounds, who did not allow the crowd to enter upon the Supreme Court grounds bearing their signs inscribed, "Save Euel Lee." The crowd, consisting of about sixty African Americans and a few whites, traveled from Baltimore in two trucks and was met in Hyattsville, in neighboring Prince Georges County, Maryland, by a contingent of police, who escorted them by motorcycle to the Capitol grounds.

James Green, one of the few white men in the crowd and its apparent leader, said that the trip to Washington had been organized by the Baltimore branch of the International Labor Defense, and come to demand that the Supreme Court accord equal rights to Negroes and hold a hearing in the Lee case. "We came in a peaceful manner and were told by the police to get the hell out of here; I was struck," Green reported. When confronted with the allegation, police denied that Green had been hit by anyone.

Earlier in the day Chief Justice Charles Evans Hughes had announced the high court's refusal to hear the case in a terse four-word order, which simply and starkly stated, "The petition is denied." In its usual fashion, the court gave no reasons for its order when it summarily refused to take up the case. It was, however, implicit in the order that, as Assistant Attorney General Henderson suggested, the court agreed with the position of the State of Maryland, that no substantial Constitutional question was present in the case. It was, in the end, a question of law for the State of Maryland to determine, and it had done so.

With the refusal of the Supreme Court to hear the issues, it was required that Governor Ritchie sign a new death warrant. That too, would have to wait, as the governor was sojourning in the resort of Hot Springs in the hills of Virginia. A new warrant could be signed without delay, said

Henderson. Therefore, from his vacation in Hot Springs, Ritchie announced that he would set the execution date for the first week in November. He had also to deal with a petition for clemency, which had been filed by Ades immediately after the Supreme Court denial. Ritchie sent a telegram to his staff setting Thursday, October 19, as a hearing date for that matter. The hearing would be held in the governor's office in the Union Trust Building in Baltimore at 3:00 p.m.

Incredibly, in the course of this time, yet another horrific event was to occur on the lower shore.

On the evening of October 16, Mrs. Mary Denston, an elderly lady of seventy-one years, was walking from the post office near her home in an isolated area of Somerset County, the county neighboring Worcester to the west and which also lies south of Wicomico, when she was attacked by a black man on the road. She was later found by two States Roads employees lying battered in a lane near her home, and an immediate search went out for George Armwood, the black man whom Mrs. Denston identified as the attacker. Before long, Armwood was caught and immediately incarcerated in the Somerset jail at Princess Anne, the county seat. Just as had occurred in Euel Lee's case, a crowd gathered around the jail, and a contingent of police and sheriff's deputies escorted Armwood out of the lockup and began the selfsame journey to Baltimore City, where he was locked up in the city jail.

What at first had appeared to be a mirror image of the Lee case, however, took an ominous turn when State's Attorney John Robins and Somerset County Circuit Court judge Robert Duer determined to order the removal of Armwood from the safety of the metropolitan area and back to the Princess Anne jail. He was removed from Baltimore about 10:00 p.m. on Monday, October 17.

In the early morning hours of Tuesday, October 18, a state police escort slipped quietly into the town, arriving at about 3:30 a.m. Shortly after arrival, Armwood was locked up in jail, with some of the state policemen remaining on duty there, though State's Attorney Robins said there was no reason to expect a reoccurrence of the mob threat.

The *Sun* reported that

> the usual hearing before a police magistrate, which is ordinarily held before an accused man's case is sent before the grand jury, will be eliminated in Armwood's case. Mr. Robins said that such a hearing might tend to arouse excitement. [A preliminary hearing is not mandated by the law when an indictment is sought in a criminal case.]
>
> Mr. Robins said that an order for the recall of the September grand jury has already been issued. The jury will reconvene Monday to hear evidence against Armwood.
>
> "We would be ready to try him Tuesday," said Mr. Robins, "if his attorney is ready. But the court hasn't appointed any attorney yet. We'll try him just as soon as possible."

Armwood had been charged with felonious assault, but Robins indicated that another charge may be yet forthcoming. An accomplice, John Richardson, a white man, also had been charged as an accessory after the fact, for the crime of spiriting Armwood away from the scene of the crime. Richardson, likewise, was locked up in the jail at Princess Anne.

At this point, it is irresistible not to speculate as to what on earth could have been in the minds of Judge Duer and State's Attorney Robins in reaching the decision to order the return of Armwood to the scene of a near riot. It is, likewise, irresistible not to draw the corollary between this case and the events of the Euel Lee matter. The two men were intimately familiar with the interminable length of time it was taking to resolve the Lee legal saga. It was a political nightmare, and surely this elected official and judge would have been irrevocably determined to avoid yet anther debacle. Even though hindsight would look aghast at the ill-conceived notion that there would not be trouble, Duer and Robins were surely intent upon trying Armwood so quickly that the Lee fiasco would not be repeated.

XXXII

Somerset's Shame

Just as surely as the sun rose over Princess Anne on Wednesday, October 18, 1933, this would be a day to stain the history of Somerset, one of the oldest and most venerable of Maryland's counties. The *Sunpapers* edition of October 19 gave the following account of the horrific event:

The following account of the mob actions at Princess Anne, when George Armwood, a Negro accused of assaulting a farm woman was lynched, was given to the Associated Press today by Captain Edward McKim Johnson, in charge of the State police defending the jail.

"The first indication we had there might be trouble appeared about 7 o'clock [p.m.] when a crowd began to gather near the jail. But it was a friendly gathering and seemed to have been drawn there out of curiosity rather than to cause us trouble. We had men picketing the vicinity to report any threatening gathering.

"About 7:30 others began to congregate on either side of the vacant lot across the street in front of the jail. They were assembling rapidly, large groups of them on each side. My men—twenty-one officers—were then drawn up in front of the prison. We had placed three automobiles in a position to throw headlights upon the crowd. Four county officers were inside the jail.

"Despite our efforts, the two crowds began to close in across the lot in front of the prison. Avalanches of bricks, stones and other missiles were hurled at us.

"It was futile for us to use our arms. We shot tear gas into the crowds, but as quickly as the fumes cleared they rushed in upon us again. They kicked the canisters of gas around like footballs.

"Our supply of gas was soon exhausted and it then became a hand-to-hand battle at the entrance to the jail.

"They had gotten heavy timbers intent upon battering down the jail door. Three of my men were struck with this battering ram at the jail entrance. Sergt. E.F. Hadaway, of Claiborne and Patrolman Clyde Serman, Salisbury, are in the Peninsula General Hospital with stomach injuries. Five other officers were treated for bruises and lacerations.

"I was struck in the head by a brick or stone at 8:10 and had no knowledge of what happened. I was taken to Dr. Lankford's office for treatment.

"It was 8:30 when they finally broke into the jail and took the prisoner. Before I was struck I saw several in the attacking crowd injured and taken away. No shots were fired. Our men have standing orders not to use their firearms except as a last resort.

"We were overwhelmingly outnumbered and were overpowered. That is the whole story. I saw Sheriff Luther Daugherty about 2 o'clock in the afternoon when he said he had to go to Crisfield and would return in a short time. He returned to the scene at 7:55.

"Between 7:30 and 8:00, Judge Duer spoke to both crowds. One crowd appeared willing to accept his admonition to leave and some of them did go away. But the other crowd was more stubborn. It is extremely difficult to estimate the number of a mob moving in waves in all directions. I would say there were between 1,500 and 2,500."

The *Evening Sun* ran another postmortem in its October 19 edition:

Princess Anne, Md. Oct. 19—A battered jail and a scorched spot on the pavement near the courthouse offered the only visual evidence of the mob outbreak here last night that sent a crowd of thousands swarming over a small band of State police to seize, hang and burn a colored prisoner.

Officialdom talked mildly and somewhat vaguely of an investigation. The body of lynching victim, George Armwood, 28 years old, had disappeared. Short lengths of the lynching rope, proudly displayed last night as souvenirs, were no longer in evidence.

Coroner Edgar Jones said he intended to hold an inquest before nightfall. He said, "I expect that it will be found that the man died by hanging." Judge Robert F. Duer, on whom Gov. Albert C. Ritchie said responsibility for apprehending the mob members rested, declared that he had not had time to determine which direction the investigation would follow.

"I intend to confer with my associates, and until I have had an opportunity to do that there is nothing much I can say," he said.

There had been some indications that Judge Duer might himself be a valuable witness in the investigation, for he addressed a crowd of 500 persons gathered around the jail shortly before the attack and reminded them that, "I know nearly all of you." Today he said that he had "no idea that any of those I addressed took part in the lynching." Sheriff Luther Daugherty, a lifelong resident of Somerset County, who went into the jail with [the] mob in an effort to halt the lynching and was surrounded by its members while the prisoner was dragged away, declared that he recognized "not a one of them. They were all strangers," the sheriff said. "I believe they came from Worcester County and maybe from down below the line in Virginia. I never saw a one of them before in my life."

He delayed the investigation until today, the sheriff said, because there was no way of getting it started last night. He went to his home in Crisfield after the lynching, but said today he was planning to return to Princess Anne to begin an inquiry. "I was right in there with them," Sheriff Daugherty said, "but I couldn't do a thing. I asked them time and time again to let the law take its course, but they went right over me. I couldn't even get to the second floor of the jail where Armwood was. He never had a chance to fight, because it was a thousand to one. I never heard him say a word, and I don't know how he got those cuts. I couldn't get near."

States Attorney John B. Robins, the Somerset county prosecutor who was charged by Capt. Edward McKim Johnson of the State police with turning down suggestions that the prisoner should be removed from Princess Anne because of the mob danger, would say nothing of plans to run down and prosecute the lynchers. In response to requests for explanations of his insistence that the prisoner be held in Princess Anne, he said: "I have no statement to make at this time."

It was reported that the police had ten tear gas bombs which were used to stand off the mob for a time. No firearms were used by the officers or by the mob in the attack. Captain Johnson said that his men used their bare hands to fight the mob, but none of them had blackjacks.

In the meantime, Governor Ritchie had, once again, a terrible situation on the lower shore to contend with. He had been in Annapolis attending the session of the Maryland legislature, which was reconsidering the repeal of the Eighteenth Amendment related to Prohibition, when he got the news that there was the likelihood of mob violence if Armwood were returned to Princess Anne. All through the afternoon, the governor was reported as being perturbed by the reports, and telephoned both Judge Duer and Mr. Robins. Both of them reportedly assured him that there was no danger. In fact, at one time during the afternoon, Captain Johnson recommended that Armwood once again be removed from Princess Anne. He said, however, that State's Attorney Robins declined to approve the removal of the prisoner. After hearing this, the governor consulted with Attorney General William Preston Lane to determine whether the State could order such a removal. No such authority existed, and it was indicated that martial law would have to be declared in order to usurp the authority of local officials.

Contrary to the assertions of the judge and the State's Attorney, Deputy Sheriff Norman Dryden sensed the oncoming turmoil early in the afternoon. He was so disturbed that he approached Edward Young, commander of the local American Legion, and asked that legionnaires be available to aid in preserving order.

Sure enough, as dark fell, automobiles began streaming into town, and the streets began filling with knots of men. The movement toward the jail began slowly and with uncertainty. The first group that approached the jail were mostly young boys, who merely shouted and attempted to peer past the state police guard and inside the barred windows. Soon, however, the crowd changed to older, grim men who moved past the boys toward the jail, and here and there ropes appeared. Just as the mob surged forward toward the cordon of police, Judge Duer drove up in his automobile and drove to the front of the mob. He stepped out of his car and motioned for silence, which rapidly descended. "My friends, why don't you disperse and go home quietly?" he asked. "The grand jury will be convened promptly. This man will have a speedy trial. Why not let the law take its course?"

He was answered with jeers and shouts, "We don't want any Euel Lee in Somerset County," voices shouted, "That was what happened in the Euel Lee case!"

"That will not happen here," replied the judge, "Let us go home quietly. I know nearly all of you, and you know me. You can depend on what I say." At that, it appeared that the judge had made a difference. The crowd receded away from the immediate area of the jail. In the mistaken impression that he had succeeded in his request, the judge got into his car and went home.

The *Evening Sun* report continued:

> *After his departure, however, the crowd, still in the area, grew more restive and surged again toward the jail. With no authority figure to dissuade them, they had only the cops to contend with. Soon, the encircling mob closed in on the entrance to the jail. Teargas was hurled, and choking fumes filled the air. From a nearby lumberyard, a group of men brought up two large timbers, fifteen feet long. They were brought forth to act a battering rams, and after a moment's hesitation, the crowd realized that there were no more teargas bombs available to the police. Bricks and sticks rained from the crowd. Hand to hand encounters took place in front of the barred door. Several police officers fell and were trampled underfoot. A group of men came forward with the large timbers and thrust them at the door, where Officer Serman and Officer Hadaway stood guard. The rams were thrust violently into the men, injuring them severely. The cops out of the way, the rams were swung into*

the locked door, and it gave way. With a whoop, the mob surged in. They got from the jailer, Deputy Sheriff Dryden, the keys to the jail cells. Several of the members of the mob seemed to be familiar with Armwood's appearance, because as Deputy Dryden urged them not to get the wrong man, they peered through jail cell bars until they reached Armwood's cell. One by one, the keys were tried in the door until it opened. Armwood was dragged out, and when the group appeared at the front door, a noose was around his neck.

As they stepped out into the night air, some looked for a nearby tree. A call came from the crowd, "Don't kill him yet!" He was knocked to the ground. Men jumped on his prostrate body and he was beaten insensible. As they dragged him down the street, the mob stopped at the house of James C. Stirling and surveyed the massive trees in his yard. He dashed from his home and pleaded with the mob to go away. "I have children in there. Please don't do it here. I don't want them to see it," he begged.

The mob moved on. It reached the home of Mrs. Thomas Bock, an elderly lady of ninety-two years who was bed-ridden with a severe illness. Her large trees suited the crowd. A young man shinnied up the tree, where the rope was tossed to him and he dropped it over a sturdy limb. The limp and apparently lifeless body of Armwood was lifted up, lowered and lifted again. The mob howled. Then came cries to take the body back to the courthouse. It was lowered and dragged to Prince William and Main Streets. The rope was thrown over a telephone wire along the street and was raised again. Then came the horrific suggestion that Armwood be burned. Gasoline was siphoned from a parked automobile and poured over the body. A match was struck and Armwood was set afire. His body lay in the street, immolated, as the crowd, its violent bent apparently satiated, slowly dispersed. Before long, the streets of Princess Anne were quiet. Deputy sheriffs ventured forth, retrieved the charred remains and removed them from the street.

The next morning it was reported that state police had the names of no less than three men who had participated in the lynching. They also had the names of several men who threw bricks and other missiles at the police guarding the jail. An investigation was launched at a conference between State's Attorney Robins, Sheriff Daugherty and state police, and Attorney General Lane. In a statement on the crime itself, an apparently infuriated Governor Ritchie laid the responsibility directly at the feet of Judge Duer and Mr. Robins. A grand jury investigation was promised.

In the *Evening Sun* edition of Friday, October 20, the day after the lynching in Princess Anne was described:

There was but one subject of conversation here last night—the lynching of George Armwood. But the affair was discussed calmly, without heat, and a note of jocularity marked most of the talk. "Well," observed one citizen, smoking a stogie in front of the Washington Hotel, "it would have cost the State $1,000, I guess, to hang that man. It only cost us 75 cents."

There isn't much of Princess Anne—just Main Street, with a handful of stores, gasoline stations and eating places, but the town seemed well populated yesterday as little groups of residents gathered to discuss the first lynching in thirty-eight years.

Men who had souvenirs of the affair attracted particular attention. One young man drew attention by displaying two of the tear gas bombs which were exploded during the battle at the jail. Another resident displayed a piece of the lynching rope. It was about 5 inches long and both ends were wrapped with cord to keep it from unraveling. During the afternoon, someone had an idea. Equipped with a saw, he went to the jail and cut up one of the long timbers which the mob used as a bettering ram to break down the jail door. A little while later several men were walking down Main Street carrying blocks of wood, about six inches square, which had been cut from the timber.

The Washington Hotel seemed to be the central "news bureau" for the town. This hotel is an ancient structure, built years before the Revolution. Some of the original Colonial dignity remains, although there are some jarring "alterations" here and there. The State police had their headquarters in the hostelry and many of the curious townsmen used the front sidewalk as an impromptu headquarters.

Some of the talkers made no secret of their attendance at the lynching. They discussed it in all its details. And the name of Euel Lee, who will be hanged next Friday morning for the murder of a Worcester county farmer, was frequently mentioned.

"If it hadn't been for that Lee affair," said one man, "this wouldn't ever have happened. They should have hanged him long ago."

Another man, who had attended the storming of the jail, said he had one regret—he was sorry about one of the State policemen who fell under the mob's barrage of brickbats. "I fought in France right alongside that cop," the man said. "He's a good fellow. I didn't like it when he went down—it made a lump come right up in my throat."

No animosity was displayed toward the State policemen who remained in town most of yesterday. Some of the townsmen even praised the officers highly.

"Those State policemen," it was observed, "deserve a lot of credit. They didn't lose their heads once. They had guns right on their hips, but there wasn't a move made to draw one. And I can tell you—it's plenty hard not to draw a gun, if you've got it, when a mob starts tossing bricks. It's a good thing too. If one of those cops had drawn a gun it would have been good-bye. There were plenty of guns in the crowd and the cops were all together. Some of the men in the back of the crowd could have stood off in the dark and popped off those cops one by one. If the shooting had ever started—well, there'd be more than one dead man today, all right."

The pending investigation of the lynching seemed to be of little importance to the townsmen.

"Did they do anything after the Salisbury lynching?" it was asked. "No, they didn't. Don't hold your breath waiting for somebody to go to jail for this one either."

Meanwhile Judge Duer also issued a statement regarding the incident:

I was badly mistaken in my judgment of what would happen. I have been sitting in court at Snow Hill every day this week and have been getting home late at night. The Governor called me at about 4:30 P.M. in Snow Hill and said he was apprehensive about conditions here. I told the Governor that I had heard nothing about a disturbance and that I had been assured by the State's Attorney that he had been all over the county and he didn't think there would be any trouble.

I told the Governor I would go immediately back to Princess Anne to ascertain conditions and call him back. I went downtown and talked to the deputy sheriffs and persons I thought would be informed as to the temper of the people. I was told they didn't think there would be any trouble. The people, I was informed, were entirely satisfied because I had ordered the grand jury reconvened on Monday and a quick trial was in prospect.

I also talked to Captain Johnson who said he had received various and conflicting reports but had not heard of any definite movements. I again held a telephone conversation with the State's Attorney at Crisfield. This was about 5:30 p.m. I called the Governor and told him exactly the impression I had received. The Governor called me back. He said the impression he received from Captain Johnson was essentially the same as that I gave him.

I was invited to dinner and, while at my hosts', I received a call from the jail authorities to come down there, as they were apprehensive of trouble. I went down and talked to a crowd of about 200. They did not strike me as being a determined crowd, rather curiosity seekers, and I went back, still satisfied that there would be no trouble. It was about 8 o'clock when I first went to the jail.

About an hour later, I was called again and told they had broken into the jail. The general impression is that the crowd was not from this section of the county. I am told that few of the persons who took the active part in the affair were recognized as residents of this section.

I was badly mistaken in my judgment, and I am deeply grieved that such a thing has happened in our county. I am grieved for the State as well. The police and authorities did everything in their power to avert this tragedy.

XXXIII

A Plea for Lee's Life

On Thursday, October 19, before the scheduled time for the governor's clemency hearing at his office in Baltimore, a rally was held in City Hall Plaza, protesting Lee's impending hanging. About fifty demonstrators, "mostly Negroes," attended, as did Ades. The *Salisbury Times* reported on the event:

> *Police Commissioner Charles D. Gaither this afternoon ordered 80 Baltimore policemen to assemble around the state executive offices here to prevent a Communist demonstration while Governor Albert Ritchie heard a plea for the life of Euel Lee, Negro convicted of murder and sentenced to hang.*
>
> *At the commissioner's office it was said that he had reports that Communists were assembling in various sections of the city to march towards the Governor's Baltimore office.*
>
> *The plea for clemency was scheduled to be made at three o'clock by Bernard Ades, attorney for the communist Labor Defense, who has defended Lee during the bitter two-year legal fight which ended when the United States Supreme Court declined to consider his appeal last week.*

The expected large crowds of demonstrators did not materialize, and after the rally, escorted by police and detectives, a handful of the group walked to the governor's office nearby, and, under an agreement, twelve of them were admitted to the office itself. Surrounded by detectives, they were allowed to group themselves around the governor's desk, where Ades presented his arguments for mercy. Arrayed in the room were, among others, Police Commissioner Charles Gaither, Inspector Stephen G. Nelson, Baltimore City State's Attorney Herbert O'Conor, William Henderson, Baltimore County State's Attorney James L. Anderson and, of course, Godfrey Child.

The October 28, 1933 edition of the *Afro-American* detailed the meeting:

> *In an impassioned and forceful plea which lasted 40 minutes Thursday afternoon before Governor Albert C. Ritchie, Defense Counsel Bernard Ades lost his two-year fight for the almost-run life of Euel Lee, 68-year old* [sic] *man charged with the murder of the four members of the Green Davis family, white, on October 12, 1931 in Taylorville, Md.*
>
> *At the Governor's Room in the Union Trust Building, Charles and Fayette Streets, Baltimore, a small group gathered for the hearing. Ades led a delegation of Communists, white and black, who silently remained through the session. Newspaper men and interested officials comprised the remainder of the group.*

At 3:00 P.M., Ades opened the hearing, with the governor seated at his desk, as he announced that he would present only two persons who would plead for the life of Lee—himself and Henry Williams, who represented the Communist party.

Williams started his remarks with a scathing criticism of the Armwood lynching at Princess Anne the night before. Governor Ritchie interrupted Williams to request that the Armwood case be left out of the discussion. "We are here to talk about Lee," said the governor.

Spiritedly, Williams dissented, asking permission to be allowed "to talk in my own way." Promptly disregarding the governor's request, Williams continued his denunciation of the Armwood lynching, stating that, "we are placing this lynching directly on you, governor."

Williams talked slowly and deliberately as he questioned the governor concerning Maryland's Jim Crow laws, seeking remedial legislation. [In another account, Williams was said to have a "West Indies accent."] *He described the Eastern Shore as "a place saturated with barbaric forms of terror…As a negro, I believe I have the right to appeal to the highest authority in the state." He then, according to this account, called for a special session of the Legislature to repeal Jim Crow laws, asserting that "these are visible signs of oppression, and a sign of the slavery under which Negroes of the state live." He continued that "all evidence proved Euel Lee innocent, that the case was a frame-up and a result of the fact that Negroes are held under the heels of certain ruling elements."*

The Afro-*American* account continued:

Concluding his appeal for the release of Lee, Williams told Governor Ritchie that executive clemency would earn for him the respect of colored citizens. "Although, I don't know if you value the respect of Negroes," he asserted.

Taking the floor, Ades talked steadily for 40 minutes, consulting notes on the table before him. Transcripts from the previous trials of Lee were used by the aged man's counsel, in his attempt to show the governor that Lee's trials had been unfair, unjust and prejudiced.

Ades asserted that his own knowledge of previous clemency hearings before the governor showed that there was no chance for a pardon unless the petitioners presented the facts.

"I have no certain policies such as you have described." interrupted Governor Ritchie.

Ades went on to show that Police Officer Allen, who arrested Lee after a two-minute investigation of the murder of the four people, himself was suspected of complicity in an abduction case. Ades contended that Allen was eager to arrest anyone in the Green Davis case, to prove his own competence as an officer and to keep off any possible investigation of his own activities. That the trials were framed was argued by Ades, as he charged that evidence produced at one trial was switched at a later one. He charged that a coat and vest found on Lee and which were the property of the murdered Davis, were apparently matched by trousers found in the Davis' home, but that while the coat and vest were old and worn, the trousers were new and unsoiled.

Ades caused a stir in the room when he directly charged Governor Ritchie with being prejudiced against Negroes. He supported this charge by reading a letter from the governor in which, he asserted, the governor spoke of Lee as committing "an atrocious murder," although at that time Lee had not been tried and was supposedly innocent before the law.

As a finale, Ades presented the governor with a petition containing ten thousand signatures requesting clemency for Lee. He was finished.

Ades and Henry Williams had argued for nearly an hour, as all the persons gathered in the room stood quietly by. At once, and without hesitation, the governor said that he was ready to render his decision.

> *The offense for which Euel Lee was convicted is an atrocious murder of four people while they lay asleep at home in their beds. Those murdered were Mr. Green Davis, his wife and two daughters. The State proved complete familiarity on the part of Euel Lee with all four members of the deceased family and their household, where he had been employed; that Lee made threats against Mr. Davis after he left the latter's employment; that Lee had been seen making his way toward the Davis house before the murder and coming away afterward; that Lee was away from his own home the night the murder was committed without any explanation of his absence; that after the crime a large number of articles belonging to the murdered man and his family were found in Lee's possession; that before the murder Lee had purchased bullets which fitted the gun with which the crime was committed, and that he had informed a reliable witness that Mr. Davis had been shot before the fact was known to the public.*
>
> *In addition to this, Lee made two confessions in the presence of reliable witnesses, the first just after his arrest, and the second a couple of days later. In both these confessions Lee gave details of the crime which could have been known to no one except the murderer and which afterward were confirmed. Lee was tried twice, and at neither trial was his confession offered in evidence. He was convicted without that. In neither case did the jury have the slightest doubt of his guilt, and every point which could be made in his favor was urged by his attorneys in both the Court of Appeals of Maryland and the Supreme Court of the United States.*
>
> *There can be no doubt in the mind of any reasonable person that Lee is guilty of the murder of the Davis family. The propaganda which has been spread to the effect that Lee is innocent has not the slightest basis to support it, and the propaganda that he was railroaded or framed is equally untrue. Every right that Lee had or could advance was fully heard and considered by the courts in which he was given every protection the law affords. There is not the slightest justification for clemency in this case, and, accordingly I will not grant the same, and I hereby fix Friday, October 27, as the date for execution.*

He sat back in his large chair, and gazed steadily at Ades.

The group stood awkwardly silent for a moment, looked to Ades for guidance, which was not forthcoming, and then, without a word, they filed out of the office and were escorted from the building.

The governor had a public announcement to make, and, later that afternoon, he stated: "This crime has been too long unpunished. But, of course, the sentence of the court could not be carried out so long as legal proceedings by way of appeal were pending. These legal proceedings were terminated just ten days ago—on October 9—and I have now given those interested in Lee the fullest opportunity to be heard on their application for clemency."

That very afternoon the death warrant was mailed to Warden Brady at the penitentiary by registered mail and was received by him that same night. The execution was to be carried out early in the morning hours on Friday, October 27, 1933.

One articulate voice was yet to be heard from. Once again, H.L. Mencken made his journalistic presence known. In a copyrighted article in the *Evening Sun* dated October 18, Mencken set forth:

It is to be hoped that the ides of November see the public and permanent conclusion of the Euel Lee case with the dispatch to parts unknown of the central luminary thereof, alias Orphan Jones. Some time ago, upset by persistent hints from Aframerican and Communist quarters that the gentleman had been framed by the Delmarva cops, a corps of men in whom I have little confidence, I read the whole record of the proceedings against him, including the two briefs on appeal of his learned counsel, the Hon. Bernard Ades, L.L.B. The result was that I came away convinced that his guilt had been proved beyond the peradventure of a doubt, not once but twice, and full of a longing to hear that Warden Brady would soon rope him…

There was absolutely no sign in either trial of any framing. The chief witness for the State was a colored woman, and her testimony alone was sufficient to connect Lee with the murders. It was not shown that he had any enemies, either white or black, or that it was to anyone's interest to swear his life away. No matter what may be alleged now, whether by Communists or Aframericans, the fact remains plain that the man confessed twice, that he was convicted without making use of his confessions, and that the evidence against him was overwhelming and unanswerable.

Well, then, why is he still on earth? Why wasn't he hanged a year or more ago? The easy reply is that he survives so long, a shame upon Maryland justice and a public nuisance, because of a legal slipup which was taken advantage by Ades, who dragged his case from Worcester county to Dorchester, and then to Baltimore county and three times to Annapolis and once to Washington. That, I take it, is what is generally believed on the lower Eastern Shore. But what is generally believed on the lower Eastern Shore is seldom true, and it is no more true this time than other times. Lee remains unhanged simply because two sets of Maryland judges neglected their plain duty, and had to be forced to do it by tedious and vexatious process.

The first to fail were Pattison, C.J., and Duer and Bailey, JJ., of the First Judicial Circuit. Lee came before the two last named on November 6, 1931, on a motion for a change of venue from Worcester county. It was his right to ask for it, and he certainly needed it, for Snow Hill was in the hands of a mob, and on the very day of the hearing Dr. Ades was manhandled by it. But the most that Duer and Bailey, JJ., would agree to was a removal to Cambridge in Dorchester county, in their own Circuit, not fifty miles away, and within easy reach of the same mob. It would be hard to imagine anything more unfair to the prisoner, yet Duer and Bailey, JJ., stuck to their decision, and presently they were supported by their chief, Pattison.

Dr. Ades naturally made an uproar: he would have been recreant to his client if he hadn't. He demanded that the case be removed to the Western Shore, where there are adequate police and mobs are put down with a strong arm. But the three judges remained immovable, though it was plain to everyone that Lee might be lynched at Cambridge, and Judge Pattison admitted that fact indirectly by making the astonishing suggestion that Lee be kept on an armed vessel in the Choptank River during the trial. The whole lower shore, in fact, was aflame, and on December 4 another Negro was actually lynched at Salisbury, in the same judicial circuit and Bible zone. So Ades sought relief from the Court of Appeals.

The Court of Appeals, obviously enough, could not interfere directly, its business is not to intrude upon cases that are still to be tried, but to review cases that have been adjudicated. But we had then, as we have now, a court at Annapolis that is happily free from pedantry, and what it couldn't do by writ it did by a declaratory judgment—an extra-constitutional proceeding, but none the less effective for that. In brief, it notified the three Shore judges that if they insisted upon trying Lee in the face of the mob, and the jury found him guilty, and his counsel entered an appeal it [the Court of Appeals] would order a new trial. So, the three judges climbed down, and Lee was tried at Towson.

At least one of the two appeals from the verdicts brought in by juries there, and all the long delays that went with it, do not lie at Dr. Ades' door but at the doors of the four learned judges of the Third Circuit, and especially that of Duncan, J., who had been acting jury commissioner. Judge Duncan had simply forgotten the Fourteenth Amendment to the Federal Constitution. No colored talesman ever appeared on his jury lists…So when the first trial ended with Lee convicted, Dr. Ades appealed to the Court of Appeals and it promptly upset the verdict and ordered a new trial, this time by a jury on which colored men, if they were otherwise eligible, would be allowed to sit.

On Lee's second conviction Dr. Ades appealed again. No colored man had been on the jury, but there were a number of colored talesmen, so that the complaint could not be made again. But now Ades alleged boldly that no colored man could ever get a fair trial there in Baltimore County. This argument the Court of Appeals dismissed as without force, and last week its view was sustained by the Supreme Court in Washington. So Lee must hang at last, more than two years after his brutal crime.

Is it fair to blame Dr. Ades for all these delays? I think not. His politics I abhor, and his manners seem to me to lack something, but as a lawyer he did his duty and kept within his prerogatives. Only his second appeal can be called frivolous, stretching the term as far as it will go. On his first two trips to Annapolis, the Court of Appeals agreed with him completely. At least three-fourths of the time that was wasted was so wasted because two sets of judges mismanaged their business sufficiently to deprive a man on trial for his life of his plain constitutional rights.

Mencken had sifted through all the rhetoric and had, once again, struck the jugular.

Remarkably, Ades was not yet done. An additional rally, much larger than before, was held on October 21, at City Hall Plaza in Baltimore. From appearances, at least two or three hundred people were in attendance, as well as a substantial delegation of policemen.

Ades was also busy on the legal front. Not dismayed by the high court rebuff and the stinging rebuke of the governor of Maryland, he filed a writ of habeas corpus with the United States District Court for the District of Maryland. On Monday, October 23, Ades and Levinson filed their writ with the district court, alleging that Lee's Constitutional rights had been violated, in that the grand jury that had indicted him had been illegally drawn, and that the petit jury panel that had convicted him had been illegally constituted. Judge Calvin Chestnut agreed to consider the case when the defense attorneys told him they were ready to argue at any moment. Judge Chestnut immediately scheduled a hearing the very afternoon of the petition, after the recess of an hour from the regular court schedule.

XXXIV

Ades Gets His Due

For Ades, however, the hearing turned out to be the nightmare of any trial lawyer. As Ades rose to introduce David Levinson, immediately after the court convened, Judge Chestnut announced that he had some remarks to make before hearing from counsel. He then said that after the petition for writ of habeas corpus was filed, he had requested Judge Coleman to participate in the case because it was so important to Lee and all involved in the proceeding.

"I wish to discuss the merits of the application for the writ," the judge announced. "And then, Judge Coleman has some remarks to make to counsel. I understand that Mr. Ades is a member of this court but that Mr. Levinson is not; for that reason what I have to say will be directed at counsel who is entitled to practice here. An application for a writ of habeas corpus presupposes that a new trial will be granted if the writ is granted because of some infringement of the defendant's rights."

The judge then went on to discuss the various trials and hearings that had already been held in the Euel Lee case and made the obvious point that two trials had resulted in convictions and that the last conviction had been affirmed by the Maryland Court of Appeals, and also had been reviewed by the Supreme Court before it rejected the petition for writ of certiorari. He also stated that the basis set forth in the application for the writ was "narrow, indeed" and, referring to the federal code, stated that there was no indication that a habeas corpus writ could be resorted to when the state courts had jurisdiction over the case.

"It is not the present view of the court that the defendant has a right of review in this court. If any invasion of the defendant's rights had taken place it would not have gone unnoticed by the Supreme Court, which goes carefully into all matters presented to it. This does not mean that a hearing will not be allowed, after Judge Coleman has spoken."

Judge Coleman then leaned over the bench looking directly at Bernard Ades. "This court cannot but take notice of the conduct of Mr. Ades in this case and in other cases. There is prima facie evidence that Mr. Ades's conduct has been unbecoming a member of the bar and not for the best interests of the accused. This court will furnish you, Mr. Ades, with a list of the facts presented to it in this connection and you will be given an opportunity to answer them at a future time. There are facts which indicate that Mr. Ades has interjected himself into this case and he will be put under an order to show cause why action should not be taken against him. Pending an investigation into these facts, the court wishes to safeguard the interests of Euel Lee and for that reason has appointed counsel who is in good standing with this court to appear for him. I wish to say, too, that Judge Chestnut concurs with all that I have said."

The judges promptly appointed a prominent member of the Federal Bar, Charles McHenry Howard, of Baltimore, to represent Lee. With Judge William C. Coleman and Judge Chestnut on the bench, Bernard Ades was suspended from the practice of law before the federal bench.

Ades rose, and looked toward Herbert R. O'Conor, Baltimore City State's Attorney, who was sitting in at the request of Godfrey Child, and his nemesis in the appeals, Assistant Attorney General William L. Henderson, and advised the court that similar charges had already been disposed of by the state court. [In fact, according to records in the archives of the Baltimore City circuit court, a petition was filed on June 25, 1934, by the Bar Association of Baltimore City against Ades, which resulted in his suspension on December 7, 1934, for a period of three months.]

"You are in federal court now, and we are handling the matter entirely independent of what may have been done in the state courts," Judge Coleman retorted.

Levinson then rose. He requested to know if he had been included in the judge's remarks. He advised the judges that he was a member of the Pennsylvania bar and was held in high regard by the judges in that state.

Judge Coleman was ready for him, also. "But you are not a member of this court and we cannot accept your introduction by a member who is not himself in good standing. In addition, Mr. Levinson, the court has certain information about your own conduct in this and other cases which it will investigate."

Judge Coleman then turned to the bailiff and curtly instructed him to adjourn court until ten o'clock the next morning. Ades was, understandably, shocked by the court's action. "I do not know what Howard's attitude will be," he said, "I do consider his appointment illegal. I intend to consult with him tomorrow morning and if he intends to file the writ the situation will not be so bad. All depends on my conference with Howard. I was so shocked in Court I couldn't make a front-page statement. I do not believe that court has the right to select counsel. In the Scottsboro case, it was decided by the United States Supreme Court that the defendant can select his own counsel. Therefore, if I were to be finally disbarred, Lee would have to be asked first what counsel he prefers and must be given a chance to select counsel before the court can select counsel. In the meantime, of course, Lee's execution must be delayed until new counsel can be selected by him."

Early the next morning, Tuesday, October 24, Ades and Levinson met with Charles McHenry Howard. A hearing on the delayed petition was set for late that same afternoon. At noon it was announced that Howard would accept Levinson as associate counsel to sit with him that afternoon. Ades, even though out of the case, was not out of press releases, and announced that if the writ were not granted, he would appeal to the Supreme Court. Howard, when asked of this, denied any knowledge of the action of Ades, though one can speculate that he was already tiring of this young upstart's ceaseless pronouncements.

Also, contrary to Ades's assertion, the execution stood for Friday, October 27. Ades still had some unplayed cards up his sleeve; on Wednesday, October 25, just one day before all would be lost (the execution, though scheduled for Friday, would take place in the wee hours of the morning, prior to any court or government office being open), Levinson petitioned the Fourth Circuit Court of Appeals (the federal appellate court for the jurisdiction of Maryland) to hear an appeal from the decision of the U.S. district court's refusal to grant a writ of habeas corpus. He would, according to Ades, ask the appellate court to issue a certificate of probable cause, which would result in the allowance of an appeal. Of course, if an appeal were allowed, a necessary stay of execution would result.

Attorney General William Preston Lane was not slacking off on his participation, either. By telegram, he replied to the allegations of the petition, and also secured a transcript of the proceedings before Judges Chestnut and Coleman, at which they denied Mr. Howard's requested relief in his presentation. His telegram said, in part, "The points relied on in the application for writ of habeas corpus are the identical points urged upon the Court of Appeals of Maryland and the Supreme Court of the United States by the petition for certiorari and there can be no doubt that the present application is solely for the purpose of delay and is, I am convinced, designed to bring the administration of justice into disrepute." He then prepared to depart, together with the ever-present William Henderson, for Richmond, where Judge Morris A. Soper, a Marylander himself, had agreed to hear arguments in the case at 8:40 p.m.

Indeed, that evening at Richmond, the location of the Federal appeals court, Judge Soper and Judge John J. Parker convened in a special night session to hear arguments from Charles McHenry Howard and Ades, who despite the bar from the U.S. district court, was allowed to participate in the arguments before the federal circuit court of appeals. General Lane and Assistant Henderson argued for the State. The combined arguments lasted almost two hours, after which the judges deliberated briefly.

Judge Parker stated the decision from the bench. "I do not know what I can add to what the judges below said, but it seems to me that the decision of the Court of Appeals of Maryland was unquestionably correct, and I can see no grounds for the argument that this man has been denied any of his rights under the Constitution. Due to the denial of the Court of Appeals and the denial of the Supreme Court, Judge Parker stated that there were no grounds for appeal. Judge Soper concurred, saying, "I do not think that I could conscientiously sign a certificate of probable cause."

However, the judges did not stop there, but engaged in some editorializing. Referring to the defendant's attorneys, Judge Parker said, "I have listened with interest to the cause so ably presented here."

Judge Soper went even further: "It is a most inspiring thing, not forgetting the seriousness of the case, that no one in this country is so poor and friendless that he cannot have the benefit of the best counsel and admission to every court in the land." One must infer that the judges were referring to Charles McHenry Howard, not Bernard Ades, and that the message from the bench was directed at the Communists who were shouting that Lee had not been given the benefit of a fair trial, when his case had in fact been reviewed by no less than four separate courts, including the highest court in the country.

It must have, in 1933, been an arduous trip back from Richmond, up Route 1 into Washington, D.C., late on that Wednesday night and into the early hours of Thursday, October 26. There was, however, as yet, no rest for the weary Ades. In fact, on Thursday three more efforts were engineered in order to delay the quickly approaching death of Euel Lee. First, Ades presented a request to Chief Justice Charles Evans Hughes asking that he issue the sought-after writ of probable cause, refused by the judges in the Fourth Circuit. Secondly, a march on the White House was staged by a group headed by William L. Patterson, secretary of the International Labor Defense, who presented a petition for the consideration of President Roosevelt to grant clemency to Lee. The president's special assistant, Louis Howe, received the delegation and accepted the petition. Thirdly, David Levinson filed in the Supreme Court yet another petition requesting that the court take original jurisdiction in the case, and to issue a writ to have Lee brought forth. Attorney General Lane prepared the State's response to the petition and late on October 26, stated that Chief Justice Hughes had denied both requests. Likewise evident was the fact that FDR was not going to get involved, either. At the meeting with Louis Howe, the delegation was informed that the president would not intervene.

XXXV

An Execution Takes Place

The last voice to be heard from on that Thursday night was that of Warden Patrick Brady, who announced that Lee would be hanged a few minutes past midnight. He related a conversation with Lee earlier that day when Lee learned from the newspaper reports that the judges had refused his attorney's request, in total. Brady revealed that Lee had told him, "I expected it. I'm satisfied—I hope everybody else is. I'm ready whenever they're ready." The warden said the services of the Reverend Edgar C. Powers, prison chaplain, would be offered to Lee that night.

The October 27 edition of the *Sunpapers* said it all. Its headline proclaimed: "Euel Lee Hangs For Murder Of Two Years Ago—Rope Ends Long Legal Fight in Behalf of Eastern Shore Slayer." The report continued:

> *Euel Lee was hanged a few minutes after midnight this morning before a closely gathered group of about fifty men, guards and officials in the Maryland Penitentiary.*
>
> *The Negro went to his death without saying a word—and bearing the same expressionless mien that marked him throughout his two trials for the murder of Green K. Davis, Taylorsville (Md.) Farmer [sic], two years and two weeks ago.*
>
> *Among those who stood in the silent crowd in the narrow, high-ceilinged whitewashed death house were four police officials from Worcester County, the scene of the killing of Davis, his wife and two daughters. The men—Sheriff Wilmer Purnell, of Berlin; Randolph Purnell, chief of police in Snow Hill, county seat of Worcester County; William Hall, deputy sheriff of Whaleyville, and Robert Lewis, of Berlin, another deputy sheriff—said little before or after the hanging.*
>
> *Bernard Ades, International Labor Defense League attorney, who carried Lee's defense from one court to another until it was finally reviewed by the Supreme Court of the United States, was also there. He was present at the invitation of the prisoner, but he stood outside the death chamber during the execution.*
>
> *"The working class will some day pay for this," he said, and quoted the last words—to him—of the convicted Negro. "I am not so much sorry for myself as I am for my race."*
>
> *Lee was led onto the scaffold at 12:05 A.M. The trap was sprung a half a minute later. It took only thirty seconds to robe and hood him in black and to affix the noose. He was pronounced dead at 12:13 A.M. and his body lowered.*
>
> *The Rev. Edgar Cordell Powers, Methodist clergyman and a chaplain at the Penitentiary, said the Lord's Prayer while Lee was being prepared for execution and continued his prayers as those in*

charge of the hanging stood by waiting for Dr. E.T. Campbell, City Jail physician to pronounce the Negro dead.

The *Afro-American* reported the event this way, with a byline by Ralph Matthews:

Euel Lee is dead.

Without a quiver of the flesh, without a tremor of the muscle, the 60-year-old man who protested to the last his innocence of the murder of Green K. Davis and his family at Taylorville, Md., on the Eastern Shore, was dashed through the trap in the death house of the Maryland penitentiary, shortly after midnight this morning.

Lee walked firmly to the trap, and without an expression of fear or emotion stood stolidly erect as officials adjusted the noose. He swayed slightly as the hood was slipped over his head, and at 12:05 the trap was sprung.

Lee apparently died instantly, as there was none of the quivering of the flesh or contortion of the muscles which usually accompany the fall of young men. The moment the body fell, the rope became taut, and eight minutes later Lee was pronounced dead by Dr. E.T. Campbell, City Jail physician. Lee was led onto the scaffold by the Rev. Edgar Cordell Powers, white Methodist, penitentiary chaplain, who quoted the Lord's prayer as the noose was affixed.

When Dr. Campbell pronounced Lee dead, Dr. Powers delivered the following prayer as the fifty-odd spectators stood with bowed heads: "Almighty God, to whom our hearts are open, from whom no secrets are hid, we pray that Thou will be graciously pleased to accept this handicapped child, to whom life has been so wretched, and forgive him and all of us for the sins we have committed. Amen."

With this, the body was cut down and carried off by waiting interns.

Bernard Ades, bushy-haired and wild-eyed, who considered himself the only friend that Lee had, arrived at the penitentiary at 11:45. He looked years older, and the buoyant air that had marked his conduct throughout the two trials at Towson was displaced by an expression of absolute dejection.

"I am here," he said, "because Lee asked me to be here. I could not go back on him, but I hate to see this sort of thing."

Suddenly, in answer to the interrogation of reporters, he momentarily regained his old fire and declared, "but someday the working class will rise up to pay for this."

Ades looked wrathfully at the assemblage gathered in the penitentiary corridor. "What are all these people here for?" he demanded. "Why have they come? Are they so anxious to see a Negro die that they relish this gruesome thing?"

He marched with the group through the penitentiary gates across the yard to the death house. Just as Lee was brought out, Ades forced his way through the witnesses and stood on the outside until after the hanging. He then disappeared. "I believe he is innocent," said Ades. "He was the bravest man I have ever known. He asked me why I was nervous and said, 'Look at me. I am not nervous. Why should you be? When I told him yesterday that I was going to Richmond to take an appeal, he said, 'You need not go, because it will not do any good. They will only phone ahead to stop you. I am not so much concerned about myself, but I am sorry for my race.'"

That Lee maintained his innocence until he stepped upon the gallows was attested to by the Rev. Mr. Powers, who said that Lee had "forgiven everybody" but swore to the last that he was not guilty of the crime.

The *Afro-American* also had an observation about the scene outside the prison. Under a byline by Clarence Mitchell, it reported:

> As the final preparations for the Euel Lee hanging were taking place on Friday morning, the chosen few who were able to view the hanging by special invitation lost no time in getting to the penitentiary. Hard-faced men from the Eastern Shore and Baltimoreans, one by one entered the iron gateway which closed behind each man to prevent any sudden or intrusive arrivals.
>
> A drunken man, who said that he was a lieutenant in the police department, kept asking for Captain Kennedy and begged the guard at the door to get him. "He is a friend of mine," said the alleged official, "and I want to talk to him." Turning to another man, he added, "I'll get you in because I have a lot of influence over here."
>
> A little after 11:30 P.M., Bernard Ades, defense counsel for the doomed man, came to the gate and offered his card of admission. This was not the Ades of two years ago, who felt sure of his client's innocence, nor was it the young man who vigorously denounced the Governor last week because of the Armwood lynching. It was a hopeless looking old man who answered to the name of Bernard Ades when the door swung open and he was permitted to enter. "I see you are here to the last, Mr. Ades," someone said. He made no reply but smiled sadly and passed into the lobby.
>
> As foot by foot of the weary last mile was covered by Euel Lee, the crowd outside made merry, even to the extent of eating peanuts and cracking many jokes. The white taxi driver who was reported to have come to the assistance of Patrolman Joseph Nemic, when the latter was being beaten by Frederick Combs, of Elder Alley, a few weeks ago, arrived and mingled with the crowd outside of the jail.
>
> A number of our people from the Communist Party stood quietly on the steps of a house just across the street from the main entrance of the penitentiary. One woman was asked by a reporter if she was sorry for Lee. "Of course," she said. "And this is not the end, either." When asked what would be the end, she smiled in a disarming way and added, "You will see and it won't be long either." Long after the trap of the hangman's scaffold had hurled Euel Lee into eternity, the crowd waited and shivered on the corners or loitered up and down the sidewalks. Many of them were waiting to see the body brought from the jail, some in order to make sure that the "N——" was dead, others to pay a last tribute of loyalty to "a brother of the crushed, working people."
>
> It was not brought out, however, and slowly the throng melted away, leaving the scene where the supreme penalty had been paid for the alleged killing of Green K. Davis and his family by a sixty-year old man, who went unflinchingly to his death.

From the *Sunpapers* report:

> A threatened Communist demonstration did not take place. Approximately 200 white and colored persons were gathered in the streets surrounding the prison, most of them standing opposite the main entrance of the penitentiary on Forrest street.
>
> Seventy policemen and a squad of detectives were on hand, under the direction of Commissioner Charles Gaither. Inspectors Steven G. Neise——, Thomas J. Mooney, Frank R. Gafe— and Captain John H. Miniens, of the detective Bureau, assisted him.

Lee's death certificate, Number E-94732 issued by the Health Department of Baltimore City, was signed by the medical examiner, John J. Aubrey, MD. Its stark contents were clinical and cold. It stated that Lee was a "Black Male-Single," with a date of birth noted as "1873?" and age noted as "60?" with a birthplace "unknown." The principal cause of death was noted as "Dislocation of 5th cervical vertebrae," and the entity providing the information for the certificate was noted as "Md. Pen."

So, it was done. It had taken two years and two weeks to finalize the quest for justice in the most difficult case the Eastern Shore and all of the state of Maryland had ever been exposed to. Yet it was finally over.

But there was yet another turn of events.

Ades promptly made an announcement that shocked even those who, in dealing with him, had thought that they had been exposed to all the twists he would muster: Lee's body would be sent to a funeral home on Druid Hill Avenue, in Baltimore City, and thereafter would be taken to Harlem, New York, where a public funeral would be held.

"Not so fast," said both Harold E. Donnell, superintendent of prisons, and Warden Patrick Brady—in accordance with Maryland law, Lee would be buried in a pauper's plot in a cemetery under contract to the State.

At this juncture, Ades produced what he claimed to be the last will and testament signed by Lee. This bizarre and remarkable document purported to will his body to one Bernard Ades!

"Lee's body is mine," said Ades. "I have Lee's written permission. His will gives me the body. I'm going to send it to New York tomorrow, it will be taken to a hall in Harlem, and a mass meeting will be held there tomorrow night."

Warden Brady was just as steadfast in his position. "Ades will not get the body. Under the law, if the hanged man has no immediate relatives, the warden is entirely responsible. We're going to give Lee a decent burial tomorrow, right here. Ades can't have the body. I'm in charge of it." The situation was further complicated when an organization of Negro women applied for the body and sent an undertaker's wagon to the penitentiary. A report soon circulated that members of a Communist organization were going to seize Lee's body when it was removed from the penitentiary. Therefore, a large contingent of police officers accompanied the body to an undertaking establishment in Druid Hill, which had been selected by prison officials. The wagon sent by the women was refused by Warden Brady and sent away. Ades placed a call to the attorney general's office to apply for assistance in retrieving the body. Deputy Attorney General Willis R. Jones consulted the statutes and ruled in favor of Brady's stance.

Ades, nevertheless, was determined to have custody of the body. On Friday, after the courts opened, he filed a petition citing the existence of the will and requesting a court order related to the disposition of the body. He also requested an injunction against the burial of the body. It was at this time that the will was produced. It stated simply, "I hereby will, devise and bequeath my dead body to Bernard Ades." It was signed, "Euel Lee." A hearing was immediately set by judge Eugene O'Dunne in the circuit court for Baltimore City. At the hearing, Deputy Attorney General Willis R. Jones argued the State's position, which was that, because Lee had no relatives, the duty of burying him fell upon Warden Patrick Brady in accordance with Maryland law. Judge O'Dunne thereupon inquired of Ades whether he knew anyone related to Lee. Ades replied in the negative. The judge then asked how long Ades had known Lee. "Two years," replied Ades, "and I have surely been a better friend to him than has the State of Maryland."

Attorney General Jones argued that the injunction should be denied, as the body of the convicted killer should not be allowed to lie in state. "We don't think this body should be used for demonstration purposes, and we don't know what will happen if it is allowed. Certainly, we don't want to be responsible."

Ades retorted that no demonstration was planned in New York, explaining only that "memorial services at which I and others will speak is scheduled in Harlem tonight. After that, the body would be buried." (In fact, Ades didn't plan just a mere demonstration—according to his daughter Janet, a Legal Aid attorney on Long Island, he intended to create a riot at the funeral in order to garner the most sensational press account of the event.)

"What's the idea of taking him up there, then?" asked Jones.

"Because there are a different kind of people up there," he replied. "I don't see why the State objects to something I might do or say in New York about the State of Maryland."

At this time, the good Reverend Powers stepped forward with yet another will, which he said had been signed by Lee and given to him at 9:00 p.m. on Thursday, about three hours before his execution. It read, "I wish the Reverend Edgar Cordell Powers to have charge of my body after my death. God will take care of my soul." One can speculate that Lee may have executed this second will so that the previous will produced by Ades would be nullified.

At this point in time, Judge O'Dunne recessed the hearing and ordered that it would reconvene at nine o'clock in the morning on Saturday. That evening, at 6:35 p.m., the doors of the funeral home of Bernard Hemsley, located in the 800 Block of Druid Hill Avenue, were thrown open. Hemsley had planned to begin the viewing at 7:00, but opened a half-hour early because a line of persons already extended over five hundred feet from the front door. In single-file the spectators' line reached from Moore Street to Biddle Street and then down Biddle a half-block. The *Sun* reported that over "8,000 Negroes filed by the casket to view Euel Lee's body."

XXXVI.

There is Nothing Further to Be Done

On Saturday morning, Judge O'Dunne was back in court with Jones and Ades. It didn't take him long to rule in the case. He based his decision on the "special jurisdiction that equity courts have over dead bodies." Whatever property the next of kin has in a dead body is not absolute, the judge held. It is subject to the trust relation of the equity court. Equity, he said, must act in the public interest in such a case to safeguard public health, public morals, public safety and public convenience. In view of Ades's confidential relationship with Lee as his client, Ades could not inherit the body in any case unless he could prove that he had not solicited the bequest. Ades, in his testimony, had admitted suggesting the will to Lee and drawing it up for him. Judge O'Dunne thereupon delivered his injunction from the bench:

> That the said Bernard Ades, claimant of the dead body of Euel Lee, is hereby restrained and permanently enjoined from interfering in any way with the body of said Euel Lee, or with the funeral or funeral arrangements of Patrick Brady, Warden of the Maryland Penitentiary regarding the burial of said body, before the burial of said body, as well as at the time of the burial of said body and after the burial of said body.

Judge O'Dunne's remarks from the bench, delivered orally, and without apparent pre-prepared written notes, are remarkable in their content. The *Daily Record*, the Warfield family legal newspaper, still published in the offices on Saratoga Street in downtown Baltimore in the year 2003, reported the judge's opinion in its October 30, 1933 edition:

> Gentlemen, for the purposes of the record, I may say this: That the petition in this case was presented to me by Mr. Ades, the petitioner, about 3 o'clock yesterday afternoon, when I was actually engaged in the work of drawing jurors from the wheel, which took about the whole afternoon. The arrangement was made to serve the Attorney-General's office with a copy of the petition before 3:30 P.M. which was only a half-hour, requiring him to answer the petition at or before 4 o'clock, coupled with my assent to give a hearing at 4 o'clock, or as close thereto as I could finish the drawing of the jury. The answer was promptly filed, as you know. The hearing was had a few minutes after 4 and testimony was taken and the will was produced and exhibited, and the circumstances of its execution testified to. At that time you also know that we did not have a stenographer present because of the lateness of the hour…Partly for that reason, I adjourned hearing until 9 A.M. today…I am frank to say that I think this is the first and only case we have had in the equity Court involving the question of a dead

body….Now, under ordinary circumstances, I do not think it can be said, as a matter of law, that a man cannot will his dead body to his lawyer. I will take an illustration to show just how I approach the question. Suppose a private citizen, a colored citizen, if you will, died of old age in this community, and he had no property, we will say, except a little plot of ground in old Virginia, where he first saw the light of day, where he was born and raised. I do think he would be entirely within the recognition of the law, if he saw fit to make a will to his lawyer, willing to him not only the little plot of ground but his dead body after death, with the directions that it was his wish that he wanted to be buried in old Virginia on the only little piece of ground that he ever owned, and asked his lawyer to carry out those instructions….Now, that is not this case…

This case is the case of Orphan Jones, or Euel Lee, who was executed in the Maryland Penitentiary as a convict of first-degree murder. He has twice been tried. [The judge then recounted the full legal proceedings involved in the matter.]

You have heard the testimony of Mr. Bernard Ades today and we recall it as of yesterday. It amounts in substance to this, if I correctly understand the testimony: That Mr. Ades was not asked and requested by this client of his, Mr. Euel Lee, to draw and prepare a will for him…The idea of preparation of the will originated in the mind of Mr. Ades and it was he who proposed going over to see Lee for the purpose of the execution. Mr. Ades says he took it over to Lee, asked him if he would sign it, read it to him and explained it to him, and asked him to execute it, and that Lee assented thereto….Now I take it that no lawyer would contend that if the subject matter of the will in this cases were property of value, that this will would be valid, because it is a well-known principle of law that any person standing in the confidential relation of attorney and client cannot be the beneficiary of his client's will, prepared and drawn by himself, unless the burden is cast upon him of showing affirmatively that it was the free and voluntary act and request of the deceased, and that it was reasonable and proper in its nature. The rule is founded on public policy and long experience; I declare this will to be void as a document executed in the confidential relationship which, under the presumption of law, invalidates it and the evidence adduced conclusively establishes the invalid nature of the instrument.

At the conclusion of his remarks from the bench, Judge O'Dunne gave the following instructions to Sheriff Joseph C. Deegan of Baltimore City:

It may be necessary for you to not only serve this restraining order but to see to it that it is literally respected and obeyed. I know from your past faithful and conscientious performance of your duties of your office that no directions from this court are necessary in the execution of its mandate. However, in view of the recent exhibition of the failure of the state constabulary, armed as they were, to understand the object of their creation and the purpose for which they are sent out for the enforcement of law and order, against mob violence if interposed, I need hardly remind you of the authority of the Sheriff in case of need to summon the entire citizenship of the community, as the posse comitatus, and compel them to act for all intents and purposes as deputy sheriffs, in case of need, in the preservation of law and order, and that side arms are not provided to the State Constabulary as a sex stimulant on the feminine mind of the fair daughters of the "Free State," but they are made to shoot with, and not intended as mere official ornament and decoration; that three or more persons engaged in common in resistance of the law, to the public disturbance, constitute a riot; that in suppression of a riot, if justified in shooting to preserve authority and suppress disorder, you are also justified in shooting to kill. The constituted authority of the State, including the police force of Baltimore City, are at your command in the execution of your duties and in carrying out the mandates of this court, and you are expected to use them if and when it becomes necessary.

The judge had made it very plain—no Communist or any other person had better interfere with the intended burial of Euel Lee.

After the judge read his order, Sheriff Deegan went immediately to Mr. Hemsley's funeral home and retrieved the body of Euel Lee. A hearse was waiting. A crowd of several hundred African Americans was present, but no demonstration was made, as if the judge's statement had been publicized to the crowd beforehand.

The hearse proceeded slowly through the streets of Baltimore, headed out to the cemetery in Anne Arundel County just south of Brooklyn in the Curtis Bay area, known as Mount Cavalry Cemetery, one of the oldest African American cemeteries in the metropolitan area. The hearse was escorted by motorcycle police, Sheriff Deegan, under-sheriff Francis Tormollan and seven deputies. At the wind-swept cemetery, located on a hilly prominence in a black neighborhood of Brooklyn, the Reverend Powers read a funeral service at the hastily dug grave. The burial was witnessed by Warden Brady as well as the assembled deputies and about fifty black residents of the neighborhood.

Waiting at the site of the grave was Sheriff Glenn Prout of Anne Arundel County, in whose jurisdiction the cemetery was sited. Sheriff Prout had gathered twenty-two Anne Arundel deputies, six uniformed Baltimore policemen recruited by Inspector Stephen G. Nelson, three state policemen and four uniformed Glen Burnie policemen. They were there because of a rumor that a band of men was going to remove the body from its grave on the forlorn hillside. All that cold windy October night, Sheriff Prout sat in his car near the grave, as his various officers, armed to the teeth, huddled around a bonfire built to ward off the chill of the breezy night. The only incident reported, however, was during the afternoon of the burial, when three unidentified well-dressed women drove into the cemetery and placed a wreath on the unmarked grave.

In its November 4 edition, though, the *Afro-American* reported:

Although Judge Eugene O'Dunne ordered Sheriff Deegan to shoot to kill any persons who attempted to molest the body of the late Euel Lee, who was hanged in the Maryland penitentiary, after Communists threatened to steal his body, the order did not prevent white vandals not Communistically inclined, from sabotage in the Mt. Calvary Cemetery Saturday night and Sunday.

A throng of white curiosity seekers disturbed the peace and quiet of the burying place on Sunday according to Mrs. Frances Brooks who lives at Moss Hill and also declares that some of those on watch shot craps over Lee's grave. Mrs. Brooks declared that an all-day crowd of ofays [defined in Webster's dictionary as "Slang, disparaging and offensive, a white person"] was permitted to enter the graveyard and wander about the place at random while members of the race were not allowed within a hundred feet of the Lee place of burial. Mrs. Brooks says she counted as many as sixty cars of whites which were allowed to enter in spite of the fact that it is a strictly colored cemetery.

As much as twenty-five dollars worth of damage has been done, according to Mrs. Brooks, because the policemen were alleged to have pulled up the identification stakes of many graves and burned them for firewood while keeping an all-night vigil over the grave of Lee. The identification stakes or markers are in the form of a cross and are above each lot. In the absence of tombstones these serve as the principal marks by which relatives and friends identify the last resting places of the dead.

No other newspaper reported any such events. One is called upon the speculate as to whether Mrs. Brooks was exaggerating or whether the other newspapers simply didn't consider the event noteworthy of reporting, due to the fact that it was the African American community that was adversely affected.

When he had been confronted with the blunt contents of Judge O'Dunne's injunction, Bernard Ades had simply said, "There is nothing further to be done." He was at last, finished.

On October 30, 1933, the county sheriff's deputies and state police officers were removed from guarding Lee's grave. All that remained of the large original contingent of officers were three Baltimore City police officers with riot guns. Soon, they too would be withdrawn to allow the wind and the grass to obliterate the unmarked resting place of Orphan Jones from view, from the writings of the press, and from the public consciousness.

At long last, the souls of Green, Ivy, Elizabeth and Mary Lee Davis were at rest.

Epilogue

Euel Lee, alias Orphan Jones, was buried in a forlorn grave on the wind-swept hillside of an African American cemetery in Brooklyn, Maryland, just north of the present-day location of the busy Baltimore beltway, and east of the highway named for Governor Albert C. Ritchie. His gravesite today, seventy years later, remains unmarked and forgotten, except in the cemetery records of the venerable and historic cemetery known as Mt. Calvary. On a cold, blustery day in November 2000, I journeyed to the cemetery to seek the location of Lee's resting place. The groundskeeper met me there and advised that the location of the grave, and in fact, Lee's identity among the interred, was unknown but would be available in the cemetery records. The next week, a journey back revealed the location of the grave—unmarked in an area down the east side of the hilly cemetery next to a family gravesite that is marked by conventional monuments. It was not, as had been speculated by the groundskeeper, in the paupers' area of the cemetery, amidst choking weeds and overgrown bushes along the western foot of the hill, but was located in the kept-up area of the cemetery, surely because of the need for the law enforcement officers' observation of the site when the body was interred in 1933. Euel Lee's resting place was not even monumented by the Communists who had made him a prominent symbol of racial oppression. Once buried, he was, indeed, forgotten.

After the death of the Green Davis family, a sad event is documented in the chancery records of the circuit court for Worcester County: Banker Calvin B. Taylor filed a foreclosure on the modest farm, which was then sold at public auction. The property was purchased by Dr. Orwin E. Howe, a Washington, D.C. physician, for the sum of $3,000. It was reported in the press that the bidding was "spirited," as there were several would-be purchasers. It was also reported in the press account that the sale was a sore disappointment to Mrs. Nellie Jennings of Bridgeville, Delaware, who had written to Berlin officials on several occasions that the "spirits of the Green Davis family wanted her to have the property."

The Green Davis homesite has long since vanished, replaced by a trailer park on what is now a side road on the way to Ocean City. Bustling U.S. Route 50 is located within sight, but few people know about the original home where the heinous crime occurred. I spent some time in the home during my high school years in the 1950s, totally unaware that I was attending a party in the locale of the most sensational crime in the history of my native Worcester County.

Green Davis, Ivy and their two daughters lie at rest in the Bishopville Cemetery in a well-tended plot that jars the senses of a visitor by the four separate gravestones with the same date of death.

Epilogue

The home of Charles Johnson, the neighbor who found the bodies, although abandoned, is still existent, as is the house of little Jack Fisher, one of the witnesses in the trial. The Berlin soda fountain in which young Charles Lynch received the phone call from the murder scene is still in business (as "Rayne's Reef") and Dr. Holland's home and office is still there (now a bed and breakfast known as "The Holland House"); the magistrate's office in Berlin now houses a realtor's office and the route from Berlin to Snow Hill traverses a new and relocated Route 113, although, as a side road, part of old 113 still exists near Newark, where, it is said by the old folks, lies the precise location where the deputies stopped and beat Lee, on the trip to the jail that first night of his arrest.

Godfrey Child, the Worcester County State's Attorney, had been born in Stockton, in the southern part of the county, in 1894. He was elected State's Attorney in 1928 and served two terms. He also maintained a private practice of law in Pocomoke since 1920, and served as attorney to the Worcester County Commissioners, and as city solicitor for Pocomoke City.

Judge Child, it is said by the elderly folks in Worcester County, was deprived of a sterling political career because of the unforgiving memory of the citizens and voters of the county, who failed to understand the legal circumstances surrounding his inability to push the trial of Euel Lee to a speedy conclusion. He later, however, became the first resident judge of the circuit court in Worcester County, being appointed in 1959, serving with quiet distinction and becoming venerated throughout the county. One quirk remained throughout his life: he refused to conduct any business on any Friday the thirteenth, electing instead to stay in bed in his Pocomoke City home.

He retired from the bench in 1964. I remember him, after he retired, as a gentle and elegant addition to the Worcester County Bar Association meetings in the late 1960s. He died November 25, 1977, and is buried in the Pitts Creek Church Cemetery in Pocomoke City.

On November 28, 1933, Governor Albert Ritchie ordered a contingent from the Maryland National Guard, stationed at the Fifth Regiment Armory in Baltimore, to Salisbury for the stated purpose of securing the arrest of nine men accused of being leaders in the Armwood lynch mob. The city came under virtual military occupation. Four of the men were taken to Baltimore with the guardsmen and locked up in the Baltimore city jail. The military-type action ordered by the governor infuriated the populace of the shore. Hundreds of stickers and signs appeared consisting of the initials NRA!—standing for "Never Ritchie Again!" At least as a partial result of this action, Governor Ritchie lost the next election for his fourth term as governor to Republican Harry Nice. Ritchie had enjoyed such heightened popularity in the early thirties, his name was mentioned as a presidential candidate, and he campaigned for the Democratic nomination against Roosevelt in 1932. Indeed, Roosevelt offered him the vice-presidency in that year. Ritchie died suddenly and unexpectedly of a cerebral hemorrhage at the age of fifty-nine in Baltimore on February 24, 1936, and is buried at Greenmount Cemetery.

Herbert O'Conor, the State's Attorney of Baltimore City, became governor of the state of Maryland in 1939, and served until 1947 when he was elected to the United States Senate. He died in Baltimore on March 4, 1960. He is buried in New Cathedral Cemetery.

When his term ended in 1934, William Preston Lane, the attorney general, did not run on the Richie ticket for re-election, stepping aside because he felt he was a liability due to of his association with the "military expedition" to Salisbury to seek arrest of the Armwood lynchers. He bided his time, however, and, after Herbert O'Conor retired as governor to serve in the Senate, Lane ran for the Democratic gubernatorial nomination against H. Street Baldwin, a Baltimore County boss, and Controller J. Millard Tawes, an Eastern Shoreman from Crisfield, in Somerset County, in the election of 1946 and became governor of the state of Maryland. Lane took office early by appointment of the legislature in 1947 when O'Conor was sworn into the Senate, served one term, and was defeated on his try for a second term by the popular mayor of Baltimore, Theodore McKeldin. Lane died in Hagerstown on February 7, 1967. He is buried at Rose Hill Cemetery in Hagerstown.

Judge Robert Duer of Somerset County had been on the bench since 1917, and, although accused by the metropolitan press as aspiring to higher office, remained a circuit court judge until his retirement in 1934. Robert Duer died on January 5, 1958. His son, E. McMaster Duer was elected State's Attorney for Somerset County and later became the judge of the circuit court in Somerset County in 1952, and by the time he retired had become the chief judge of the First Judicial Circuit. He died on September 13, 1993. Father and son are buried at St. Andrews Episcopal Church Cemetery at Princess Anne, just down the street from the scene of the Armwood lynching.

Henry L. Mencken remained with the Baltimore *Sunpapers* throughout his journalistic career. He never got over his contempt for the Eastern Shore. During his career, he wrote several manuscripts, which he bequeathed in his will to the Enoch Pratt Library in Baltimore. One of these was entitled *Thirty-Five Years of Newspaper Work*, which, under the terms of his will, remained sealed until thirty-five years after his death. The manuscript was finally published in January 1991. (Mencken died on January 29, 1956.) Interestingly, in the book, edited by Fred Hobson, Vincent Fitzpatrick and Bradford Jacobs, Mencken writes of the events in this story. On page 210 of the published version, he describes his involvement in the furor caused by the publication of "The Eastern Shore Kultur."

My contributions to the editorial page of the Evening Sun *in 1931 were mainly of small importance for I was already beginning to lose interest in both the page and my job…nevertheless, I helped, in December, to lead the* Sunpapers *into a row which raged savagely for years afterward, and still [in 1942] has repercussions. The uproar followed a lynching in Salisbury, on the Eastern Shore of Maryland, on December 4—the first lynching in the State for twenty years. The gentleman hanged and burned was a blackamoor named Matthew Williams, and he well deserved his fate, for he had murdered his employer, a white man named Daniel J. Elliott, in a barbaric manner. Nor were the people of Salisbury without some excuse, at least by their lights, in taking the law into their own hands, for another atrocious murder on the Shore, performed by a Negro named Euel Lee some time before, was still unavenged, and the intervention of various highly dubious busybodies, including some Jewish Communists in Baltimore, made it seem likely that the culprit would escape the gallows for a long while, despite the fact that he had twice confessed. But though I was more or less sympathetic with the lynchers in the specific case I was strongly against them in general, and with them the whole Eastern Shore scheme of things. For some years past, I had actually been proposing that the Shore be detached from Maryland, and joined with Delaware and the Eastern Shore of Virginia in a new state called Delmarva…I therefore seized the chance that the butchering of Williams provided for whooping up the scheme, and on December 7 printed on the editorial page, "The Eastern Shore Kultur," an article which made every Eastern Shoreman, at least below the Choptank River, my sworn enemy forever…For weeks afterward I was denounced violently in every country paper south of the Choptank, and from almost every pulpit. The main charge was that I was an apologist for drunkards, whores and murderers, but there were also correlative charges that I was both a Communist and a German spy…To this day, in fact, I am persona non grata there, to put it mildly, and so recently as March 1942, Paul Palmer found I was still remembered and detested in Ocean City, which is on the ocean front about 25 miles from Salisbury. Inasmuch as I have no desire to be admired by morons I let the Shoremen howl.*

Mencken also honed in on the effort of Governor Ritchie to bring the Princess Anne lynchers to justice, commenting (on page 234 of *Thirty Five Years*) on the arrest of the four alleged ringleaders by the state police, aided by the Maryland militia, at Salisbury:

After the show was over, Ritchie employed Pinkerton detectives to track down the lynchers, and in a little while four of them were collared and brought to Baltimore—a druggist named William H. Thompson, who was the leader of the mob; Irving Atkins [Adkins], one of the town constables; William S. McQuade, a chain-store clerk from the nearby town of Pocomoke City; and William P Hearn, a truck driver from the hamlet of Shad Point…Unhappily, it [the arrests] came to nothing, for a local judge eager for higher office, Robert F. Duer by name, ordered the four suspects—they were obviously guilty—brought before him on a writ of Habeas Corpus, and released them for "lack of evidence." A curious feature of the whole uproar was that public opinion in Baltimore seemed to be predominately on the side of the lynchers; in fact I got more threatening letters from city people than from the simians of the Lower Shore itself.

Thus Henry Mencken, who had excoriated the shore and its lynchings with righteous indignation, acknowledged a decade later that he had, in fact, sympathized with the events, but admitted that he had used the story to further the reading public's acceptance of his prejudice and resentment toward the Eastern Shore.

State policeman Carroll Serman—one of the officers who stood heroically before the mob—was injured by the battering ram at the Somerset jailhouse door during the Armwood lynching, and was, indeed, severely injured. His name was erroneously reported in the newspaper account as "Clyde." He later became a sitting magistrate in Worcester County, where he lived at Public Landing, a village near Snow Hill. He was later elected sheriff for Worcester County and served ably, but he retained a limp resulting from his injuries all his life. I knew Sheriff Serman well, but didn't realize, until his daughter Pat advised me, that he had been involved in the historical events of this story.

After the four accused lynchers of George Armwood had traveled to Baltimore in the National Guard convoy, Somerset Sheriff Luther Daugherty, armed with a writ of habeas corpus signed by Judge Robert Duer, motored to Baltimore and removed them from the Baltimore city jail, and took them to Princess Anne. On November 29, 1933, they were brought before Chief Judge John R. Pattison, who found that State's Attorney John Robins had filed no charges. He thereupon dismissed the case (to the tumultuous cheer of all those assembled), and a Somerset County grand jury failed to return any indictments against the accused. The Somerset County courthouse, unlike those in Worcester and Wicomico, which each have been expanded several times, is precisely the same as it was in 1933, when George Armwood was hanged and then immolated nearby. The Somerset County jail from which Armwood was dragged to be hanged still stands stoically on a quiet and peaceful side street in Princess Anne, two blocks from the courthouse, and now used by the Princess Anne police department.

Not one person was ever indicted or charged for the lynch murder of Matthew Williams on the Wicomico County courthouse lawn on December 4, 1931. The courthouse is still in use, although greatly expanded. On the spot reputed as the lynching location and denoted by a large arrow in photos of Salisbury in the *Afro-American* edition of December 12, 1931, a venerable old tree still exists.

Bernard Ades was the subject of a disbarment proceeding in the federal courts in 1934. Judge Morris Soper presided. Ades was represented by Dr. Charles H. Houston, dean of Howard University Law School, and later-to-become Supreme Court Justice Thurgood Marshall—the first time in the history of Maryland that black lawyers had ever represented a white lawyer. (Ades's daughter, Janet, remarked that when she talked to her father about this, he invariably referred to the later-to-be justice as "young Thurgood.") The U.S. district court for the District of Maryland declined to disbar Ades, but wrote a scathing opinion (reported as "*In re Ades*" in the Federal Reports at 6 F. Supp. 467):

> *The respondent, however, has gone to such extremes of action and statement in some respects as to merit the condemnation of the court. After all his efforts on behalf of Lee had failed, he brought an action against the warden of the Maryland penitentiary on the day after the execution had taken place in order to require the delivery of Lee's body to him. He filed with the papers in the case a will of the deceased, executed the day before his death, in which the deceased bequeathed his body to Ades. The latter testified that the idea of such a will originated with him, and that it was his purpose to take the body to New York city for a memorial service to be held in Harlem under the auspices of the International Labor Defense so as to show that Euel Lee was in fact innocent and that in his case there had been a "legal lynching" by the officials of Maryland; that the purpose was not to stir up race prejudice, but to show that the State of Maryland oppresses the colored race and does not recognize their legal rights. It was also brought up that Ades did not tell Lee of the intended disposition of his body, and that after signing the will, Lee also signed a statement requesting that the chaplain of the penitentiary have charge of the body after death and had expressed a desire that there be no spectacle made either of his death or his funeral. [The will is existent in the Maryland Hall of Records.] The petition in this case was dismissed after hearing, and Ades himself was enjoined from interfering with the body…His conduct was not merely offensive to every instinct of good taste. It was to a high degree, reprehensible in that he withheld from Lee the real purpose that he had in mind in obtaining the body…He has to his credit, however, [ensured] that actions of the trial court detrimental to the defendant in the Lee*

Epilogue

case were corrected, because they were regarded as improper, not merely by him or by the organization which employed him, but by the Court of Appeals of Maryland…Much that is blameworthy in the respondent's conduct carries its own antidote, for no one can succeed at the bar who comports himself as he has done.

Ades was suspended from the practice of law in the federal courts for five months, awaiting the evidentiary hearing on the disciplinary issues. The order of the court was that he be publicly reprimanded.

In 1934, he ran as the Communist Party candidate for governor of Maryland, and even though the office of the Maryland secretary of state recorded a nomination petition containing 2,465 signatures, he only garnered about 800 votes.

He later fought in the Washington and Lincoln Brigades in the Spanish Civil War in the late 1930s. According to his daughter, Janet, the family was ostracized and had to leave Baltimore for Washington, where Ades worked as a government auditor. Congressman Thomas D'Alesandro, later mayor of Baltimore, upon finding out that Ades held a government job, saw to it that he was fired, and the family moved to the Bronx, where Ades practiced as an accountant, maintaining an office at 505 Fifth Avenue. He died on May 27, 1984, in New York. His obituary in the *New York Times* stated: "He represented black defendants in Maryland, winning their right to unsegregated jury panels, and to obtain counsel through organizations." He is buried at the Cemetery of Baltimore Hebrew Congregation.

The obituary also noted that his survivors included "a daughter, Janet." With the aid of the Internet, I tracked Janet down at an address in a Legal Aid office on Long Island. I wrote to her and advised her of my quest. She responded, and we began a correspondence that led to a visit by her to Worcester County in 2001. She arrived with another attorney from her office, and we spent most of a week together. [One of the evenings we spent together was a dinner with my wife, Susan, and other guests at the Atlantic Hotel in Berlin. As we entered the front door, by chance we encountered Judge Alfred T. Truitt, from Salisbury, who, as a small child of five or six, had witnessed part of the Salisbury lynching of Williams. I introduced Janet as the daughter of the lawyer who represented Euel Lee. Without a pause, the judge said, "My goodness, honey, you're not a Communist too, are you?]

During her visit, I took her to all the sites of her father's travails in the county. We arrived in the county seat of Snow Hill on a stiflingly hot day and typically, the town was still and quiet. We stood in front of the courthouse where Brimer's luncheonette had been located in 1931, and the building, although empty, is still there. I pointed out to her the location of her father's automobile on Washington Street in front of the Methodist Church, the exact location of the mob attack upon him, and showed her the location of the jail in which Ades and Helen Mays had been housed to protect them from the presence of the mob. Janet stood there for a long, silent moment and then said, "So, this is Snow Hill. I have been terrified of this place for my entire life, because of what my father told me happened here."

We then visited the courtroom where Ades first interjected himself into the defense of Lee, and she met with two of the present judges of the First Circuit, Judge Theodore Eschenburg and retired Judge Lloyd "Hot Dog" Simpkins from Somerset County, both of whom were familiar with the facts of the case, although from a historical perspective only. Before she left the area, Janet advised me of many of the difficulties Ades's politics had caused her family. She stated to me: "I loved my father, but I detested his politics." She has absolutely no use for the Communists, calling them, very forthrightly, "those bastards."

Later, after she had sent me the archives records involving Ades, I inquired of her whether she had read the confessions that had been reproduced in their entirety. Her response cinched my conclusion that Euel Lee had, indeed, committed the crime. Her reply: "Why should I bother? My father told me he was guilty."

Statement of Orphan Jones
October 13, 1931

T he following Statement was made on Tuesday, October 13, 1931, at 2:00 p.m. at Snow Hill, Maryland, in the presence of John H. Farlow of Salisbury, Maryland; W.R. Purnell, chief of police, Snow Hill, Maryland; Lieutenant Joseph H. Itzel of Baltimore; Sheriff Wilmer S. Purnell of Snow Hill, Maryland; Robert Allen, chief of police of Ocean City, Maryland; State's Attorney Godfrey Child; and Corporal M.D. Brubaker of the Maryland State Police.

MR. CHILD:

Q: Jones, we want you to tell us all about the shooting of these four people on Saturday night or Sunday morning but we have nothing to promise you if you tell us and we have nothing to threaten you with if you don't tell us and if you make a statement I want it all to be the truth. Under these circumstances are you willing to make a statement?

A: Yes sir.

Q: You are willing to tell us the truth regardless of the fact that what you might tell us might be used against you?

A: I am going to tell you the truth. I don't know what time it was, anyhow, it was on Saturday night I went up to the Davis' place—I had been drinking and I taken my handbag and my gun.

Q: You mean your pistol?

A: My gun too, and a lot of shells, a Winchester Pump gun, and I shoots Mr. Davis and his wife and his children. I takes the cigar box of money. I had $30.00 of my own money and the rest of it belonged to him and the change was in the pouch. I takes these things down to where I stayed and I come back Sunday night and I feeds his stock and watered them and throwed corn out for the chickens the next morning. I left the door not fastened, just pulled it to. I have the key to the little store and I goes down there and packs up a lot of things in a basket I got out of a corn crib and I leaves it there—it is there now. Nobody was with me, I did it all myself. I am sorry. The man was good to me. The whiskey caused me to commit the worst crime ever been in the history of the world.

Q: Why did you kill this man?

A: I don't know except it was mean whiskey and the devil in me. He never done nothing to me, he was a kind man.

Q: When did you first plan to do it?

A: Must have been Saturday night because I came out there Saturday and done it Sunday morning just before day, just light enough to see them in their room.

Q: Do you remember throwing any coal oil over the place?

A: No, sir.

Q: You don't remember doing that?

A: No, sir. No lamp exploded up there did it? I did not leave no lamp burning, not that I can remember. I remember everything I done because after I did it I was awful sorry and was afraid too.

By Mr. Itzel:

Q: Jones was any of the bed clothing afire anytime you were there?

A: Yes, sir, from the gun. Must have been from the gun because I put out the fire.

Q: Was it a small blaze or a smother?

A: Just a smother in the cotton or wool.

Q: You did the shooting with a pump gun?

A: I shot that gun until it hung up with me.

Q: Who did you shoot with it?

A: I think Mr. Davis.

Q: Anyone else?

A: And his wife.

Q: What did you use when you shot the two girls?

A: I think I must have used my revolver because I did not have but two more bullets in it.

Q: What caliber revolver is it?

A: Colt D.A. 41.

Q: After the shooting what did you do with the pump gun and pistol?

A: Taken them and fastened them up like I brought them and put the pistol in the handbag.

Q: Did you take them back to your room?

A: Yes, sir and then Monday I cleaned them—went and got a gallon of oil and cleaned them.

Q: Where were you when you cleaned them?

A: Right across from this man's place.

Q: Did you not have some difficulty with Mr. Davis about a dollar in your pay?

A: I will tell you how it was. When I went there he promised to give me $2.75 a day, that is, if I boarded myself and he boarded me $1.75. I worked there I suppose about 14 or 15 days and he gave me some money every Saturday night. $8.50, but when he come to settle up I claimed he owed me $12.00 and he said it was only eleven days and he only owed me $11.00. I said, "you owe me twelve." He said, "I don't think so." I did not say no more about it and when I was going down the road home I come to Mr. Lewis' place. He said, "Hello." I said "Hello." He said, "where are you going?" I said, "Ocean City." He said, "are you done work at Green's now?" I said, "no he has got some more corn for me to cut in two weeks." I said, "I don't know, I guess I will get even with him and not cut the corn" then I said, "he is a good old scout" and I went on. On Thursday when I come back to bring some clothes to get them washed I meets Mr. Davis, he had been hauling sand and he said "hello, Orphan." He said, "How are you getting along?" I said, "all right." He said, "I want you to come up Thursday or Friday and start cutting corn." That was the last time I laid eyes on him until I shot him. I told him I would be up. How come me to shoot him I cannot say only the devil got in me.

Q: After you shot Mr. & Mrs. Davis, did that awaken the two girls?

A: They were lying down when I shot in there just like their father and mother. I was looking for them to be up.

Q: When you left your own house or your room you took your shotgun and pistol with you?

A: Yes, sir.

Q: Were you planning then to go to the house and kill these people?

A: No, sir, my plan was to go down to James A. Long's who lives down to Western, Maryland and when I come by there half drunk I got the devil in me and goes on up to the house—my intention was to wait until he got up and ask him about cutting the corn. He was a man that snored loud and when I heard him snoring the devil jumped in me and I shot them all.

Q: Did you touch any of the bodies after you killed them?

A: No, sir.

Q: Are you sure about that?

A: Yes, sir. I don't remember touching no bodies.

Q: Try to think back now, if you did?

A: When I put out that fire.

Q: Do you remember any clothing laying around there?

A: No, sir.

Q: How old are you?

A: I was born in 1872. Will be 60 years old my next birthday.

Q: Do you remember anything about the coal oil?

A: No, sir. He asked me about that.

Q: Can you account for all the bed clothing lying on the floor?

A: They were searching them.

Q: Can you account for all the clothing, bed clothing and other clothes lying on the floor being saturated with coal oil?

A: No, sir.

Q: When the lamp exploded—you said the lamp exploded?

A: That caused the fire or the gun, I don't know which. It wasn't a lamp, it was one of his gasoline lights. When I went back up there it was out.

Q: There wasn't no fire?

A: No, sir.

Q: You don't recall saturating anything with coal oil?

A: No, sir.

Q: What did you want with the money if you had $30.00?

A: Just natural devil and a thief that is all. I knew where it was. I knew it was in a cigar box.

Q: Did you have any immediate use for that money?

A: No, sir.

Q: Any big bills coming due that you needed it?

A: No, sir. If I needed money I could have come to Mr. Davis and he would have advanced me money before I cut his corn. He was good to me.

Q: Was the front door unlocked?

A: Yes, sir.

Q: Did you go through that door?

A: He never locked that door day and night.

Q: You went in there and immediately went up stairs?

A: Yes, sir.

Q: Did you drink anything in Davis' home while you were searching?

A: Yes, sir.

Q: What did you drink?

A: Got out some wine. She had given me some before, it was in a closet.

Q: In the kitchen?

A: No, sir up stairs.

Q: Did you drink that wine after you shot these people?

A: Yes, sir.

Q: And that wine was on the second floor in one of the bedrooms?

A: Yes, sir in one of the little preserve jars and I put a handkerchief over it and drank through that to strain it.

Q: Where was the cigar box?

A: Sitting on the dresser.

Q: In the old man's room?

A: Yes, sir and a pouch.

Q: What was in the cigar box?

A: Money.

Q: How much?

A: About $50.00.

Q: What else?

A: That was all. The change was in the pouch, nickels and dimes.

Q: Where was the jewelry?

A: In a jewelry box on the table.

Q: In the same room?

A: No, sir in the girl's room.

Q: When you had the articles and the money, what did you do with them?

A: Put them in the handbag.

Q: Where is the handbag?

A: I think he has it. Haven't you Mr. Child?

By Mr. Child:

Q: Orphan you say this was your pump gun?

A: Yes, sir.

Q: Where did you get it?

A: I bought it in Baltimore, the same place I bought my revolver.

Q: What place?

A: I don't even know the street but it was where they sell a lot of fruit, people come there with wagons.

By Mr. Itzel:

Q: Is it Market place?

A: Yes, sir. There is only two Jews there you can pond *[pawn]* stuff.

Q: How much did you pay for the gun?

A: $29.50.

Q: How long ago did you buy it?

A: It was in May.

Q: This past May?

A: Yes, sir.

Q: How much did you pay for the pistol?

A: $15.00

Q: Did you buy it at the same place?

A: Yes, sir but not at the same time.

Q: How long ago did you buy that?

A: I had that pistol about ten years. I got it off some guy that came from the army. I bought the revolver in 1920 or '22.

Q: What money did you use when you bought the shot gun?

A: My own money and also the revolver.

By Mr. Child:

Q: When you left home on Saturday afternoon with that gun and pistol with you, was the gun put together?

A: No, sir I took it apart and wrapped it up with paper.

Q: That is when you started out from home?

A: Yes, sir.

Q: Where were you when you put the gun together?

A: Right there by the little fruit stand. There is some benches and tables there, I set down there and put it together.

Q: That is about two hundred yards from Mr. Green Davis' house, isn't it?

A: Yes, sir.

Q: Why did you put it together in back of that fruit stand?

A: To keep anybody from seeing me.

Q: Had you planned then to go in and shoot Mr. Davis?

A: No, sir not then.

Q: Why did you put this gun together?

A: I was going to put it up. He needed me to cut the other corn. I generally go there and work on Sunday anyhow, pick tomatoes and beans, whatever anybody wanted. I would go down in the field and get watermelons.

Q: You were going to wake him up about three o'clock in the morning to ask him about cutting corn?

A: It wasn't three o'clock.

Q: What time was it?

A: Getting light. When I went up there and heard him snoring I got the gun and shot him.

Q: Did you take the gun apart?

A: Yes, sir.

Q: Where did you do that?

A: In the same place.

Q: After you had shot all four of them?

A: Yes, sir.

By MR. ITZEL:

Q: Did you ever carry that gun there before?

A: Yes, sir. Mr. Davis used to keep that gun there to watch the watermelon patch and used to keep the revolver. When I first went there I gave him the revolver to keep. When I left Mr. James A. Long's some colored named Archie had stole my gun and Mr. Long made him go get it and I left it there because I said that man would steal something and say I was with him and I told Mr. Long I did not want to stay there because Archie was there.

Q: You left something in the store, did you not?

A: Basket with cigars, peanut candy, chewing gum and Mr. Davis' shoes.

Q: Did you collect all that stuff in the store and put it in the basket?

A: Up to the house I got the towels and put them in there.

Q: Why did you take them with you?

A: To throw the suspicion on someone else.

Q: You left it there to show suspicion on someone else?

A: Yes, sir.

Q: What did you do with the key?

A: Throwed it down in the road.

Q: How far away from the store?

A: From here to those people standing out there—about 100 yards, right in the rut. It had a brass piece on the end with a hole in each end.

Q: Where did you get the key?

A: I used to keep that key. I would go down there and open up and put out everything. He never asked me for it when I left and I had it. There was two of them.

Appendix 1

By Mr. Child:

Q: About how long did you work for Mr. Green Davis?

A: I think somewhere in the middle of September.

Q: Did you sleep in the house when you come there?

A: Yes, sir in the front room where the pump is.

By Mr. Itzel:

Q: Did you sleep on the floor?

A: Yes, sir I had two horse blankets and another blanket and some rugs. He was going to get me a mattress.

Q: Where are you from?

A: From Maryland.

Q: Where were you born?

A: East [*sic*] Virginia.

Q: How long have you been in Maryland?

A: I came here in 1901 and worked at Sparrows Point, Maryland.

Q: Were you ever married?

A: No, Sir.

Q: Where are your folks, do you have any relatives?

A: No, sir, that is the reason they call me Orphan Jones. White people raised me and they are all dead now.

Q: Do you assume this entire responsibility?

A: Yes, sir.

Q: Are you alone responsible for this crime?

A: Nobody else but me.

Q: If you are not, we want you to tell us.

A: I would not tell a lie. Nobody responsible but me alone.

Q: Did you use any other instrument, did you use an ax or a hatchet in addition to shooting them?

A: No, sir. The gun was fully loaded. I don't know how many times I shot and I loaded it again. She hung up on me and I took the revolver and the gentlemen said the balls out of the gun was in them people.

Q: Who did you shoot first, Mr. Davis?

A: Yes, sir, he was in the front of the bed.

Q: And then you shot his wife?

A: Yes, sir.

Q: Did you reload the gun?

A: She shoots six times.

Q: You had four good shots in it?

A: I don't know how many times I shot them before I went in the other room. I pushed the door open and the girls had not got up and I shot and the gun hung up and I taken the revolver.

Q: You think you used the pump gun in the girls' room too?

A: Yes, sir

Q: Did it go off?

A: Yes, sir.

Q: But you did shoot both of them with the revolver?

A: Yes, sir I think so.

Q: You know where you shot these two girls with the revolver?

A: No, sir. Just aimed over and shot them.

Q: I mean with the revolver.

A: I shot at their head, just the same as I had the parents. I am going to tell the truth.

Q: Both the girls are shot right over the heart, now you must have been sober enough to take that aim?

A: I did not say real staggering drunk, but just had enough whiskey to make you mean, no good, a murderer.

Q: But you were sober enough to take that aim?

A: Yes, sir or I could not shoot them people like that.

Q: On the way to the house Jones when you came from your room did you meet anyone on the road you know?

A: Not coming up.

Q: Did you meet Mr. Robert Davis or Mr. Levin Baker?

A: I don't know them. If I met anyone I did not know their names.

Q: Did you meet a Mr. Lewis?

A: Yes, sir I passed by his place.

Q: Did you see Mr. Lewis?

A: Yes, sir.

Q: That was after the crime?

A: Yes, sir and I had the handbag.

Q: What did you say?

A: He said, "Hello, where are you going?" I said "Down to Ocean City" and just what he said to me I cannot recall. That is all I remember.

Q: Does he know you?

A: Yes, sir. Just the same as I know this officer here now.

Q: Did you have your handbag with you then?

A: Yes, sir.

Q: You had already put the basket in the store?

A: Yes, sir.

Q: You did not meet anyone going toward the place?

A: I would not like to say. I know I did not meet nobody walking and nobody said anything to me but Mr. Lewis.

Q: Was Mr. Lewis walking?

A: No, sir he was at his porch.

Q: How far is Mr. Lewis' home from Mr. Davis'?

A: I would say five hundred yards.

Q: This was Monday morning?

Appendix 1

A: No, sir Sunday morning.

Q: Now you went back again Monday?

A: Sunday night and fed the stock and I did not leave there until Monday morning.

Q: How long did you hang around there?

A: All night.

Q: Where did you sleep?

A: Did not sleep, just waited up there in the store. That is the reason I packed the things in the basket and locked the store.

Q: Locked yourself in there?

A: No, sir you cannot lock yourself in there. I drank soda pop in there and packed the basket and left it in there.

Q: Did you go into the house proper, where the people were?

A: No, sir because I had searched in there Sunday morning before I left. I took all the stuff I need when I was in there.

Q: Where did you make your search, in the two bedrooms?

A: Yes, sir.

Q: Did you search anywhere else?

A: In the attic.

Q: Down stairs anywhere?

A: Yes, sir all the drawers and everything.

Q: You were familiar with the entire house?

A: I had never been upstairs before until I shot them people. I had never been in the room downstairs next to me. I had been to the door and talked to Mr. Davis when he was putting on his shoes every morning because I had been up and watered the things.

Q: You never were up-stairs before?

A: No, sir.

Q: How did you know where he kept his money?

A: Because when sometimes he would forget it and I would go back down to the store and bring it up in the cigar box. They trusted me, they went to the show and left me to the whole house. You know when the show was in Berlin, the circus. The devil got in me when I done that.

Q: What did you use to put the fire out in the bed clothing?

A: Take some more clothes and smothered it out and it got blazing and I went down and got some more water and throwed on it.

Q: Jones, one of the girls, Elizabeth is the youngest girl?

A: Oldest.

Q: And she was lying on the right side of the bed, the side nearest the door?

A: I don't know which side she was laying on, I did not see.

Q: She had a pair of bloomers on and one leg was out entirely and the other leg in the bloomers, did you do that?

A: No, sir.

Q: Did you take her bloomers partly off?

223

A: No, sir did not touch none of them, only when that fire was there and I put the fire out.

Q: And none of the four saw you in the room at all?

A: I don't think so.

Q: There was no outcry?

A: No, sir nobody said nothing.

Q: What was your sole purpose in this case?

A: When I heard him snoring the devil jumped in me and said go rob them and shoot them and I did it.

Q: Jones when you are telling this story you are sure you know what you are talking about?

A: Yes, sir. I have no whiskey now and I have no dope. My conscious [sic] is clear when I tell the truth about it, a dirty crime like that.

By MR. CHILD:

Q: You realize everything?

A: Yes, sir.

Q: Realize this statement might be used against you?

A: Yes, sir.

Q: And have realized it since you started this statement?

A: Yes, sir.

By MR. ITZEL:

Q: How long did you stay around the place after the shooting?

A: It was getting light. Maybe twenty-five minutes. I got the money and put the things in my handbag and fixed my gun again.

Q: That was Sunday morning?

A: Yes, sir.

Q: Where did you put in all day Sunday?

A: Went down to Ocean City

Q: Did you talk to anyone down there?

A: Only the people I boarded with.

Q: You live at Ocean City?

A: Yes, sir

By CHIEF PURNELL:

Q: You stated you went home and went to bed and slept all day?

A: Yes, sir.

Q: Did you tell these people that you board with where you got this stuff?

A: No, sir, they never asked me nothing about it.

Q: Did you tell anybody anything about taking any of this property from Mr. Davis' place?

A: No, sir.

Appendix 1

Q: Tell anybody about this crime at all?

A: No, sir.

Q: Nobody knew it?

A: No, sir.

By Mr. Itzel:

Q: Did you say that you got that revolver or pistol from somebody who was in the army?

A: No, sir. I had one gun just like that and I bought this gun at the Jew place.

Q: The one you did buy from somebody in the army somebody stole it?

A: Yes, sir.

Q: Was this a little store?

A: No, sir it run from the front down to the back.

Q: Was it on the corner?

A: No, sir it was between two stores. They sell flowers and all kind of wagons come in there.

By Chief Purnell:

Q: You gave your right name when you bought both of those guns?

A: Yes, sir.

By Mr. Itzel:

Q: What address did you give when you bought the shotgun?

A: Fulton Hotel, Belair Road.

Q: Did you ever stay there?

A: Yes, sir with Mrs. Sheppard. We call him Mack but his name is Fred A. Weisner.

By Sheriff Purnell:

Q: What did you do with the shirt you were wearing that day?

A: The same clothes I have on now. You see all that blood on me.

Q: Leading from the house to the woods there were tracks there in the woods where somebody had eaten some watermelon?

A: Yes, sir.

By Mr. Itzel:

Q: You say you eat some watermelon?

A: Yes, sir.

Q: When?

A: Monday. Monday morning after twelve o'clock.

Q: At noon

A: No, sir.

Q: Midnight?

A: In the morning.

Q: Monday morning after midnight?

A: Yes, sir.

Q: Where did you get it?

A: In the patch.

Q: Anybody with you?

A: No, sir alone.

Q: Jones after you had a few drinks did it occur to you that Davis owed you a dollar?

A: No, sir he had done and paid me.

Q: There was some disagreement over a dollar?

A: I did not have anything against him.

Q: Did you tell someone he gave you a dollar short?

A: I told Lewis he shortened my pay that is the reason I am going to leave.

Q: Did that occur to you while you were drinking?

A: No, sir.

Q: Did you not feel at anytime before or after that you could have robbed the house without killing the people?

A: Yes, sir. I don't know what made me do it only the whiskey and the devil. They used to trust me with the money and go up town.

Q: Mr. Davis owned a pistol too did he not, a .38?

A: No, sir. He used to keep mine there. Mr. Davis owned an old automatic that would not work.

Q: What became of it?

A: Left in the house. When I was searching the bureau drawer I saw it there.

Q: Did you take it?

A: No, sir. I don't know whether it was a .22 or .32.

Q: How close were you when you fired the shot at Mr. Davis?

A: Just coming up to the head of the step.

Q: Were you standing on the step?

A: One foot on the step and one on top.

Q: One on the step and one on the platform?

A: Yes, sir.

Q: Did you ever go hunting?

A: Yes, sir, I was what they call a regular nimrod.

Q: You were a good shot?

A: Yes, sir used to be. I am getting old and nervous now.

Q: Both Mr. & Mrs. Davis are shot in the head and you must be a good shot because you hit both in the head, you could not have been so drunk when you fired those shots were you?

A: I was drunk enough to have the devil in me.

Q: You were not too drunk to take a good aim?

A: I could not tell that. I just had a mean disposition. That is all I can say.

Q: The way the folks are shot it is a self-evident fact that you were a good aimer, that is so isn't it?

A: The gun is a good gun. I guess I could take half sight on some things and hit it.

Q: Did you ever fire that gun before when you were drunk?

A: I have never been drunk. I don't drink no whiskey to amount to anything. That is what was wrong.

Q: Where did you get the whiskey?

A: Down in Ocean City.

Q: Were you ever in trouble before?

A: No, sir.

Q: Ever been arrested in Virginia?

A: No, sir. I left Virginia when I was eleven years old.

Q: Never in trouble in Baltimore County?

A: No, sir.

Q: The girls' bed started a fire?

A: Yes, sir.

Q: How did you extinguish it?

A: Water.

Q: Where did you get the water?

A: Down stairs to the pump.

Q: Was there any coal oil in the bucket?

A: He generally takes coal oil down to the store and put in the coal oil stove.

Q: In other words, the same bucket he used for coal oil purposes you used that bucket for water and threw it on the girls' bed?

A: I did not notice what kind of bucket it was.

Q: After you had thrown the water on the fire did you smell coal oil?

A: No, sir, there was so much gun powder in there you could not distinguish it.

Q: Were the windows open in the house?

A: Yes, sir.

Q: You know how many?

A: No, sir I did not pay no attention. They always slept with their windows up.

Q: When you entered the room was any lamp burning?

A: I don't remember. I don't think it was because I waited until it was getting light.

Q: How do you account for explaining before one of the lamps might have exploded?

A: I don't think that now because there wasn't none burning.

Q: You were mistaken about that?

A: Yes, sir.

Q: You did not set fire to anything with a match did you?

A: No, sir.

Q: This explanation accounts for the coal oil on the bed and up-stairs, how do you account for the place downstairs on the first floor being saturated with coal oil?

A: May have run through the floor is all I know.

Q: If you did that Jones you might as well give that to us to.

A: That is the only way I know, by me throwing water on it and there was coal oil in the bucket.

By Mr. Child:

Q: When we found the bucket it was down stairs—after you threw this water or coal oil, whatever it was in the bucket on the two beds what did you do with the bucket?

A: I took it back down stairs.

Q: Where did you put it?

A: I don't know. I think by the sink some place.

By Sheriff Purnell:

Q: Did you tell the woman where you were boarding not to go into your room?

A: No, sir. She makes up my bed all the time.

Q: She told us you told her not to go in your room. She said you told her that Friday. I don't want you to come in my room?

A: No, sir I did not tell her.

By Lieut. Itzel:

Q: You took this basket to the store and filled it up after you had filled it up you left it there?

A: Yes, sir.

Q: What was your reason for leaving it there?

A: So that they would not think anything about me. His shoes were in there and they were too small, they were five or six and I wear seven.

Q: Did you have anything in mind to notify the authorities about the crime?

A: Yes, sir, but I wasn't going to tell the name. I wasn't going to tell them who did it.

Q: Just how did you plan to tell them this?

A: Write to the State Barracks.

Q: And tell them what?

A: And tell them Mr. Green Davis and his wife and children were killed over on his farm and his house sets back from his fruit stand on the road.

Q: What else were you going to tell them?

A: That was all.

Q: You were not going to sign your name?

A: No, sir.

Q: Going to mail it?

A: Yes, sir going to send it special delivery.

Q: Why were you going to do that?

A: So that somebody would come there and care for those people. I was sorry after I did it.

Q: You did not plan a crime like that just because Mr. Davis was snoring did you?

A: The devil was in me.

Q: Is your mind clear now as to exactly what took place?

A: Yes, sir, if I ever had my right mind I think it is right now.

Q: Then you could not have been so drunk?

A: I got sobered up after I got that devil in me.

Q: Jones when did you take your Winchester to Davis' place the last time prior to the crime?

A: On Sunday evening when I went up there.

Q: Before this occasion?

A: Never did take it up there.

Q: This has got nothing to do with the time you were living there?

A: Yes, sir.

Q: Since you were living there I mean.

A: Yes, sir.

Q: After you moved away from Mr. Davis' home you took the shotgun with you to your room, did you ever go back to Davis' house with that shotgun anytime than the one last Sunday?

A: Only Sunday night.

Q: Why did you take the gun apart and wrap it in paper?

A: That is where I always carried it when I was on the road.

Q: The pistol you had in your pocket, is that right?

A: No, sir had it in the handbag.

Q: Is that handbag your property?

A: Yes, sir I brought it to Mr. Davis'.

Q: When you left home with that Winchester and that pistol what then was your intention doing with it?

A: The pistol was to protect me. Colored fellows had robbed me down in Virginia about six months previous and State Officers told me on the highway in Virginia, said you can carry that pistol in your handbag but you must never carry it in your pocket. When I got the shot gun my intention was to go home to Mrs. Sheppard's and I went to Mr. Long's and went to work. He never knew I had it. I kept it hid in the hay. This guy steals my pistol and Mr. Long made him go get it.

Q: Why did you take the gun with you that day?

A: I was going to Mr. Long's—leaving Ocean City and going to Mr. Long's to live and that is how come me with it. I was looking at the corn and it was getting yellow and I said maybe he will want it cut in a few days and I said I will stop here. I went up there and he was up there snoring and the devil jumped in me and I killed the whole family.

Q: What did you take a shotgun with you to go to Long's for?

A: I was traveling. He told me anytime I come back I could get a job with him.

Q: You intended to go back to your room in Ocean City?

A: No, sir. I had all my clothes with me.

Q: Jones on a number of different occasions you walked around the house and peeped in the windows and you were seen and the party this information comes from is reliable, absolutely honest and has no feeling against you and we are sure it is true?

A: And you are sure it was me?

Q: Yes, sir he knows you. Do you acknowledge that or deny it?

A: No, sir I did not do it.

Q: Did you peep in the windows on this particular Sunday night?

A: No, sir. I looked in the window and there wasn't much light in there and I opened the door. There was a window from the South and it showed light on the bed and I could see to shoot them.

Q: You immediately walked in the front door?

A: Yes, sir.

Q: And immediately went up-stairs?

A: Yes, sir.

Q: Were you careful not to make much noise?

A: Shoes like this don't keep much noise.

Q: Are they the only shoes you have?

A: Yes, sir.

Q: When did you buy the shot for the gun?

A: Different kinds, some yellow, some red.

Q: When did you get them?

A: Buy them pretty much every month when I was at home.

By MR. JOHN FARLOW:

Q: What do you call your home?

A: Fulton Hotel.

Q: How long did you work for Mrs. Sheppard up there?

A: From May on up.

CONCLUSION OF STATEMENT

(Signed; Orphan Jones)

Statement of Orphan Jones
October 15, 1931

T his statement of Orphan Jones was made at Baltimore city jail, October 15, 1931, at 9:45 p.m. in the presence of Captain J. McKim Johnson, Maryland State Police; Warden Harry C. Martin; Corporal M.D. Brubaker, Maryland State Police; Detective Lieutenant Joseph H. Itzel; and Detective Sergeant William J. Flynn.

LIEUT. ITZEL.

Q: Jones you made a statement at Snow Hill, Md. several days ago, both in the form of a confession and a statement. Do you recall that?

A: I do.

Q: Can you read?

A: Yes, sir, but not without glasses.

Q: Well, we can save time, I will read it to you and will you follow me carefully?

A: Yes, sir.

[Statement read by Lieut. Itzel]

Q: Are these correct?

A: Yes, sir.

Q: No mistakes?

A: No, sir.

Q: Jones, I am going to ask you if you will sign this statement?

A: Will I sign it, sure I'll sign it, I was the one that made it. But I never told what caused the whole business, I never said that.

Q: Just a minute Jones, I want to warn you of your rights. We have nothing to promise you if you tell us anything in addition to what you have already told us. You will not be threatened or harmed if you don't tell us anything, and we want you to thoroughly understand that anything you do tell us may be used against you at your trial. Do you thoroughly understand now what I say?

A: I will tell you the whole story.

SERGT. FLYNN:

Q: What did cause all the trouble?

A: When I first went there I gave him my money and my gun to keep for me and he said he lost it in the Ocean City Bank, and he tried to drive me away and if I didn't leave there he would have the girls say I attacked them.

Q: What did the girls say?

A: Just what their father told them.

Q: What was that?

A: He had me working for him and he just gave me the money I worked for and when I asked him for my other money he said he was sorry that he had lost it in the Ocean City Bank, but I knew he didn't lose it, he wanted to beat me out of it.

Q: How much money did you give him?

A: Davis had $250.00. When I went to work for him I had $268.00 and I kept the $18.00 in my pocket and gave him the $250.00.

Q: Are you sure that was the amount of money you gave him? When did you give it to him to keep?

A: When I first went there in September, I gave him my revolver and my money to keep. I make my money and I don't want to get done out of it. I always gets work when I am out of money. He told me he lost the money in the bank, he was going to rob me out of it.

Q: According to that you really had that on your mind when you left Ocean City?

A: Yes, sir.

Q: You had it on your mind to get your money?

A: To collect the money or I was going to fight him.

Q: Did you have this intention when you went to ask him for the money and he couldn't give you a reasonable excuse, what did you intend to do to him?

A: I intended to fight him.

Q: Did you intend to kill him?

A: No, I didn't.

Q: Orphan, did these girls ever say anything?

A: Yes, sir, they said something down around the store about running him away from here.

Q: When you left Ocean City you had your bag and your clothing, why did you go back to Ocean City?

A: I went back because I changed my mind.

Q: After you killed the family?

A: Yes, sir.

Q: What bank did you get that money out of that you say you gave to Mr. Davis to hold?

A: I didn't have it in any bank.

Q: Where did you keep it?

A: Kept it on myself all the time.

Q: When did you give it to him, last September?

A: When I went to work for him, I gave him my pistol and my money to keep.

Q: When did you ask for the money the first time?

A: On Saturday, October 3rd, he said he would have it for me, he would get the money for me, so on Monday he told me he had lost it in the Ocean City Bank, and I said "what's the use of telling me that, the bank has been busted over a week, and I didn't give you the money to put in the bank, I could have put it in the bank," and it just came to me he was trying to beat me out of it.

Q: That was the 3rd of October?

A: That was the 3rd of October when he was talking to me.

Q: Then when did you go back to him?

A: I didn't leave. Monday he said he had more corn to cut, I didn't know he had another field to cut so I worked Monday and Tuesday I asked for the money and he just gave me the money I had been working for, he made me sore, he didn't lose my money in the bank, he didn't put it in any bank.

Q: That was on Tuesday?

A: On Tuesday, that's when I left there.

Q: When did you go back again?

A: Following Saturday that week.

Q: Did you have any conversation with him?

A: I had seen him before then, he owed me a dollar and he paid me the dollar and he said about losing the money in the bank, but I knew he didn't lose the money, he was trying to beat me out of it.

Q: That is what you think?

A: Yes, sir.

LIEUT. ITZEL:

Q: When you say he owed you a dollar in your previous statement, that isn't true?

A: Sure it is, but he paid me the dollar.

Q: He had paid you the dollar?

A: He gave me $2.00, but I told him he only owed me $1.00. Davis intended to beat me out of the $250.00.

Q: Did anyone see you turn the money over to him?

A: The wife and family was there.

Q: Anyone know you had that money?

A: Mrs. Sheppard, but she didn't know how much money I had.

Q: Did you ever keep any money around the house at Mrs. Sheppard's?

A: Kept it in my pocket.

Q: You kept it in your pocket?

A: Yes, kept it in my pocket. Sheppard gave me money and Mac gave me money.

SERGT. FLYNN:

Q: When did you first ask him to give you the money back?

A: I didn't ask him, he just said he didn't have the money.

Q: That was Saturday before this happened?

A: Same week. I asked Mr. Davis for money and he said "Sure, but I didn't think you were finished," and I worked until I was finished and I wanted to go to Berlin to get some shoes and some other things and I asked for part of the money, but he didn't come across, he said he had lost it in the bank at Ocean City, and I said "I didn't tell you to put the money in the bank, I could have put it in myself."

LIEUT. ITZEL:

Q: Orphan, what did you do with the shells that were ejected from the gun?

A: I had the shells in my pocket, I guess I threw them away.

Q: Did you take them out of the house in your pocket?

A: I did.

Q: Do you think you threw them away on Davis' land on your way down to the store?

A: I threw them away in the grass. As you leave the house, there is some planting near there, and I might have thrown them in there.

SERGT. FLYNN:

Q: Down where the pumpkins are?

A: There are no pumpkins, they are watermelons.

Q: Down in the same direction?

A: No, there is planking to keep the truck from going over the bank and I might have thrown in the grass down there.

LIEUT. ITZEL:

Q: You tell about throwing the key away, can you picture the 2 signs, one immediately alongside of the store and the other about 200 yards away.

A: You know that wooden horse down there along that same place in the gutter, that is the place. The key was on a piece of brass about 2 inches long (indicating), and had a hole cut in it like a diamond, I threw it down there in the gutter.

Q: Do you recall when you came up if you took the shot gun and pistol from your home in Ocean City, when you were going to the Long's to work?

A: Yes, sir.

Q: And you really moved from your room in Ocean City and had taken all your belongings?

A: Yes, sir.

Q: Well tell us why you went back there after you killed them?

A: Had too many things to carry. My intentions were to go back and catch a train for Baltimore or Love Point.

Q: Was Long's home closer to Davis' than your home in Ocean City?

A: No, sir.

Q: The reason I ask you that is I am not familiar with the section.

A: Ocean City is 5 miles from Davis'.

Q: Where is Long's?

A: Lives up near some little place, about 30 miles up.

Q: Who washed your clothes?

A: Some lady down near Lewis's going toward Ocean City, I guess about 250 yards from Mrs. Lewis', about ¾ of a mile.

Q: What is her name?

A: I don't know her name. There is a big willow tree standing in front of her house on the right hand side going to Ocean City.

Q: Have you any clothes there now?

A: No, sir.

Q: Have you any clothes in your room in Ocean City?

A: Didn't the officers go there and take all the clothes I had?

Q: Did you also have a new suit that Davis bought recently?

A: No, not any new suit.

Q: Did you take any clothes out?

A: Only the shirts he gave me, had cuff buttons in it and he said they were gold.

SERGT. FLYNN:

Q: You didn't take any clothes?

A: No, sir.

Q: Did you ever know him to own several suits of clothing?

A: I saw him with a light suit.

Q: Who put the clothes in that basket just as you go in the door?

A: They were washed clothes, they had just washed one day that week and I seen them 2 or 3 baskets full.

LIEUT. ITZEL:

Q: The autopsy shows very distinctly and clear that the younger girl had a fracture of the skull right in front, as shows as if she had been struck by some blunt instrument. Did you hit her with the butt of the gun?

A: No, indeed, I never hit any of them with nothing.

Q: Are you sure of that?

A: Certainly I am sure.

Q: What do you suppose caused the injury?

A: I don't know. I didn't hit her with anything.

Q: She was struck with some blunt instrument.

A: Could it have been a glancing shot?

Q: No, the skin wasn't broken, but the bone was broken in the skull.

A: Maybe the doctor was wrong.

SERGT. FLYNN:

Q: After you had shot the 2 children with the pump gun, why was it necessary to use the pistol on both the children?

A: I don't know why it was.

Q: You remember doing it?

A: Sure I done it.

Q: You had 4 shells, you killed Davis and his wife and then shot both children with the pump gun and then you used the pistol. Why was that necessary?

A: I don't know. I can't remember.

Q: You shot them with the revolver?

A: The gun jammed and I took the revolver and shot them, I don't know for what reason.

Lieut. Itzel:

Q: You shot each one of the persons with the shot gun, that was 4 shots and the gun didn't jamb [*sic*] on any of those 4 shots?

A: I can't remember, I don't know maybe I reloaded the gun and started shooting again when it jammed.

Sergt. Flynn:

Q: How many shots in the gun when you first started to shoot?

A: 6.

Q: You emptied all 6 and it jammed on the second loading?

A: That is right.

Q: And you took the pistol and shot both of the girls?

A: Yes, sir.

Lieut. Itzel:

Q: Do you recall distinctly doing it?

A: I must have done it.

Sergt. Flynn:

Q: Do you recall which you shot first, the older or younger girl?

A: The older girl.

Q: Where did you shoot her?

A: I shot her in the head on time and over the left breast.

Q: The left breast was a pump gun wound, I mean with the revolver?

A: I think in the head.

Q: How close were you when you fired the pump gun?

A: Just inside the door.

Q: Were they awake?

A: I didn't take time to notice, nobody said anything.

Lieut. Itzel:

Q: Do you know Edward B. Gray of West Ocean City, keeps a store?

A: Gray, lives back there.

Q: Gray, the man you asked to get a license?

A: Yes, sir, I asked him to get me a license.

Q: Do you recall seeing him last Sunday while you were going toward Ocean City about 9 o'clock?

A: I remember seeing him, I went to get some soda pop.

Q: Where?

A: In Gray's.

Q: What time was that?

A: Sunday evening, one day last week.

Q: Gray said it was about 9 o'clock and you were going toward Ocean City on Sunday.

A: Sure, he was right.

Q: Did you see him?

A: No, sir, I seen him in the store.

Q: You did go to Ocean City about 9 o'clock Sunday morning?

A: I must have.

Q: And did you return about 3 o'clock in the afternoon?

A: Later than that, I went up to bed and slept.

Q: Did you have the gun wrapped in news paper when you passed him at 9 o'clock?

A: Sure.

Q: Did you have it when you went past in the afternoon?

A: No sir.

Q: You went back and forth past Gray's house at least 3 times.

A: He may have seen me pass up and down, but not on the same day.

Q: On the same day?

A: No.

Q: Do you remember talking to Allen Chief of Police?

A: Yes, sir.

Q: When were you arrested?

A: Monday.

Q: Do you recall talking to Allen on Monday?

A: Yes, sir.

Q: Will you tell us just what you told Allen?

A: I will tell you what he said. He called Martha Miller, then he called me and asked if I worked for Green Davis, and I said "yes sir'" and he said you come with me all of those people were found dead in their beds.

Q: Is this true, did you ask Allen this question: "What do you want with me, I didn't murder anyone"?

A: Allen is a liar, I didn't say that.

Q: Did you want to buy some .38 calibre bullets from Gray?

A: Sure.

Q: When?

A: On Monday when Willie Miller went to get the license.

Q: For what purpose?

A: I wanted to have them, I only had 2 left.

Q: Did you want them for any particular purpose?

A: No sir, I thought maybe I would want to shoot something.

Q: Do you know where Davis kept the gun when you had it at his house?

A: I didn't know, but he took it to town with him.

Q: I mean the big rifle, the Winchester, he didn't take that?

A: I kept that up in the barn.

Q: When did you have it in his house?

A: Not in his house.

Q: Did you have the Winchester in Davis' house?

A: No, had it in the barn up in the rafters.

Q: Did you ever take it apart?

A: Yes, sir.

Q: Do you know Robert J. Lewis of Taylorsville?

A: Yes, I know him, he lives about 500 yards from Davis' place going toward Ocean City.

Q: Describe him?

A: He is silvery grey, not as old as I am, he is on the right hand side toward Ocean City, he runs a place like Davis'.

Q: How tall is Mr. Lewis?

A: Something like the Warden (meaning Warden Martin) (about 5ft. 6in.) He hasn't as much stomach.

Q: Did you ever tell Mr. Lewis you had a quarrel with Davis?

A: The only thing I said to him was I didn't work there any more because he wouldn't pay me my money.

Q: Did you go over to Lewis' house on Thursday and talk with him?

A: Over to his house?

Q: Walked over to see him?

A: No, sir.

Q: Did you have a conversation with Mr. Lewis and tell Lewis that "our friend is not the man you take him to be"?

A: No the only conversation I had I told you about.

Q: Did you tell Lewis that "them wenches called you 'coon' and 'negro'"?

A: I didn't.

SERGT. FLYNN:

Q: What did you tell him?

A: Too much coon and negro in their mouth, they made a remark that there goes more negroes down there, and I said they had just as much rights as the white people.

Q: Did you mention to him about wenches?

A: No, sir.

Q: Did Mrs. Lewis hear the conversation?

A: She was around there and might have heard it, she went around the house.

Q: Were 2 other men there listening to the conversation?

A: No, sir.

Q: Was there another colored man sitting there on the bumper of a car?

A: No, I was the only colored man.

Q: Were you sitting on the bumper of the car?

A: I was standing on the side walk.

Q: Did you see Lewis about 8 o'clock coming from the Davis house?

A: I did.

Q: That was after the crime was committed?

A: That's right.

Q: Did you pass Lewis' house again about one hour after dark coming from Ocean City going toward Davis' house?

A: I did.

Q: On Sunday night?

A: No.

Q: On Sunday night, one hour after dark coming from Ocean City going toward Davis'?

A: He might have seen me.

Q: Lewis said he saw you on Sunday night an hour after dark going in the direction of Davis'.

A: Sure, I went there to feed the stock.

Q: You say the shooting took place about twilight, or about daybreak Sunday morning?

A: Sometime in the morning, the light was shining in the window.

Q: And about 25 minutes or a half hour after you had all things fixed ready to leave?

A: I didn't leave until the sun was way up.

Q: What were you doing?

A: I pumped water for the stock and fed the pigs.

Sergt. Flynn:

Q: After you did the shooting?

A: Sure.

Lieut. Itzel:

Q: When you went to Ocean City, did you stop anywhere from Davis' to where you were staying in Ocean City?

A: No, indeed.

Q: Did you have any conversation, or stop at any place in that territory while you were on your way to Ocean City?

A: No, sir, I tell you I never visit anybody, when I am working I stay by myself, I don't visit my own people, I don't have any women, I stays to myself and reads.

Q: What time did you get back to Ocean City?

A: Sometime after 9 o'clock. I told you it was around about 5 ½ miles, it is 7 ½ miles to Berlin where the roads come together and I lives about 2 miles from there, or 5 miles from Ocean City.

Q: After you got home to Ocean City, did you go to your room?

A: Yes, sir.

Q: And you took the gun and pistol there?

A: Sure.

Q: What did you do then?

A: Got some breakfast, than came back and went to bed.

Q: How long did you sleep?

A: Sometime after noon.

Q: About what time did you get up?

A: About one hour before the sun gets down in the west, I was at Lewis's at about 8 o'clock, when I was going back to feed the cattle.

Sergt. Flynn:

Q: Then you went back to feed the cattle?

A: Sure.

Q: Then what did you do?

A: Stayed there.

Q: Where?

A: In the store room, that is where I took them things.

Q: Then you took the things and threw the key in the road and what did you do?

A: Came on down to Ocean City.

Q: Did you go home and go to sleep?

A: I guess it was about 6 or 6:30 in the morning. That was the last time I was up there until I was arrested and carried up there.

Q: Did you go up in the room anytime after you left it on Sunday morning?

A: No indeed.

Q: You never went back up there after feeding the cattle and going to Ocean City?

A: No.

Q: Did you go up Sunday night?

A: No.

Q: You came back Sunday night?

A: I fed the cattle and stayed in the store and got some towels out of basket.

Lieut. Itzel:

Q: We spoke to a number of relatives of Davis and we have quite a lot of information at the fact that the Winchester rifle or shot gun belonged to Davis. Was that Davis' gun?

A: That was my own gun. If you can't find the man I bought it from, that's your hard luck.

Q: Was the pistol silver or nickle [sic] plated?

A: Nickle plated, but is [sic] was rusted.

Q: It was a colt?

A: A Colt DA-41, left hand wheel.

Q: Did you ever take a pistol or steal a pistol from Mr. Crowe?

A: What Crowe?

Q: A man who was working at one of the canning camps about 3 or 4 weeks ago.

A: He's a liar, I had the pistol long before that, I had the pistol up at Mrs. Sheppard's.

Q: Does Long know the pistol?

A: Sure he does.

SERGT. FLYNN:

Q: Does Long know the pump gun?

A: No, I didn't have it then.

Q: Who knows it?

A: I don't know if Mrs. Sheppard saw it, but Francis Sheppard saw it.

LIEUT. ITZEL:

Q: You told us that coming up, going to Long's you had the gun and pistol with you, and that you had moved everything you had?

A: I did.

Q: And you had all the belongings you had?

A: I did.

Q: You didn't have all your clothes with you?

A: Why not?

Q: How much?

A: I had all of them.

Q: How many suits?

A: 2 suits, 2 vests, I don't know how many underwear 2 or 3 sets, and shirts, I don't know how many.

Q: What did you carry the clothes in?

A: Some in the suit case and some in a package hanging on the handle.

Q: Where did you have that stuff placed while you were committing this crime?

A: Down stairs on the table.

Q: And you say you have all the clothing down there belonging to Davis?

A: Only the shirt that he gave me and a pair of shoes.

Q: The cuff buttons Davis gave you are they good buttons?

A: He claims they were.

Q: Did you ever wear the shirt?

A: No.

Q: When did he give you the shirt?

A: Saturday after the show.

Q: After the circus was in town?

A: Yes, sir.

Q: Orphan, can you recall if you hit the girl over the head?

A: I can't recall hitting anybody.

Q: If you hit her you would know it, and you had the presence of mind to know it?

A: I think I would, I don't think I did. Who was the doctor who said that?

SERGT. FLYNN:

Q: Where did you load the gun?

A: What gun?

Q: The pump gun, where did you load that?

A: When I took the gun out and put it together I loaded it.

Q: Then you had 6 shots in that gun?

A: Sure.

Q: You fired the gun, all 6 shots, where did you get the shots to reload?

A: I had over 2 boxes in my suit case, some #4 and some #2.

Q: You didn't have the suit case with you?

A: I had my pockets filled up.

Q: Where did Davis keep his shells in the house?

A: I didn't see him have any at all.

Q: You put shells in your pocket going up stairs?

A: I told you that.

Q: Do you recall Davis keeping shells on a board near the water pump?

A: No, not on the ledge.

Q: Where did he keep the shells?

A: I never seen him have any shells, the only thing he had was an automatic and I don't know what kind.

Q: Did you go to the oil boiler and draw any?

A: I didn't draw any oil.

Q: Was there oil there?

A: I didn't see any.

Q: How do you account for the oil being all over the place?

A: I think I must have used the bucket with oil in it and pumped water on top of it.

LIEUT. ITZEL:

Q: There were a pair of bloomers lying on the bed, pair of lady's bloomers, lying under the feet of Mrs. Davis, I think they were pink, they were under the comfort or blanket and this blanket or comfort had oil on it from the bloomers and the bloomers were entirely saturated with oil. How can you account for that?

A: I don't know, unless somebody else done it.

Q: Let us assume you took the bucket to put the fire out the fire on the girls' bed, how do you account for the room being so thoroughly saturated with oil?

A: Search me.

Q: That oil didn't come through the ceiling, there are no marks on the ceiling and the floor down stairs was full of oil.

A: Who found the people?

Q: Some neighbors.

A: Don't you know who the neighbors was, they may have been the ones that put the oil around.

Q: Those people got out as quick as they could, they were friends of the Davises, who they were I don't know, they were neighbors and they had missed the Davis family because they had not opened the store.

SERGT. FLYNN:

Q: You say you shot the older girl, she was the one on the outside of the bed, first?

A: I can't recall, I may have, I don't know.

Q: This little girl was lying in the bed, and she had a pair of pink bloomers on, her left leg was out of the bloomers and the right leg was in the bloomers and her under gown was up above the navel.

A: I don't know anything about that I didn't put my hands on anything at all.

Q: The left breast of the girl on the right side near the window, her breast was exposed and the night gown was torn entirely away from the breast.

A: I thought you said they were shot through the breast?

LIEUT. ITZEL:

Q: Both of the girls were shot directly through the left breast, the older's night gown had a hole just big enough for the shot to go through, but the younger one had her entire breast exposed and the night gown torn away.

A: It might have been done before, did you look to see if it was a new rent?

Q: How much distance would you have to stand away from a person to show powder marks?

A: I don't know.

Q: Did you know that the blanket on Mr. Davis' bed was burned?

A: I put out all the fires.

Q: You put the fire out on their bed too?

A: I am not sure.

Q: How much time did you consume in killing the whole 4?

A: A minute, not quite a minute, as fast as I could shoot, I can't estimate the time, I just kept shooting, didn't stop.

Q: How much wine did you drink after shooting those people?

A: I didn't drink but very little, I went up stair and got it.

Q: Did you drink the wine in the same room where the shooting took place?

A: I went down stairs and drank the wine, mixed it with some water.

Q: You said you drank that wine up in the room where the shooting took place?

A: I didn't say that.

Q: You did say it, I'll read it to you.

(Taken from the previous statement)

(Q: Did you drink anything in Davis' home while you were searching?

(A: Yes, sir.

(Q: What did you drink?

(A: Got some wine. She had given me some before, it was in a closet.

(Q: In the kitchen?

(A: No, sir up stairs.

(Q: Did you drink that wine after you shot these people?

(A: Yes, sir.

(Q: And that wine was on the second floor in one of the bedrooms?

(A: Yes, sir, in one of the little preserve jars and I put a handkerchief over it and drank through that to strain it.

A: I didn't say where I drank it.

Q: If you drank it down stairs, why did you carry the jar upstairs with wine in it?

A: There were only dregs in there, that is why I put my handkerchief over it.

Q: Why did you carry it upstairs again?

A: I got it up in the attic.

Q: When you took it back, why did you go back, just to take it up?

A: I don't know why.

Q: Did you get any of the girl's clothing?

A: No, indeed. They say they found a lot of stockings, I must have stuck them in there for something else.

Q: We have that little jar and that little jar has some wine in it. In addition to the dregs. Where did you put it when you took it back up stairs?

A: I put it on the second floor.

Q: Did you put it near the bureau?

A: Maybe I had.

Q: One other important thing I want to clear, where [sic] you standing directly in front of the bed when you did the shooting?

A: I told you that I came up to the head of the stairs and I was standing with one foot on the stairs and the other on the platform.

Q: I'll show you a picture (Exhibit #1), show you the stairs, do you recall this point, the different articles, were you standing here when you did the shooting?

A: I must have been there.

Q: Your statement that you had one foot on the landing and one foot on the step, assuming you did stand over her, you could not have shot the man in the right side of the head?

A: I must have been in farther.

Q: You had to be in if you did that?

A: When you come to the head of the stairs, isn't that at the foot of the bed?

Q: You have saw this picture, and it is physically impossible to have hit the man from the head of the steps. Do you recall where you were?

A: I recall a trunk or box just coming around the corner.

Q: Well that was in front of the bed. Where were you standing in the other room?

A: I told you I just pushed the door open.

Q: Mr. Davis' truck, was that standing there (Shown a picture of the outside of the house).

A: It generally stands there.

Q: The shells, did you throw them away before you got to the road proper?

A: I don't know, I threw them in the grass down there somewhere.

Q: These bloomers were lying on the bed at Mrs. Davis' feet, and they were soaked in coal oil and the covers, don't you recall what you did with them?

A: Just assume she didn't sleep in any. I went down and got the bucket and it might have looked like water in it, but maybe it was coal oil that he brought back from the store, and I put more water on it and put it on the fire.

Q: Did you have anything against these girls?

A: They had too much coon and nigger in their mouths, and they were told by their father they were going to keep my money and say I attacked them.

Q: Did you kill them because they called you nigger, did you kill them for that?

A: No, they were just as nice as could be.

Q: Did they call other colored people names?

A: I never heard them.

Q: When did you first conceive the idea to kill this family?

A: When I went up there, I went up to the house, that is the first time I thought of it, I thought I could get him to give me my money, or either he or I would get done up.

Q: You must have conceived this idea before, that was your intention when you loaded the gun?

A: I loaded the gun when I got up to the store.

Q: When you got to the store, you made up your mind to kill them?

A: Sure.

Q: When you took the gun up to Davis' from your home, you didn't take it up there for the purpose of taking care of the watermelon patch?

A: I didn't have any home then.

Q: I am talking about Sunday.

A: On the Sunday, I was taking it back to work.

Q: You said you always carried the gun, you had the gun to take care of the watermelon patch, you had the gun in your room in Ocean City.

A: I wasn't staying in Ocean City.

Q: You didn't take this gun with you to take care of the watermelon patch?

A: I was on the way to Long's, I told him I would come up he had some corn to cut.

Q: What is your correct name?

A: Orphan Jones.

Q: Where [sic] you ever baptized?

A: I must have been baptized when I was a baby.

Q: Nobody baptized you "Orphan."

A: That is my name, the people that raised me called me that.

Q: What is your right name?

A: Euel Lee.

Q: What was your father's name?

A: Joe.

Q: Mother's name.

A: Jane.

Q: And you were born in Virginia?

A: Lynchburg.

Q: How long have you been using the name of Jones?

A: Ever since I can remember.

Q: Your foster parents' name was Jones, that is why you took it?

A: Yes, they were white people.

Q: Did you consider the white people your foster parents?

A: Yes, sir.

SERGT. FLYNN:

Q: How long have your foster parents been dead?

A: I don't know if Miss Alice is dead or not, she went over to France.

Q: Did they have any children?

A: Stella, John and Alice.

Q: What was their father's name?

A: Clay.

Q: Why did you drop your right name?

A: Because people thought I didn't have any right to use that name.

LIEUT. ITZEL:

Q: Orphan, you made one answer to a question and the question is this: "Jones when you are telling this story you are sure you know what you are talking about?" and your answer was:

"Yes, sir. I have no whiskey now and no dope. My conscience is clear when I tell the truth about it, a dirty crime like that." Were you referring to dope, are you a narcotic?

A: I just wanted you to know I had a clear head.

Q: When you make this statement is your mind clear and what you are telling us is the absolute truth?

A: Yes, sir.

Q: And are you willing to sign this statement?

A: Sure.

Q: And so you realize this statement might be used against you?

A: I know all of them will be used against me, that is why you are taking them.

Q: Did you tell anybody at all about this crime after you committed it?

A: Who should I tell?

Q: Have you spoken to any of the guards in the jail about the crime?

A: No, indeed.

Q: Have you spoken to the warden about the crime?

A: No, he hasn't asked me any questions.

Q: Jones, after you had this whiskey, which you bought, received or got in some manner in Ocean City, was it then that these facts concerning the money Davis was supposed to have owed you, brought more clearly in your mind?

A: No body had better bother with my money, my eats or my women if I have any.

Q: When you took this whiskey, drank the whiskey that you received in Ocean City, you state that the money matters concerning Davis impressed itself on your mind, is that true?

A: I don't know whether it impressed itself on my mind more then [*sic*] it did at any other time, it was my money and I wanted it.

Q: You say you don't want a lawyer?

A: What good is a lawyer going to do, it only means additional expense.

Q: You asked someone at Snow Hill to send you a Baptist minister to baptize you.

A: The chief of police said he was going to send me one and I told him all right.

SERGT. FLYNN:

Q: You know they were buried today, all of them and they couldn't find any clothing for them.

A: God knows they had enough clothing, somebody got the clothing, the girls had all kinds of clothing hanging up there.

Q: All the stuff you had in the basket, the 2 towels are the only things you got out of the house?

A: His shoes, I brought them down in the basket.

Q: How about the pocket book, the little brown pocket book?

A: That belonged to one of the girls, I think it had a dollar in it.

Q: This is what was in the basket; 2 towels, a pair of shoes, 1 egg, 1 face powder compact, 6 boxes matches and 1 extra box of matches, 1 black leather hat—

A: The hat belonged to him, it was a gum hat.

Q: 1 brown imitation book, containing 2 lead pencils, 1 child's school compass, 2 fountain pens, a woman's ring, 1 child's compact, 1 box of lead for pencil, 1 automatic pencil, 1 child's pencil, pearl handle nail file, 7 bars milky way, 6 bars Peter Pauls Chocolate mounds, 20 packages of chewing gum. I want to ask you where you got the towels?

A: Out of the house.

Q: And shoes out of the house?

A: Sure.

Q: The brown initial pocket book?

A: In the store, she left it there.

Q: Got the egg in the store?

A: Sure, I had a dozen of them.

Q: Do you want counsel, or a lawyer?

A: I don't see where a lawyer can do anything about it.

Q: Are you sure you don't want a lawyer?

A: That is up to the court, I am perfectly satisfied to let the court take care of it.

Q: Orphan, we want to close this statement. Have you anything else to tell us?

A: I have told you all I know.

Q: Do you thoroughly understand everything you have told us, and do you thoroughly understand the questions that have been asked you and do you make your answers voluntarily of your own free will, not expecting any immunity or reward?

A: I understand everything, please don't ask me any more questions, I am satisfied.

Statement completed 12:30 a.m., Friday, October 16, 1931
(Signed) Orphan Jones
(SEAL)

Joseph H. Itzel, Lieut.
M. D. Brubaker, Corp.
Wm. J. Flynn, Sergt.

Bibliography

Archival Sources

Albin O. Kuhn Library, University of Maryland Baltimore County, Catonsville, Maryland.

Baltimore *Sunpapers* Library, Baltimore, Maryland.

Cemetery Records. Mt. Cavalry Cemetery, Brooklyn, Maryland.

Cemetery Records. Bishopville Cemetery, Bishopville, Maryland.

Enoch Pratt Free Library, Baltimore, Maryland. Periodical Room, Mencken Room and Maryland Room records.

FBI Records re: Bernard Ades. File No. 100-1541-1A. Baltimore office of FBI.

Franklin D. Roosevelt Library, Hyde Park, New York. Various newspaper records.

Johns Hopkins University. Admission records for Bernard Ades, 1919; records of College For Teachers, 1929–30.

National Archives and Record Administration. Federal disbarment proceedings for Bernard Ades. (Mid-Atlantic Region Archives Facility, Philadelphia, Pennsylvania.)

Maryland State Archives.

University of Maryland School of Law, Baltimore, Maryland. Academic Record of Bernard Ades, 1928.

Wicomico County Library, Salisbury. Maryland Room.

Legal Proceedings

Bernard Ades v. Patrick Brady, Warden of Maryland Penitentiary. Baltimore City Circuit Court No. 2, October 1933. (Regarding the will of Euel Lee.)

Euel Lee alias Orphan Jones v. State of Maryland. 54 S. Ct. 56, 1933. (Denial of petition for writ of certiorari.)

In Re: Ades. 6 F. Supp. 467, United States District Court for the District of Maryland, 1934. (Federal disbarment proceedings.)

In the Matter of The Bar Association of Baltimore City v. Bernard Ades. Baltimore City Supreme Bench. 1934. (Disbarment proceedings.) Maryland Archives.

Lee v. State. MD Ct. App., No. 105, October Term, 1931. (Record abstract.) 161 Md 430.

Lee v. State. MD Ct. App., No. 64, October Term, 1932. (Record abstract.) 163 Md 56.

Lee v. State. MD Ct. App., No. 46, April Term, 1933. (Record abstract.) 164 Md 550.

State of Maryland v. Euel Lee, alias Orphan Jones, Worcester County Criminal Court Records, Snow Hill, Maryland. (Indictments, motions, etc.)

Newspapers

Baltimore Afro-American

Baltimore Evening Sun

Berlin-Ocean City News

Centreville Record

Crisfield Times

Easton Journal

New York Times

Salisbury Times

Worcester Democrat

Baltimore American (later the *Baltimore News-American*)

Baltimore Sunpapers

Cecil County Star

Chestertown Enterprise

Democratic Messenger (Snow Hill)

Federalsburg Times

Princess Anne Marylander and Herald

Washington Post

Books, Treatises, Articles

Clark, Charles J. *History of the Eastern Shore of Maryland and Virginia*. New York: Lewis Historical Publishing Co., 1950.

Cooper, Richard. *Salisbury in Times Gone By*. Baltimore: Gateway Press, 1991.

Corddrey, George H. *Wicomico County History*. Salisbury, MD: Peninsula Press, 1981.

Fenton, John H. *Politics in the Border States—A study of the Patterns of Political Organization, and Political Change Common to the Border States—Maryland, West Virginia, Kentucky and Missouri*. New Orleans, Hauser, 1957.

Hayman, John C. *Rails Along the Chesapeake*. Marvadel Publishers, 1979.

Manchester, William. *Disturber Of The Peace*. New York: Harper & Brothers, 1951.

Mencken, Henry L. *Thirty-Five Years in Newspaper Work*. Edited by Fred Hobson, Vincent Fitzpatrick and Bradford Jacobs. Baltimore: Johns Hopkins University Press, 1994.

Nock, Mary L. *It Was a Joy and a Pleasure*. Salisbury, MD: Nock, 1979.

Rodgers, Marion Elizabeth. *The Impossible H.L. Mencken*. New York: Doubleday, 1991.

Skotnes, Andor. "The Communist Party, Anti-Racism, and the Freedom Movement in Baltimore, 1930–1934." *Science & Society Magazine* 60 (1997).

Truitt, Charles J. *Historic Salisbury Updated; 1662–1982*. Salisbury, MD: Historical Books, Inc., 1982.

Truitt, Reginald, and Millard LesCallette. *Worcester County, Maryland's Arcadia*. Snow Hill, MD: Worcester County Historical Society, 1977.

Wennersten, John R. *Maryland's Eastern Shore, A Journey in Time and Place*. Centreville, MD: Tidewater Publishers, 1992.

Williams, Juan. *Thurgood Marshall, American Revolutionary*. New York: Random House, 1998.

Wycherely, H. Alan. *H.L. Mencken vs. The Eastern Shore*. Bulletin of the New York Public Library, June 1970.

Index

About the Author

Joseph Moore was born in Berlin, Worcester County, Maryland, the location of the events reported in this book. Educated in the Worcester County school system, he received a BA degree from the University of Maryland, College Park, and an LLB from the University of Maryland School of Law.

Mr. Moore is the senior partner in the law firm of Williams, Moore, Shockley & Harrison, LLP, in Ocean City, Maryland, where he has practiced law since 1969.

Mr. Moore served as deputy State's Attorney for Worcester County from 1972 to1978 and was thereafter elected to the office of State's Attorney. He is a former member of the Maryland State Bar Association Board of Governors and presently serves as co-chairman of the First Appellate Circuit Character Committee of the Maryland State Board of Law Examiners. In 2003, Joe was admitted as a Fellow of the American College of Trial Lawyers, one of the premier legal organizations in the country. He is also on several boards of local historical organizations.

Joe and his wife, Susan, live in Berlin, and they have two daughters and two grandchildren.